ORCHIDS
FOR EVERYONE

Above: *Odontoglossum* Sunpahia   *Photo x 1¼*

Above: *Miltonia* Peach Blossom   *Photo x 1½*

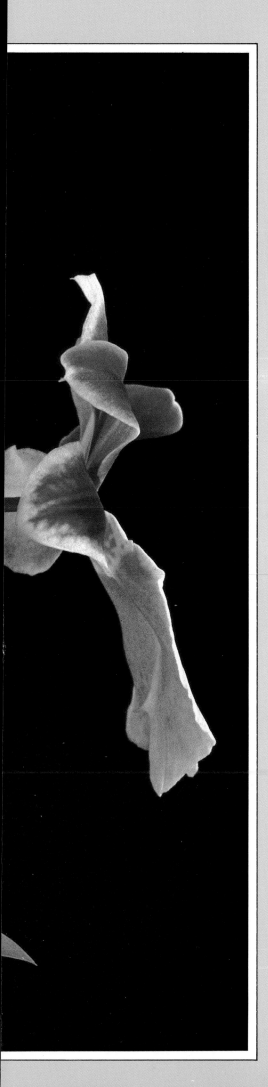

ORCHIDS
FOR EVERYONE

*A practical guide to the home cultivation of over
200 of the world's most beautiful varieties*

Principal author: Brian Williams
Consultant: Jack Kramer

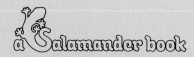

Published by Herbert Michelman Books
Crown Publishers, Inc.
NEW YORK

A Salamander Book

First published in the
United Kingdom in 1980 by
Salamander Books Ltd.

© Salamander Books Ltd, 1980
Salamander House,
27 Old Gloucester Street,
London WC1N 3AF,
United Kingdom.

First published in the United
States in 1980 by Herbert
Michelman Books, a division of
Crown Publishers, Inc.,
One Park Avenue,
New York, N.Y. 10016,
United States of America.

All correspondence concerning the
content of this volume should be
addressed to Salamander Books Ltd.

Library of Congress Cataloging in Publication
Data   Main entry under title:

Orchids for everyone.
    'A Herbert Michelman Book,
    Includes index.
    1. Orchid culture. 2. Orchids. I. Williams.
Brian, 1934- II. Kramer, Jack, 1927-
SB409.069 1980 635.9'34'15 79-20021
ISBN 0-517-539896

Credits

Editor: Valerie Noel-Finch
Designers: Mark Holt, Roger Hyde

Colour reproductions: Scansets Ltd,
    Middlesex, England
Monochrome: Tenreck, London, England

Filmset: Modern Text Typesetting Ltd,
    Essex, England

Printed in Belgium by
Henri Proost et Cie, Turnhout

Above: *Coelogyne intermedia*   Photo x 1¼

THE AUTHORS

Brian Williams A professional horticulturalist for over 20 years, Brian Williams has for the past 14 years built up and been responsible for an extremely varied private orchid collection, which has become noted for cultural awards. From 1974 to 1978, Brian was Editor of The Orchid Review, the world's oldest international orchid journal. He frequently lectures to national and international orchid societies, has appeared on television programmes, and was the chairman of lecture sessions at the 9th World Orchid Conference in Bangkok in 1978.

Peter Dumbelton has spent the whole of his professional life growing orchids and for the past 12 years has been working for a commercial orchid company, where he is now nursery manager. He lectures to a wide range of societies and often judges at orchid shows.

Ray Bilton An acknowledged expert on cymbidiums, Ray Bilton has given papers on the breeding of cymbidiums at the World Orchid Conferences in Australia and Thailand and has contributed to orchid periodicals throughout the world.

Wilma Rittershausen continues the family orchid business set up by her father P R C Rittershausen. She is now Editor of The Orchid Review and, with her brother Brian, is author of two orchid books and frequently contributes articles to orchid magazines.

David Stead An experienced professional grower with a particular interest in breeding odontoglossums, and former Chairman of the British Orchid Growers Association, David Stead is a regular contributor to orchid journals and international conferences.

Paul Phillips One of the foremost breeders of paphiopedilums in the world, and Chairman of the British Orchid Growers Association, Paul Phillips has lectured on paphiopedilums in many countries and has written for orchid magazines in Australia, America, Britain and Germany.

Keith Andrew A commercial orchid grower for 25 years, Keith Andrew has a special interest in breeding phalaenopsis and miniature cymbidiums. He has given papers at conferences in California and exhibited orchids in Germany and throughout Britain.

Alan Greatwood Learning his trade from one of the established orchid growing firms, Alan Greatwood has grown orchids for over 30 years. His main interest today is growing species on into specimen plants, for which he has won many awards.

THE CONSULTANT

Jack Kramer A well known and highly respected horticulturalist writer, Jack Kramer has a personal collection of species orchids and has written and contributed to many orchid books appealing to a wide readership.

PHOTOGRAPHY

The majority of photographs within *Orchids for Everyone,* and all those on the cover have been taken specially for the book by Eric Crichton.

Above: *Pleione formosana* 'Iris'   *Photo x 2¾*

CONTENTS

Part One: 10-99
Orchids in Cultivation

Part Two: 100-197
Orchids in Close-up

Key to symbols
Temperature categories for growing orchids:
● = Warm—minimum 15.5°C (60°F)
◐ = Intermediate—minimum 13°C (55°F)
○ = Cool—minimum 10°C (50°F)

❀ = Flowering season

Above: *Cymbidium* Gymer 'Cooksbridge'   *Photo x1¼*

FOREWORD

It was with very great pleasure that I accepted the invitation to write the foreword to 'ORCHIDS FOR EVERYONE'. The authors are all personal friends of mine, dedicated to orchids and their culture, and I am confident that this book will do much to increase the popularity of the subject.

Orchids are probably the most misunderstood of all nature's creations. During the past two centuries countless myths have developed to surround these fascinating flowers with an aura of mystery to the extent that, in many people's eyes, they are either weird or exotic and quite impossible to grow.

The flowers of orchids are notorious mimics and their common names often refer to this similarity: monkey orchid, bee orchid, lady's slipper, dove orchid and many more. The plant form is also very varied, and caused much confusion to early botanists. The flowers of some species are as small as one millimetre and others up to 25 centimetres in diameter. Some have single flowers and others many hundreds on a spray. Some remain in flower for less than a day and others for more than six months.

In nature there may be more than 25,000 different species and these are native to almost every part of the world, growing at elevations from sea level up to 3,000 metres. They are found in continents covered with ice and snow for many months of the year, but are particularly prolific in the tropical forests of the world. Some orchids even grow and flower beneath the ground and never see the light of day, and a few have no leaves at all.

From selected species the hybridist has, over the past 100 years, produced more than 30,000 hybrids to delight and amaze with their vast spectrum of colours and forms.

To write about a little-known specialist subject, about which there are so many misconceptions, in a style understandable to the layman, it is necessary to use a basic uncomplicated language. To educate the novice and to be of interest to the more experienced grower, it is important that the text is accurate. The authors have managed to meet both these requirements, and the result is a compilation that is more than just a reference book, although each subject is complete in itself.

The working lives of the authors have been entirely spent in practical horticulture and all are at present closely involved with some of the world's leading orchid nurseries. They have all travelled extensively to see orchids either in nature or in cultivation in many parts of the globe. The knowledge gained by day-to-day contact with the plants has been put before the reader in such a way that success in cultivation with the minimum of effort is assured.

The text is complemented not only with superb photographs of plants and flowers but also with illustrations of cultural techniques. The majority of the pictures were especially commissioned for this work.

If you are new to orchids, start to grow them with every confidence. Your new hobby can be started with a very modest outlay and many varieties can be grown in an ordinary room. If you are already 'hooked' I need say no more! You are already a member of that great fraternity of orchid lovers to be found in every country of the world. You are already an addict, but this addiction will bring you only pleasure and friendship, and each day will be a new day with the thrill of looking at treasures that bloom in your collection.

Eric E. Young

Eric E. Young
President, Orchid Society of Great Britain
President, British Orchid Council

Part One
Orchids in Cultivation

Orchids are parasites. They are also carnivorous, insectivorous, and possess mystic—usually evil—powers. Additionally they are extremely expensive and need to be grown in very hot and humid conditions which are costly to provide. In cultivation orchids are short-lived plants.

These are just some of the many myths that in the past have surrounded orchids, and inhibited all but the very wealthy from growing what is surely nature's most extravagant family of flowering plants. With an almost worldwide distribution that includes every conceivable ecological niche, orchids stand supreme in the plant kingdom for their beauty and diversity, and are unrivalled for their willingness to adapt to a wide variety of conditions under cultivation.

This adaptability is one of the main reasons why orchids are fast becoming *the* plant, not only for greenhouse owners but also for apartment dwellers—many of whom are growing orchids very successfully as pot plants. With their long-lasting flowers and often attractive foliage, many of the more compact growing orchids are ideal plants for the windowsill. With a greenhouse at your disposal, all 70,000 species and hybrid orchids are potentially available to you, whilst a few genera may be treated as 'alpine' plants and grown without heat. In subtropical, tropical and equatorial areas of the world, a far wider range of orchids may be grown as garden plants, thus adding another dimension to the uses of this great family.

As decorative plants, orchids are without peers. Although in the past many non-ornamental uses—including both contraceptive and aphrodisiac qualities—have been ascribed to them, there is but one 'orchid of commerce', *Vanilla planifolia*. This primarily Central American species, a vine that can in nature climb to 15-23m (50-75ft), produces seed pods that are the beans of true vanilla.

Although now largely replaced by artificial flavouring, Vanillin, it remains an important crop in many tropical countries.

But it is to lovers of flowering plants that this book is dedicated, especially those who yearn for perennial plants that produce their flowers during the dull days of winter, as many orchids do.

This first part of the book opens with an introduction to the botany of the orchid family. Then follows a brief historical look at orchid collecting and breeding, which leads on to a detailed practical guide to the successful cultivation of these fascinating plants. The first consideration in this section is where to grow orchids, with discussion of greenhouses, their ideal shapes and sizes, and their correct positioning in the garden. This is followed by a review of the greenhouse equipment and gadgetry available to assist the amateur grower, not forgetting the garden lover without the space for a greenhouse, for whom there is guidance on cultivating orchids on windowsills, in growing cases, cellars and lofts.

The provision of temperature and light requirements prefaces the section on how to cultivate orchids, which compares the merits of the various composts, discusses methods of potting and vegetative propagation and provides instructions on watering, feeding and pest control. For those interested in the decorative uses of orchids, there is a section on corsage-making and preparing plants for exhibition, and for the more ambitious, the final section gives instructions on artificial pollination, seed raising and tissue culture.

The aim of this first part is to whet the appetite for the cultivation of these wonderful flowers, by introducing new growers to a few of the many methods currently in use. One word of warning: although orchids are not parasitic by nature, they do have the infectious habit of growing on the casual onlooker.

Left: Orchids can be grown almost anywhere, providing a few basic requirements are met. Many—like these paphiopedilums—flower in winter, brightening your home on the dull days.

UNRAVELLING THE LEGEND

Orchids are seldom mediocre: people either love them or loathe them. However, once they have become acquainted with orchids, most people are fascinated by them—occasionally to the point of obsession. Loathing often stems from an ignorance of the enormous orchid family and may be based on an elementary fear or dislike of the unknown. Of course, some orchid growers do give up, but almost certainly not because the flowers repulse them.

Over the years orchids have been the focus of many stories, some of which descend to the depths of absurdity. One such, recounted by a former orchid grower exhibiting at a Chelsea Flower Show in the 1930s, alleges that an elegantly dressed lady, misled by a newspaper article on orchids, enquired the whereabouts of 'the meat-eating orchid'. Without hesitation the exhibitor apologized for the absence of this orchid from his stand, explaining: 'It has gone to lunch!'—a reply which appeared to satisfy the gullible enquirer. Considering the strength of the myths about orchids at that time, her innocence was at least partially understandable.

The aims of this book are to unravel the web of legend and half-truths surrounding orchids and to encourage a better understanding of the characteristics and attractions of the astonishing orchid family.

Above: This spectacular terrestrial species of *Caladenia* comes from Western Australia. Although not in general cultivation, there are many species, all brightly coloured.

Above: *Calypso bulbosa* is a terrestrial orchid found wild in North America, Europe and Asia. It produces a single leaf and flower.

Right: The leafless orchid, *Epipogium aphylla*, thrives on the decomposing leaves of the forest floor. It is found from Europe to Japan.

What is an orchid?

There is no simple answer to the question 'What is an orchid?' No clearcut statement is possible: there is no single country of origin, no single habit of growth, and no single shape and colour of flower.

The Orchidaceae form the largest family of flowering plants known to science. Estimates of the number of native species range from around 15,000 to as many as 35,000, but it is generally accepted that there are at least 25,000 native species, derived from approximately 750 genera grouped in numerous tribes and subtribes. And, despite intensive exploration of large areas of the world during the past 200 years, new species are still being found. Most of these are members of established genera, but occasionally even a new genus is discovered.

Orchids are perennial plants found growing in a wide variety of situations and with different growth habits. Members of one large group grow in or near the surface of the ground and are known as *terrestrials*. Plants in the other of the two main groups grow on trees or shrubs and are known as *epiphytes*. The name is derived from 'epi' (above or on), and 'phyte' (plant), hence epiphyte: a plant growing on another plant. Members of

Above: This large epiphytic *Epidendrum* from Mexico has heavy leaves and pendent stems. An attractive species. It is easily cultivated.

Left: Epiphytic cattleyas growing on trees near the light in a Florida forest. Aerial roots anchor the plants and search for food.

Below: Although this African orchid, *Ansellia africana* is found as an epiphyte in trees, it also grows on rocks as a lithophyte.

this group are not parasites; they do not draw food from their host, but merely obtain anchorage. They draw moisture and nourishment from the air and from humus collected in the angles of branches or in the crevices of the bark. Occasionally, epiphytic orchids are found growing on rocks, when they are more correctly termed *lithophytes*. In general terms, most orchids from temperate zones are terrestrial, whereas most coming from the tropics are epiphytic.

Orchids' flowers vary in size from those requiring a magnifying glass to appreciate their full beauty, to blooms up to 20cm (8in) in diameter. And flowers may vary considerably in size and shape within a single genus, thus complicating species identification, even for an expert. Although all orchid flowers are made up of six basic segments (see page 16),

there are countless variations on this pattern. Breeders of hybrids have produced a large number of varieties, introducing new colours or broadening the segments of the flowers to produce a more rounded shape.

'New' orchids to fascinate the grower are constantly being created by hybridization between two different species or two or more different genera. Those crossed between more than one genus are known as *inter-* or *multigeneric hybrids.* Up to the present a maximum of seven different genera have been combined, over several generations, into a single multigeneric hybrid. Doubtless the future will yield even more complicated breeding.

Growing orchids

This extreme diversity is one of the main attractions of orchid growing, and main-

tains the fascination indefinitely. However long a grower has been cultivating orchids, there are always thousands more that will present a challenge to his growing skills and eventually delight him with yet a different shape or colour combination. Most amateur growers prefer a very mixed collection, but this will really test cultural abilities; invariably requirements of one group must be compromised to satisfy the needs of the majority. New growers would do better to limit the range of orchids they grow at first; it is advisable to master the basic skills needed to cultivate one group before progressing to another. This does not mean that the initial choice must be made between one or two types, for such is the variety available that there is bound to be a group just right for any particular set of growing conditions.

Patterns of Growth

To the layman, orchid plants often present a bewildering variety of shapes, but in reality they have only two basic types of growth: sympodial and monopodial.

Sympodial orchids

The majority of orchids have a sympodial growth pattern. These plants produce their new growth from the base of previous growths, rather in the manner of most herbaceous perennial plants. Many sympodial orchids have *pseudobulbs,* so called because they are not true bulbs (as in narcissus, for example), but are merely thickened stems that have become adapted to store moisture and food. These pseudobulbs enable the plant to withstand periods of dryness, and indicate that in nature the species grows in an area of seasonal drought.

Pseudobulbs show great diversity. The common egg-shaped ones of, for example,

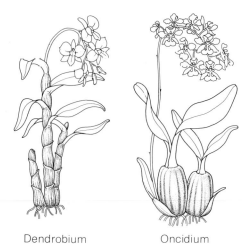
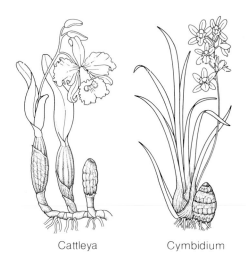

Dendrobium   Oncidium   Cattleya   Cymbidium

Above: Pseudobulbs vary greatly in size and shape. Each is beautifully suited to its environment, having adapted to varying habitats.

Right: Paphiopedilums have no need for pseudobulbs. They grow in the ground in moist climates where drought conditions do not occur.

Left: The typical sympodial orchid has several pseudobulbs joined by a rhizome, which is not always visible between them. Each bulb may support one or more leaves.

Right: *Coelogyne cristata* produces many closely packed pseudobulbs. When a few leaves are shed the old bulbs survive to provide food for the younger ones.

Lycaste, Cymbidium and *Odontoglossum* may vary from a few millimetres to 15-20cm (6-8in) in height. They can be very flattened, as in some *Oncidium* species, or almost round, as in several species of *Encyclia.* At the other end of the scale there are the thin, cane-like pseudobulbs of *Dendrobium* and *Epidendrum* which, although they may seldom exceed 3-4 cm (1.2-1.6in) in diameter, will frequently grow to 2 or 3m (up to 10ft) in height. In between these are the club- or spindle-shaped pseudobulbs of cattleyas and some laelias, which may range in height from 5-30cm (2-12in), but are generally comparatively plump.

As if this variety were not sufficient to cause confusion, even to growers beyond the very early stages, the rhizomes (the woody parts of the rootstock that join one pseudobulb to the next) may vary even within one genus from practically non-existent to 15cm (6in) or more in length. The pseudobulbs of *Coelogyne cristata,* for example, are produced very close together; a mature specimen frequently has the appearance of a bunch of large, shrivelled grapes. By contrast, the rhizome of *Coelogyne pandurata,* which grows in warmer conditions, scrambles over the surface of the ground, producing a new pseudobulb only every 10cm (4 in).

There are also sympodial orchids without pseudobulbs. Generally speaking, these inhabit areas where the seasonal supply of moisture is more constant. Perhaps the best known of these are *Paphiopedilum* from Southeast Asia and the related *Phragmipedium* from South America. Although both these groups may be deciduous in nature, they are seldom so when grown under glass. They produce large fans of leaves with the flower stem emerging from the centre.

Despite their apparently different growth habits, *all* sympodial orchids have at least one thing in common: the new growth is always produced from the base of previous ones.

Monopodial orchids

The principal direction of growth of monopodial orchids is upwards, new growth being an extension of the growth of previous years. Leaves are produced alternately on either side of a central stem, the interval between the leaves ranging from minimal to many centimetres. Although growth variation is less obvious among monopodial than sympodial orchids, it still exists. One extreme is shown by the genus *Arachnis,* which is often described as having a climbing habit, the vigorous stems reach-

ing the higher tree branches 10 or even 20m (33-65ft) above ground. Such vigorous *Arachnis* species from tropical areas of Asia are not suited to pot culture in temperate zones, but the related genera *Phalaenopsis* and *Doritis* are ideal. In these, the broad leaves are produced from an abbreviated stem, and the plant remains compact for many years.

Occasionally, certain monopodial orchids will freely produce side growths from the leaf axils; some species of *Aerides* and *Angraecum* are particularly noted for this and often develop into bushy, multi-lead plants. But always the new growth is an extension of previous years, and pseudobulbs are never present.

Right: The typical monopodial grows from an upright stem from which the leaves grow outwards in pairs. New leaves are produced from the apex. Aerial roots grow from the sides and base. The plants vary in height according to genus. Vandas, as illustrated, can grow to more than 1m (3ft) while phalaenopsis are usually restricted to three or four leaves on a plant at any one time.

Orchid roots

The roots of orchids, particularly epiphytic orchids, are usually much thicker than in other plants, and the root system may appear compact when compared with the fibrous root system of a more familiar plant. Many terrestrial orchids possess a comparatively finer root system and some spherical tubers (sometimes incorrectly called pseudobulbs). This is particularly the case with temperate species, many of which are herbaceous. These underground tubers enable the plant to survive periods of cold weather, with a resurgence of new growth when conditions are favourable. Terrestrial orchids from warmer areas usually produce the thicker roots characteristic of epiphytic orchids. Epiphytes need strong, thick roots for several reasons; they secure the plant to its host, and their thickness helps the plant to

Above: Exposed aerial roots can only exist in warm moist climates. The green tip shows that the root is active and absorbing moisture.

survive temporary periods of drought.

The roots of monopodial orchids are produced at intervals between the leaves on the main stems, whereas in sympodial orchids the roots develop from beneath each new growth. The outer layer of the root, called the *velamen*, consists of several layers of spongy cells that are capable of absorbing and storing considerable quantities of moisture. Recent research on monopodials has shown that nutrients can also be absorbed in this way.

The growing tip of the root is often green (or white if under the surface of the

compost) for the first 2-3cm. Away from the tip the velamen gives the root a whitish or tan colour, although when saturated it will assume a greenish hue. When the orchid is in its least active stage of growth or resting, the velamen will completely cover the growing point.

Foliage and flowers

The leaves of orchid plants vary in size from microscopic to 1m (39in) or more in length. They can be broad or pencil-shaped and range in texture from thin, papery leaves designed to last a single season, to thick, almost succulent leaves that persist for a great many years. In some orchids the leaves are attractively tessellated — marked into small squares like a mosaic — and in the 'jewel' orchids, such as *Haemaria, Macodes* and *Anoectochilus,* the velvety leaves in shades of rich brown or green with a contrasting network of silver, gold or reddish veins, become the principal attraction. The flowers of these orchids are generally whitish or grey-green, and are small and relatively insignificant.

Most orchids, however, are grown for the intricate beauty of their flowers. The variety of flower form is far greater than that of plant habit, with almost every colour except black represented — even a

Above: An odontoglossum hybrid which shows the typical well balanced flower with all segments similar in size. Right: A non-typical orchid shape is represented by the masdevallia whose kite-shaped flowers consist of enlarged sepals fused together at the base to form a tube. The petals and lip are diminutive and remain hidden at the centre of the flower.

true blue is found. The flowers may be flat to almost tubular; in most the petals are the showiest parts but in others these segments are reduced and the sepals become the dominant feature. Flowers may be spotted, blotched or striped with a contrasting colour, or they may be a pure single colour. The lip is usually the most colourful and spectacular part of the flower, and has often developed an intricate, occasionally even bizarre, shape.

These adaptations are part of an efficient design that helps to ensure reproduction of the species (see page 18). Scent, which is present in many species and may vary from slight to overpowering, is another part of this mechanism.

The Orchid Flower

The typical orchid flower has six segments: an outer ring of three sepals and an inner ring of three petals. These six segments are all coloured, whereas in most flowers—a rose, for example—the protective outer sepals (here called the calyx) are green and like small leaves or bracts beneath the significantly more conspicuous coloured petals.

The uppermost, or dorsal, sepal of an orchid is symmetrical and slightly larger than the other two. This has been exploited by plant breeders with considerable success, particularly in the genus *Paphiopedilum*. The two lower, or lateral, sepals are equal in size and shape, usually separate and held at an angle between the petals. In *Paphiopedilum*, however, and also in its cousins, *Cypripedium* from the northern hemisphere and the South American *Phragmipedium*, the two lateral sepals are usually fused together to form a ventral sepal behind the lower petal. In certain other orchids, such as *Masdevallia*, all three sepals are united for the greater part of their length to form a tube. But these are exceptions. The majority of horticulturally interesting orchids have three separate sepals spaced symmetrically at the back of the flower.

The inner ring of segments consists of three petals, the lowest of which is frequently greatly enlarged and highly coloured. This larger petal is known as the *labellum*, or lip, and is the principal visual attraction for pollinating insects. Some genera, including, among others, *Coryanthes*, *Paphiopedilum* and *Acineta*, have developed the lip into a bucket or pouchlike structure. Once a visiting insect has climbed or fallen into this the only exit is past the sexual parts of the flower and pollination is assured. This natural tendency to elaboration of the lip has been developed by plant breeders into the most significant part of hybrid flowers. Indeed, many judges at orchid shows have commented that, with cymbidiums in particular, the absence of a brightly coloured lip precludes consideration!

At the bud stage the lip is the uppermost petal but as the bud develops to flowering the lip becomes the lowest segment by a 180° twist of the flower stalk, or *pedicel*. This process is known as *resupination* and is common to most orchids, although in most encyclias, among others, the lip remains uppermost.

The other two petals are usually held across the horizontal axis and are the most variable of all the segments. In some species the petals are broad, often frilled, and extremely flamboyant.

A distinctive feature common to all orchid flowers is that they can be divided into two equal halves in a vertical plane only. This feature has been one of the criteria used by botanists in deciding whether a flower new to science is a member of the orchid family.

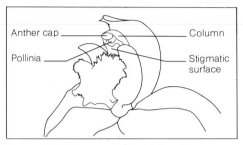

Above: This close up of *Cymbidium traceyanum* clearly shows the structure of the column, which carries the reproductive organs of the flower.

The reproductive system

The most significant difference between orchids and other flowers is in their reproductive apparatus. Like most flowers, the majority of orchids are bisexual, the male and female organs being present in each flower, but the structure and operation of the reproductive parts are different from the conventional system.

In a more familiar flower the female part of the flower (the pistil with the receptive stigma) is situated in the centre and the male parts (the stamens, each with anthers containing pollen grains) are arranged in a ring around it. In an orchid flower, however, the male and female sexual parts are combined into a fingerlike structure in the centre called the column or, more correctly, the *gynostemium*.

The pollen grains, the male part of the flower, are usually at the front end of the column. They are combined into waxy masses called *pollinia* and protected by a cap that represents the anther of 'conventional' flowers. The female part of the flower is represented by a stigmatic surface situated on the underside of the column a little way back from the tip. The relative position of the male and female parts is of critical importance for insect pollination to be successful.

Although most orchids have bisexual flowers, many species of the genus *Catasetum* have unisexual flowers, with male and female organs on separate flowers or even on separate inflorescences. These male and female flowers are often superficially different and early taxonomists named them as different species. As these peculiarities have become known, revised botanical names have been ascribed to many of these plants.

The Structure of an Orchid Flower
The drawings on this page show the typical flower shapes of six groups of orchids widely grown around the world. They share the following features common to all orchid flowers:

1 **Sepals** Usually three of approximately equal size—the uppermost or dorsal sepal, and two lateral sepals below.

2 **Petals** Always three—two similar petals either side of the centre and one lower petal which has become the lip.

3 **Lip or Labellum** Formed from the lower petal, this is the most ornamental segment of the flower. It acts as a 'landing platform' for pollinators.

4 **Column** The fingerlike structure that carries the reproductive parts—the pollinia and stigmatic surface.

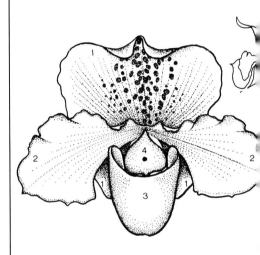

Paphiopedilum
Above: Heavily textured, almost 'varnished' blooms with a distinctive pouchlike lip and fused lateral sepals. Most flowers are borne singly on a strong 15-25cm (6-10in) stem and will remain on the plant in good condition for a period of three months or more.

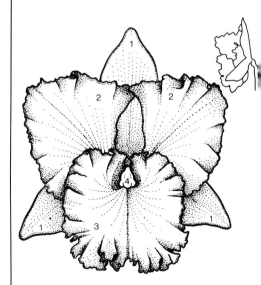

Cattleya
Above: The broad petals and large, wavy lip, which is often of a contrasting colour, combine to produce blooms of up to 15cm (6in) in diameter. Cattleya flowers are often heavily scented but tend to be weak in texture; they seldom last for more than three weeks.

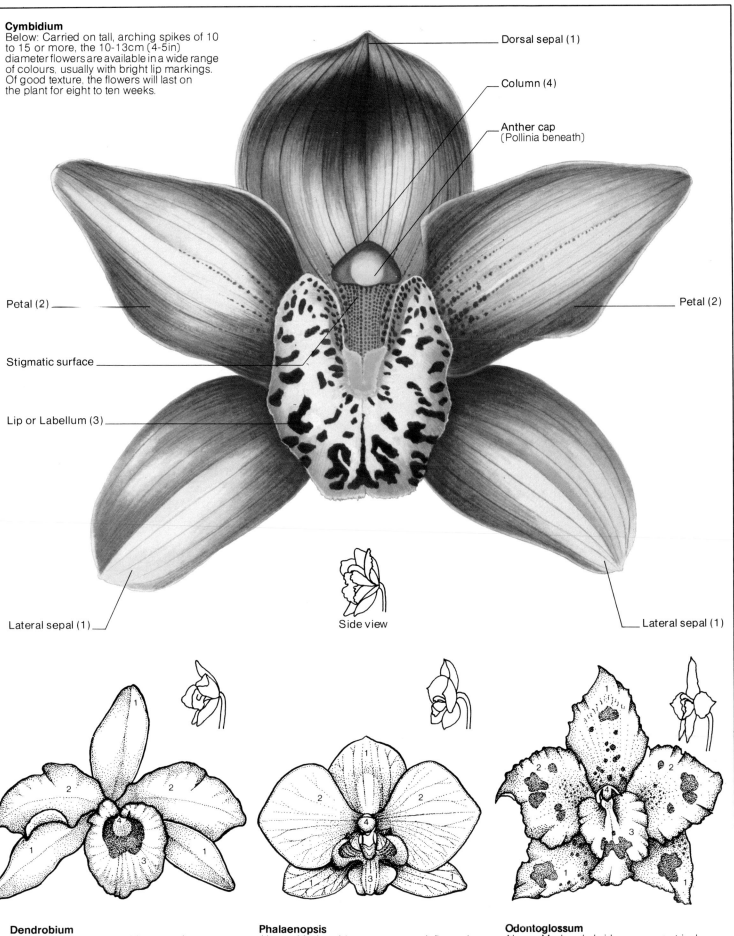

Cymbidium
Below: Carried on tall, arching spikes of 10 to 15 or more, the 10-13cm (4-5in) diameter flowers are available in a wide range of colours, usually with bright lip markings. Of good texture, the flowers will last on the plant for eight to ten weeks.

Dorsal sepal (1)

Column (4)

Anther cap
(Pollinia beneath)

Petal (2)

Petal (2)

Stigmatic surface

Lip or Labellum (3)

Lateral sepal (1)

Side view

Lateral sepal (1)

Dendrobium
Above: Brightly coloured flowers, about 4cm (1.5in) in diameter, carried on a variety of erect, arching or pendent spikes depending on type. The lateral petals are fused at the base, sometimes forming a short spur. The flowers will last on the plant for three to eight weeks.

Phalaenopsis
Above: Modern blooms are round, flat and produced on tall, branching stems each carrying 15 to 20 flowers. Colours are white, yellow or pink, often with spots and/or stripes. Deceptively fragile in appearance, the flowers will easily last for seven to eight weeks.

Odontoglossum
Above: Modern hybrids are symmetrical and usually circular in outline. The markings often contrast boldly with the base colour. Each flower spike carries 8 to 12 or more flowers, of attractive shape and held well clear of the foliage. The flowers will last for four to five weeks.

Pollination

The shape, colour or scent of a species orchid undoubtedly gives great pleasure to man, but this is purely incidental to its natural objective. The sole purpose of any ornamentation of an orchid flower is to attract a suitable pollinating agent, which in addition to the more 'normal' insects, such as flies, wasps and bees, includes such creatures as snails, bats, humming-birds and moths.

Cross-pollination

In order to improve vigour and variety in a species—an important survival factor where the 'law of the jungle' rules—it is desirable that the pollen of a flower is not used to fertilize that same flower (termed as *selfing*) but is transferred to a flower of the same species on a different plant. This process of *cross-pollination*, resulting in *cross-fertilization*, ensures continual redistribution of the various genes present in the entire population of the species; whereas self-pollination may lead to the accumulation of bad characteristics that usually occurs with inbreeding.

To achieve cross-pollination, the orchid flower has developed many intricate mechanisms to ensure that the pollen taken from one flower is not, in the majority of cases, deposited on the stigma of the same flower. This is particularly so where the flowers are pollinated by insects, and since orchids are predominantly plants of the tropics, where insect life is highly developed and abundant, we can see immediately why orchids—if left to their own devices — are efficient at reproduction.

Of course, insects do not visit flowers merely to transfer pollen from one flower to the next, but in a search for nectar or pollen on which to feed. Thus, in most cases, the provision of nectar is a vital part of the pollination mechanism. Colour is also significant in attracting specific pollinators and, at close range, the shape and markings of the lip and/or column play an important role in ensuring efficient pollination. But the initial attraction is probably one of scent, which to the human nose is not always sweet and is occasionally decidedly repugnant!

Purpose-built pollinators

Most orchids growing in natural environments are pollinated by one species of insect only and the entire structure of the flower is delicately balanced to match the visiting insect. Many orchids, for example,

store nectar within the walls of a hollow spur, which is an extension at the back of the lip, and only insects with a tongue, or proboscis, of a suitable length are able to reach this liquid. Significantly, it is these insects that have the correctly-shaped head to ensure pollination; as the insect pushes its proboscis down the spur it flips back the anther cap and the pollinia become attached in an upright position to the top of its head or body.

As the insect flies off in search of another flower, the pollinia play their part in the process. If the pollinia were to

Below: This flower produces a scent of aphid honeydew and fools the fly into laying its eggs inside the flower, at the same time removing the pollinia and effecting pollination. These flies normally feed on honeydew and lay their eggs near aphid colonies.

remain in an upright position they would merely come into contact with the anther cap or stamen of the next flower, but as the insect moves from flower to flower, possibly collecting further pollinia on the way, the pollinial stalk (*caudicle* or *stipe*) curls so that the pollinia pivot to a forward-facing position. When the insect alights on another flower the pollinia are brought into contact with the underside of the column and become attached to the sticky surface of the stigma. Where the orchid has laterally placed stigmas the pollinia do not pivot forward into a horizontal position but diverge slightly to each side. Again, this serves to bring them into precise contact with the stigmas of another flower.

Pollinating insects appear to be naturally selected by the length of the orchids'

spur; bees, with their comparatively short tongues, for example, are effective in pollinating short spurred orchids such as the British native *Orchis mascula;* whereas moths and butterflies, with their longer probosces, are the pollinating agents for the longer spurred orchids, which include most of the tropical angraecoids. Indeed, the pollinia of the latter have frequently been seen attached to the proboscis of visiting insects, particularly where the orchid has laterally placed stigmas. Not only would a bee's tongue be too short to reach into these longer spurs, but its head would be too broad to enter the opening in the flower centre.

The above are two perfect examples of flowers and pollinators that are balanced one to another. But the most famous and often cited example is the Madagascan orchid *Angraecum sesquipedale,* which has a spur of 30-35cm (10-12in) in length. Charles Darwin, in his book *On the Various Contrivances by which British and Foreign Orchids are Fertilized by Insects* (1862) concluded that only a very large and strong moth with a suitably long proboscis could effect pollination, but his theory was not proved until the discovery of just such an insect, *Xanthopan morgani praedicta,* in Madagascar many years later.

The tender trap

In many orchids, including paphiopedilums, cypripediums, coryanthes and stanhopeas, the lip has evolved into a pouch or slipper-like organ; again, the structure of the flower is aimed at efficient cross-pollination. A bee, probably initially attracted by scent, alights on the front edge of the pouch in search of nectar or occasionally, as in *Coryanthes macrantha,* to eat the interior brim of the pouch. Frequently, either through intoxication or accident, the poor unsuspecting bee tumbles in and, because of the angle of the pouch and its slippery interior surface, cannot make its exit through the pouch opening. Instead, assisted by hairs suitably placed on the surface of the pouch, it crawls up the back interior wall towards one of the small openings on either side of the column. These exits are a fairly tight fit and often considerable effort is required before the bee can escape. In doing so it rubs against the stamen, removing the pollinia onto its back. The bee then visits another flower where the 'tumbling in' process is repeated. This time, on crawling

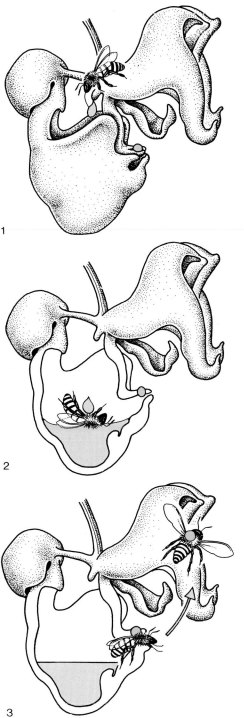

1

2

3

Left: (1) Bees are attracted to the flower of *Coryanthes* by the fleshy lip which they gnaw with relish. (2) While investigating the flower the bee may be knocked into the 'bucket' by the droplet of liquid secreted by the lobes. (3) The exit for the bee is through the small opening in the lip. It has to push very hard to get through and while doing so collects the pollinia on its back.

up the back wall of the pouch, the bee's back comes into contact with the stigmatic surface, leaving the pollen behind. As it completes its escape it collects additional pollen, which will then be transferred to another flower.

Several points are important here. First, the design of the flower ensures that the bee passes under the stigmatic surface before reaching the pollen, thus making self-pollination extremely unlikely. Second, if a smaller insect visits the flower, possibly with pollinia from a different species on its back, it is able to pass with ease beneath the stigma and stamen, thus not interfering with the natural processes. Unfortunately, if a larger insect is unwise enough to enter the flower it cannot make its exit through the small side holes and dies miserably in the base of the pouch.

This is another example of an orchid flower which is in exact harmony with its pollinator.

Scent and colour

Scent has been mentioned as the probable initial attractant, and it certainly plays an important part in the pollination mechanism of many orchids. For example, where orchids are pollinated by moths the scent is virtually absent during daylight hours, but visit the greenhouse during the evening or night and it is a different story! Most of the angraecoids from tropical Africa, such as *Angraecum* and *Aerangis* species, fall within this category, and one can imagine the almost overpowering scent given off by a colony of these plants on a humid night.

Colour, too, plays its part. There would be little point in a dark or dull-coloured orchid giving off scent during the hours of darkness: the poor half-blind moth, attracted by the scent, would blunder round vainly in search of its source and might never find it. Nature is not so careless. Night-scented orchids are generally of glistening white and possess a well-defined shape. Thus the combination of scent, colour and shape ensures that the moths do not waste their time.

Not all scents that attract insects, however, are so sweet. Many tropical orchids, *Bulbophyllum fletcherianum* among them, emit a foetid smell of bad meat that attracts carrion flies. The British lizard orchid, *Himantoglossum hircinum,* is said to smell of goats and also attracts flies, several of which have been observed carrying pollinia on their heads. But there is little evidence that flies are the sole pollinators of any orchid species.

Mimicry

The common name applied to many orchids often alludes to the animal that part of the flower resembles. In the national flower of Panama, *Peristeria elata,* for example, the column bears a

Above: The brightly coloured area at the centre of this *Miltonia* flower acts as a map, guiding a visiting insect to the source of the nectar.

Below: The spider-like flowers of *Ophrys sphegodes* attract male spiders which remove the pollinia when 'mating'. Pseudocopulation with another flower ensures pollination.

by some growers using this system, there is little evidence to suggest that the plants are fooled by this adjustment to the number and length of days, or that the results in flowering obtained are any better than those from plants grown under more conventional conditions.

What does seem possible with culture under lights is the virtual elimination of the dull, short winter's day. By maintaining the day length at 16 hours, with perhaps only slight seasonal adjustments, the plants respond by growing vigorously almost throughout the year. The more regular supply of light and warmth also means that the orchids can be watered and fertilized at summer levels, with the inevitable result of steady, year-round growth.

In most homes there are at least two or three areas that could be converted fairly easily into a 'growing room' suitable for orchids. Any recess or alcove, such as that formed by a staircase, would be ideal. Rather than hide all your 'rubbish' in the loft, you can put this area to good use at very little expense. Similarly, your basement or cellar, with its excellent insulative qualities, could be transformed into an Aladdin's cave by the addition of a modest collection of orchids.

The size of your indoor growing area will be dictated by the dimensions of the alcove or window recess, although most lofts and cellars will be larger than the space required. In these situations it will therefore be necessary to build a suitable 'room' in order to confine the orchid-growing activities to a predetermined area. As artificial heating will almost certainly be needed, the restricted space will also be less costly to maintain at correct temperatures.

Basic rules for under-lights growing apply to all three areas, but where these differ for one or more of the locations, this will obviously be mentioned.

Rule one is safety! To grow plants under artificial lights you need two ingredients that do not mix: water and electricity. Therefore, unless you are qualified, have an electrician install the wiring, ensuring that he knows that water will never be far away once the plants have moved in.

Water

Water will, of course, remain a problem when growing plants indoors, and it is essential to provide thorough and adequate facilities to drain off the surplus water. This will be most difficult in the loft, but it should be possible to arrange a drainage pipe out of the trough that forms the floor of your growing area. This drainage pipe could be linked with the bathroom overflow pipe, since although it *must* be available, it will not carry much water under normal operating conditions. Drainage in a cellar is usually installed when the house is built but, if not, a small soakaway will suffice.

If running only a small installation in an alcove or window recess off one of the living rooms, the base or floor area must be made waterproof. This can be achieved by building a wall from timber (10 x 7.5cm; 4 x 3in is suitable) round the perimeter of the floor area, and then lining the entire floor space with plastic

Above and Left: A garden room built on to the house makes a perfect winter home for orchids, which, in warmer areas, can stand outside during the growing season.

Right: Flourescent tubes arranged on an adjustable board will provide sufficient light to grow many orchids successfully in attic or cellar. Fans are essential to provide adequate ventilation.

sheeting to form a trough. When fitting the sluice, ensure that the surplus water can either drain safely through an outside wall or be drained into a suitable container which can then be emptied.

Another major cultural difference with indoor growing as opposed to culture in the greenhouse, is the amount of watering necessary. Generally speaking, lofts or cellars, with their more constant temperatures and comparative lack of ventilation, will maintain higher average (relative) humidity than most greenhouses. This means that the compost in the pots will remain moist for a longer period after watering. Indeed, many growers only water the pots occasionally, relying instead on a fairly heavy misting once or twice each day, depending upon day-to-day conditions.

To protect the fabric and furnishings of the house from the excess of moisture produced by spraying, the walls and roof of the growing areas should be lined. In a window recess, use polyethylene, as this will allow the natural light to reach the plants, and also reflect any artificial light used back onto the growing area. An alcove away from a window, or the area within either loft or cellar, should be lined with silver foil or painted white in order to make the interior surfaces reflective. Where the area concerned is comparatively small, such as the window recess or alcove, the front of the unit should be left open to prevent a build-up of excessive humidity around the plants.

Light
Many types of commercial light fittings are available, and most makes of fluorescent tube have proved satisfactory. Select a length of tube suited to the dimensions of your growing area, then attach the light fixtures to a stout piece of plywood or similar material, setting the fluorescent tubes approximately 7.5cm (3in) apart. This density of tubes will provide a light output of 2,000 foot candles about 5cm (2in) from the tubes, where plants with a high light requirement should be placed. Orchids satisfied with lower light conditions, eg paphiopedilums and—to a lesser extent—phalaenopsis, could be set at a slightly lower level (achieved by standing the light-loving plants on top of an inverted pot), or placed towards the perimeter of your shelves, where inevitably the intensity of light is lower.

Plants with similar light requirements should be grouped together, and the lights then suspended at the appropriate height above the plants. This is more easily achieved if the boards to which the light fixtures are attached are suspended on chains from the ceiling. By altering the length of the chains, the correct level will be achieved.

It is impossible to give hard and fast

ORCHIDS FOR INDOOR CULTIVATION

Windowsill	Growing case	Attic or Cellar
Brassolaeliocattleya Norman's Bay	Brassia verrucosa	Ada aurantiaca
Cattleya aurantiaca	Brassolaeliocattleya Norman's Bay	Aerides fieldingii
Cattleya bowringiana	Cattleya aurantiaca	Bifrenaria harrisoniae
Coelogyne cristata	Cattleya Bow Bells	Brassia verrucosa
Cymbidium devonianum		Calanthe vestita
Cymbidium Peter Pan	Dendrobium phalaenopsis	Cattleya Bow Bells
Cymbidium Touchstone	Epidendrum cochliatum	Chysis bractescens
Dendrobium nobile		Dendrobium phalaenopsis
Epidendrum cochliatum	Paphiopedilum callosum	Dendrochilum glumaceum
Laelia anceps	Paphiopedilum fairieanum	Gomesa crispa
Maxillaria luteo-alba	Paphiopedilum Honey Gorse	Lycaste aromatica
Maxillaria tenuifolia	Paphiopedilum Silvara	Masdevallia coccinea
Miltonia clowesii	Paphiopedilum Small World	Miltonia endresii
Odontoglossum grande		Odontoglossum crispum
Paphiopedilum callosum	Phalaenopsis equestris	Paphiopedilum Small World
Paphiopedilum fairieanum	Phalaenopsis lueddemanniana	Phalaenopsis equestris
Paphiopedilum Honey Gorse	Phalaenopsis Party Dress	Rhynchostylis gigantea
Paphiopedilum Silvara	Phalaenopsis sanderiana	Trichopilia suavis
Pleione formosana	Phalaenopsis Temple Cloud	Vanda coerulea
Vanda cristata	Phalaenopsis Zada	Zygopetalum intermedium

Above: Paphiopedilums and phalaenopsis are good subjects for permanent culture in a growing case.

rules on subjects related to culture, as no two situations are identical. The important point to watch is that the light, water, temperature, nutriment and air movement are as near correctly balanced as possible. With certain reservations, when the temperature and light density are higher than normal, more food and water can with safety be applied to the orchids, which will respond by maintaining growth for most of the year.

Temperature
However, this increased temperature and light system must be kept within reason. Cool-growing orchids, such as cymbidiums, odontoglossums and most coelogynes, may make good vegetative growth under warmer conditions, but almost certainly will not flower. Likewise, the warm-growing types will not appreciate daytime temperatures of much

above 24-27°C (75-81°F). The temperatures recommended for each genus or group of orchids when growing in a greenhouse apply equally to plants grown under artificial light conditions, the only major difference being that under lights, orchids enjoy almost perpetual summer.

Ventilation
In the early days of growing under lights —especially where the area was lined with polyethylene—many orchids grew too fast, with the result that leaves became soft and floppy, and were usually pale green in colour. This soft growth, especially in what was virtually a polyethylene tent, fell prone to numerous diseases, particularly botrytis and general rotting problems. It was considered that air movement would solve the latter fault, thus it became standard practice to install circulation fans. In the event, this vigorous air movement that caused leaves to almost snap in the breeze, also cured the unbalanced growth and dispersed excess

is that each shelf may be given a different light intensity. However, the problems of growing plants in any restricted area are intensified where space is really limited, and it was found necessary to install two small fans on each shelf of the unit. It is also essential to ensure that the light fittings below each shelf are perfectly insulated from the water above—best achieved by fixing a lead sheet between the light fittings and the shelf to which these are screwed.

Growing cases

Modern homes and open-plan offices lend themselves very well to room dividers, which often take the form of a shelf unit or bamboo lattice panel. A more original method of defining boundaries within a large area could be achieved by the use of a growing case. These miniature indoor greenhouses—the modern counterpart to last century's Wardian case—are available in a great variety of sizes to suit any location. A typical case would be about 2m (6.5ft) high, 1.5-1.8m (5-6ft) long and approximately 61cm (2ft) wide. They are constructed either in traditional materials, using a wooden framework for the plate glass sides, or with stainless steel or aluminium frames to suit a modern setting. These cases usually stand on short legs, a waterproof tray being set into the base in order to prevent carpets being ruined by water. Several inches of moisture-retentive material should be placed in the bottom of this tray, and the orchids stood on this material. Other plants could be attached to a suitably positioned 'tree' mounted within the case to give a natural effect, and a few small foliage plants would complete the picture.

A heating cable is usually installed beneath the gravel tray, and lights recessed into the top panel of the case. As both heating and lighting are controlled automatically, it is possible to leave the orchids for many days without harm coming to them. Humidity within the case remains high, and ventilators are provided both in the base and the roof, thus creating a chimney effect which ensures good air movement. This type of growing may not satisfy the compulsive gardener, but it does enable orchid lovers with very limited time to have an aesthetically pleasing, albeit restricted collection. A growing case is also the perfect answer for flat dwellers, or handicapped people who may not be able to go into the garden. Most of the locations suggested as suitable areas for growing orchids will require similar cultural techniques. The same basic principles, adapted to suit each location, apply whether orchids are being grown on the windowsill or in the greenhouse. Success can be obtained under most conditions, and the next chapter should help prospective growers avoid some of the pitfalls.

humidity. Circulation fans, running continuously, have proved to be more essential in a restricted environment, ie in a comparatively small area under lights, than in conventional greenhouse culture.

Although it may not be possible to ventilate in the true sense of the word whenever possible, fresh air should be admitted daily into the loft or cellar, either through a conveniently positioned window or by making a small vent hole through to the outside.

Supplementary heating

Provision should also be made in the loft or cellar for some form of heating, which may be necessary during winter nights. The domestic central heating boiler is often located in a basement or cellar, in which case it may even be necessary to lower the temperature at night by opening the window or ventilator. In unheated cellars or in lofts, a thermostatically controlled fan-heater is probably the best supplier of warmth, as the fan can be left

Above: This attractive Wardian growing case, with its automatic heating and lighting, doubles as a useful piece of furniture.

running continuously to circulate the air, with the heating element only switching in when the thermostat calls for heat.

Where the orchids are growing in a recess or alcove off the living area, it is unlikely that supplementary heating will be needed. Although the floor size of the chosen recess may not be large, this need not restrict your orchid-growing activities. In the window recess of a New York apartment, over 400 orchids were once grown in an area only 91cm (3ft) deep, 106cm (3.5ft) wide and 2.4 m (8ft) high! These orchids were not all miniature types or 'botanicals', but included paphiopedilums, phalaenopsis, oncidiums, cattleyas and even vandas. The owner-designed-and-built unit contained five shelves, the light fittings for one shelf being fixed to the underside of the shelf immediately above it. Apart from space an obvious advantage of this type of unit

BASIC EQUIPMENT AND TECHNIQUES

To make full and economic use of your greenhouse, it will be necessary to arrange the layout carefully so that all the different kinds of orchids in your collection receive the best possible environment. But there is more to layout than just the height of the staging, and whether or not shelves will be needed. Position of the heat source, and the various methods of heating available, number and position of ventilators, practical and efficient ways of supplying shade during summer months: these are just some of the questions to answer if the grower is to obtain maximum satisfaction from a greenhouse.

Equipment for a greenhouse falls into two different categories: basic necessities without which it will be difficult (though not impossible) to grow plants successfully, and extra equipment, or labour-saving gadgetry, that may either be installed when the greenhouse is erected, or introduced as the collection develops or circumstances change.

Heating systems

Heating a greenhouse is one of those topics that often evokes definite views, which are frequently based less on scientific knowledge of what is needed in terms of heat input, than on personal preferences. As always, it is best to consider the various options, and then decide which method is most suited to the particular situation.

The first priority required of a heating system is adequate heat output to maintain the desired temperature even when the outside temperature is below freezing point. At these times many heating systems will be unable to keep the greenhouse sufficiently warm, but providing such lapses are neither too severe nor occur too frequently, little harm will come to the plants.

Convenient methods of measuring heat include British Thermal Units, calories (4.2 BTUs per calorie) or watts (3.4 BTUs per watt), but to use three systems here will be needlessly complicated. Heat always flows from a high to a lower temperature, thus the warm air in a greenhouse will flow through the glass, brickwork and floor to the outside. The rate of flow depends upon the areas of each surface, the insulation properties of the various component materials and the difference in temperature. As it is generally accepted that the flow of heat through glass is twice the rate of flow through brickwork, it is immediately obvious that a glass-to-ground greenhouse will be more costly to heat than one with at least some brick walls.

If, for example, your greenhouse is the conventional 3.7 x 2.4m (12 x 8ft) size, with solid walls to 76cm (29in) in height, and the average required temperature 'lift' is 11°C (20°F) above that outside, the approximate heat input

needed to replace the lost heat would be 7,000 BTUs per hour. This could be supplied by 2kw of electricity, so a 2.5-3kw fan-heater is required in order to have some margin of safety. Alternatively, about 10.3m (34ft) of 10cm (4in) hot water pipe heated to 55.5°C (100°F) hotter than the required air temperature would suffice. A portable oil-burning greenhouse heater would use approximately 300ml (0.5pt) of paraffin (kerosene) per hour to achieve a similar result.

Thermostatic control

A second priority is that the heating system must be thermostatically controlled in order to achieve maximum economy — there is little point in supplying artificial heat once there is sufficient sun heat or radiation to maintain the desired temperature. Also during the night when there is unlikely to be any manual control of the heating system, a thermostat will do the job. Any system that cannot be controlled automatically, will probably prove more costly to run despite the apparent lower costs per unit.

Although they are not cheap to install, thermostatically controlled valves are the most efficient method of controlling the flow of hot water, where this system is adopted. Likewise with electric heating systems. Do not be satisfied with the type of thermostat that is commonly used in

Left: This greenhouse is heated by hot water circulating in a system of cast iron pipes beneath the staging. The boiler is controlled by a thermostat positioned just above head height in the centre of the greenhouse.

Above: By building a greenhouse on the roof of a garden room or conservatory, it is possible to grow almost any orchid successfully, particularly the sun-loving types, such as vandas.

domestic central heating systems, or worse still the very small thermostats that are frequently built in to electric fan-heaters. The degree of tolerance with these types of small thermostats, especially after several years use, may be as great as + or − 3°C (5°F), an unnecessarily high margin of error. It would be preferable — and certainly more economical — to incorporate into the system a rod-type thermostat that has much finer settings.

Thermostats are generally positioned at between two-thirds and three-quarters of the greenhouse height, i.e. approximately 1.8m (6ft) high in the average 2.4m (8ft) height-to-ridge house. The position should be such that there is a good flow of air around the thermostat, which should not be directly affected either by the warm air rising from the heating system or the direct rays of the sun. To counteract this latter tendency, some rod-type thermostats are encased in a perforated sleeve through which a gentle flow of air is circulated. In this way the thermostat becomes more sensitive to the air temperature within the greenhouse, and the heating system is more responsive.

To ensure that preselected temperatures are maintained throughout the night and day, a reliable thermometer should be used. If this is the manually reset minimum/maximum type, both the lowest and highest temperatures over a given period of time will be recorded. In this way the grower will easily discover whether or not the overnight temperature dropped below the preselected minimum. This thermometer should be hung at the approximate height of the plants, as it is in this area that the correct temperature is most critical. Even in the average smaller greenhouse of, say, 2.3-2.4m (7.5-8ft) high at the ridge, recent experiments have shown that, since cool air sinks and hot air rises, the temperature difference between floor level and the top third of the greenhouse can be as much as 5.5-6.5°C (10-12°F), and the installation of air circulating fans can only reduce this temperature gradient by about half.

Natural convection

Several growers have used natural convection to advantage, and by installing tiered staging have been able to grow plants preferring cool conditions, such as cymbidiums and odontoglossums, together with their warmth-loving cousins, the cattleyas and phalaenopsis. One internationally known and successful grower from the United States built his greenhouse at an angle of 45° on the roof of a south-facing garage. The staging consisted of narrow-stepped shelves from floor level up to the roof, with access by a central staircase. Plants from the high mountains of the Andes were housed on the lower shelves whilst the heat and sun-loving vandas occupied the uppermost areas. In this approximately 4.5-5.5m (15-18ft) high greenhouse, conditions ranged from a cool and shady 10°C (50°F) to a much brighter and less humid 21°C (70°F).

Hot-water systems

Given the choice, most growers would select a heating method using hot water circulated through a system of pipes. Although modern thinking decrees that 5cm (2in) pipes have a greater surface area and thus higher heat output than a single 10cm (4in) pipe, there is much in favour of the older 10cm pipe for the amateur. These larger pipes can be used in a location where electricity is not available, the water circulating around the pipes by natural convection, whereas a system using 5cm piping will need a water-circulating pump incorporated into the flow pipe. A second advantage is the reservoir of hot water stored within the pipes (obviously much greater in a larger pipe), thereby maintaining temperatures for a longer period of time after a boiler

Heating and Staging

By carefully planning the layout of staging and heating pipes, maximum use is made of the available area. To illustrate the possible alternatives available to the orchidist, both low and standard level walls are shown.

A rod-type thermostat is adequate for most greenhouses. It should be positioned where it will not be influenced either by the sun or the heating apparatus.

An upturned pot is a simple yet effective way of placing nearer to the glass those orchids that require more light.

For accurate readings, thermometers and/or hygrometers should be placed at plant level in a position where they are not affected by the sun, as this would produce spurious results.

Tiered staging has many advantages: it enables a greater number of plants to be accommodated, and also allows you to reach every plant more easily. The higher temperature, created by natural convection, on the upper shelf will permit warmer growing orchids to share the same greenhouse as cool growing ones.

Lower walls on at least one side will allow more light into the greenhouse. This is an advantage where some form of multitiered staging is in use, and will also benefit cymbidiums and the sun-loving vandaceous orchids.

Hot water pipes have an advantage over most other heating systems because they stay warm during temporary breakdowns. A large overall surface area of pipe will permit the boiler (water) temperature to be set lower, thus creating the gentle heat supply so desirous to good culture.

Water 'troughs' below the staging and/or at floor level should be filled with Lytag (perlite) or a similar water-retentive material, which, if kept moist, will help to maintain the correct relative humidity.

Although pathways should be sufficiently wide to allow room to work, they should not occupy too much of the greenhouse area. A hard, easily cleaned surface is preferable.

Useful for topping up the temperature when the boiler is not in use, fan heaters have the added advantage of providing a portable supply of either heat or moving air.

Boiler capacity should be sufficient to maintain required temperatures even during very cold weather. By placing the boiler inside the greenhouse, the boiler surface heat can be utilized. But in this position it is essential to use some form of external flue.

breakdown. Against these advantages must be measured the more rapid response of the small bore system, together with relative ease of greenhouse installation.

The water within the pipes may be heated by a variety of energy sources. Four fuels are generally available in most countries: oil, gas, electricity and solid fuel. Gas or oil-fired boilers can be completely automatically controlled and, apart from regular servicing by experienced engineers, are virtually maintenance free. As a fuel in the UK and the US, natural gas has the advantage of being readily available and favourably priced, but many rural areas are not supplied with gas and have thus found oil or propane gas good substitutes. Solid fuel

boilers are now better designed than previously, when cleaning at least two to three times each day coupled with adding extra fuel, made heating a greenhouse an onerous chore! A more sophisticated boiler, 'automatically' loaded with a modern solid fuel, has reduced this chore to once each day but can never eliminate daily attention. However, this type of boiler is independent of an electricity supply and, therefore, will maintain greenhouse temperatures during power failures. Electric immersion heaters may also be used but, although installation costs are low, the 6kw needed to maintain 10°C (50°F) in a 6 x 3.5m (20 x 12ft) greenhouse will mean high electricity costs!

Electric heating

An alternative method of electric heating that has been popular in the past for the smaller greenhouse, is tubular-heating. This system consists of metal tubes of various lengths, containing an electrically heated element rated at approximately 60watts per 30cm (1ft). Although this form of heating is relatively inexpensive to install and can be fully controlled by means of a thermostat, the surface temperature of the tubes becomes very high. This means that the areas near the heaters are frequently above the present temperature, whilst other areas within the greenhouse are too cool. Some form of air movement would certainly reduce this differential, but because of the localized

Right: Tiered staging is easy to construct. The three shelves offer varying degrees of light and temperature, permitting the cultivation of a high density of plants.

If it is not possible to have a potting shed, a portable potting bench can usually be accommodated in the greenhouse. This layout has the advantage of bringing plants and working area into close proximity, but a high degree of cleanliness should be observed.

Below Right: In this greenhouse, designed and built by an amateur orchidist, the high level shelf, curving path and hanging space for orchids mounted on rafts, have created both interest and extra space in this conventional 3m (10ft) wide greenhouse.

heat output tubular heaters have lost favour in recent years. As with all forms of direct heating that rely on an external power supply, the grower is at the mercy of breakdowns and other problems beyond his control, and without the reservoir of heat contained in a hot water pipe system, temperatures within the greenhouse drop very rapidly in the event of any interruption to the supply of heat.

Gas or oil-fired heaters

Gas or oil used as fuels in direct burners within the greenhouse need very careful handling. Close attention must be paid to the cleanliness and correct adjustment of the burner or wick, as a slight malfunction of the burner will result in the incomplete combustion of the gas or oil (usually paraffin or kerosene) with the subsequent build-up of fumes. But even a correctly operating greenhouse heater of this type will be harmful to plants unless adequate ventilation is supplied. A flame uses oxygen during burning, and the 'fumes' produced are, in fact, a build-up of carbon dioxide. Therefore, a supply of air to the burner is essential (some portable modern burners have a pipe leading to the outside for this purpose), but it is also necessary to have a small ventilator open near the floor of the greenhouse in order to allow the heavier carbon dioxide to escape. Gas and oil-fired convector heaters with a flue to extract the burnt gases are now available, and are preferable to the fully portable but flueless greenhouse heaters. These may have worked satisfactorily in the past

when greenhouses were less airtight, but greenhouses are now lined with polyurethane and have thus become virtually sealed units.

Hot air

The greenhouse may also be heated by circulating warm air either by means of a simple fan-heater or through a system of polyethylene tubes. With this latter method, a boiler (fueled by any of the energy sources previously mentioned) is used to heat a network of 'radiators'. Air is drawn through and over these heated surfaces, and then blown down one or more polyethylene tubes which have small holes at irregular intervals. Using this method, the warm air is very rapidly

circulated around the entire greenhouse area, with the added bonus of a buoyant atmosphere created by the moving air.

A less satisfactory result is obtained by using a fan-heater, as any plant directly in the current of hot air will experience some degree of dehydration. It is preferable to direct the hot air down the centre path or under the staging, ensuring that all plants in front of the heater are at least 2m away. Despite this potential hazard, electric fan-heaters have many points in their favour for use in small greenhouses. They are not too expensive initially, can be installed without expert attention (a 'power-point' or outlet is adequate for the supply of electricity), are thermostatically controlled, thus only produce heat when the temperature drops below the preselected level (especially sensitive if fitted with a rod-type thermostat), and the fan may be used independently during warmer weather to help maintain a better atmosphere within the house.

Staging

Staging is the term used to describe the tabling, or stage, on which plants are frequently stood. The amount and type of staging used depend upon the type of orchids being grown and the design of the greenhouse, ranging from its absence to a form of tiered shelving, with or without a moisture bench beneath. Cool-growing orchids, such as cymbidiums and laelias, grow more successfully on an open-mesh staging where there is a good circulation of fresh air around the pot and plant.

Moisture staging

With some orchids, such as odonto-glossums, it is advisable to install a moisture staging several inches below the shelves on which the plants stand.

This moisture staging consists of a solid base, such as sheets of corrugated iron, asbestos or similarly durable material covered with a moisture retentive substance. Many years ago the clinker from the solid fuel boilers was used, giving not only a retentive material, but also one that was disliked by slugs. Now that clinker is a product of the past, the modern equivalents are expanded light-weight aggregate, such as Lytag (perlite), crushed volcanic rock, pumice, or pea-gravel. Surplus water draining from the pots after each watering, or water that is applied directly to the moisture staging, ensures that the material remains moist. This moisture slowly evaporates, particularly in warm conditions, resulting in the desired humid atmosphere.

Another purpose of a solid staging, with or without the moisture retentive material, is to act as a 'baffle' to the heat rising from the hot water pipes. It is therefore more important to have this moisture staging in warm houses than in those where the temperature is allowed to drop to 10-12°C (50-52°F). In greenhouses built on a heavy or naturally wet soil, it will not be necessary to cover the solid staging as reasonably high humidity will be maintained.

In the cool house, cymbidiums prefer the more airy and slightly drier atmosphere of a greenhouse without a moisture staging, but in situations where it is then difficult to retain sufficient humidity, a layer of Lytag or similar material should be spread on the greenhouse floor beneath the staging. Alternatively, odontoglossums and many other genera are happiest where the air is moist and buoyant, and thus will benefit from the humid air rising off the moisture staging. Similarly, the warmer-growing paphiopedilums and

phalaenopsis like humid conditions; whilst vandas, most angraecoids and some cattleyas grow best in conditions of good air circulation and less constant humidity.

Ensuring drainage and stability

When a plant pot is standing on a flat surface, a watertight seal may be made between pot and bench during watering, with the result that the all-important drainage becomes ineffective. Also where slatted staging is used, the smaller sizes of pot can very easily be knocked over. Both of these potential problems will be prevented if the slatted or mesh staging is covered with a material such as the extruded polyurethane network (Netlon) sold as a windbreak. This means that the base of even the smallest plant pot is in partial contact with many surfaces, and as a result drainage cannot be impaired and stability is ensured.

This emphasis on fresh air being circulated not only around the plants but also the pots, may seem strange to the non-orchid grower. But remember that most orchids being grown in greenhouses are of epiphytic origin, and even the terrestrials have comparatively thick roots. Almost without exception, orchid roots will suffer if air is excluded from the compost, and even orchids cannot live for more than a year or two without roots! Thus if an abundance of air moves around the entire plant, the orchid will thrive and produce even better flowers.

For this reason, orchids have not proved too successful on a capillary bench where the supply of water to the plant is constant. The continuously wet conditions in the lower part of the pot tend to rot away roots in that area. Also the very open composts used by most growers do not lend themselves to capillary attraction.

Above: Circulation of air by means of an electric fan will greatly reduce the chance of hot or cold air pockets forming in parts of the greenhouse.

Above: Tiered staging enables you to see every plant clearly, and it is easy to see which are in need of water. Watering can be simplified with the help of a system that pumps water from the storage tank to a trigger-operated watering lance.

Experimental staging

Experiments are currently being carried out, on a small commercial scale, into the feasibility of growing orchids by hydro-culture. With this method, the staging is a shallow trough containing approximately 2.5cm (1in) of water, in which the basket or mesh-pot grown plants are stood. The water is continuously circulating, and on its journey is both oxygenated and adjusted to a predetermined chemical formula. Although a wide range of foliage and flowering plants are now grown successfully by this method, there are no great expectations that orchids—with their peculiar epiphytic root systems—will eventually be grown in this manner.

Ventilation

That orchids need an abundance of fresh air is not a new concept, and it was realized over a century ago that epiphytic plants need air as much as any other commodity in order to thrive. Yet as recently as 1964, it was stated in a book on orchid culture—when referring to the warm house—that 'the air must be admitted only with the greatest care and in small quantities'. Whilst it is true that it would be unwise to open the ventilators into a cold prevailing wind, it is equally true to state that fresh air should be admitted liberally on every possible occasion. To achieve this, an efficient system of ventilators is required. The smaller the greenhouse, the more critical are the size, position and operation of the ventilating system. Regrettably, it is in this type of greenhouse that manufacturers almost seem to forget ventilation, relying on a gullible purchaser to modify the ventilators later.

The average standard greenhouse of, say, 9.3m² (100ft²) floor area, is often fitted with just two roof ventilators plus one at staging height in each side wall. In almost all circumstances, these are not only of inadequate size, but are also wrongly positioned! To achieve good air flow through the greenhouse, it is necessary to be able to admit air at floor level (or at least from below staging level). There are several ways of doing this, but only two basic methods.

Box ventilators

Most plant houses have solid walls up to staging height—approximately 84cm (33in) from floor level—giving ample opportunity to fit some form of box ventilator. It is normal to install these when building the brick base, as the standard size of these ventilators is 61cm (24in) long x 15cm (6in) high. Box ventilators are fitted either with a door which hinges open and shut by a system of internally operated ropes and pulleys, or with two manually adjustable sliding doors which are fitted to the outside of the greenhouse wall. Where unheated frames are built as 'lean-tos' on the greenhouse base wall, the ventilator doors should be fitted to the inside wall. During very cold weather, the box ventilators opening into the cold frames can be left open—thus giving an element of frost protection to the plants growing within the frames. As with all ventilators, at least one is needed on each side wall, in order to avoid opening any ventilator into the wind.

With wooden base greenhouses low-level ventilators can be fitted easily at any time: simply cut a hole to the required size as low as possible in the base wall, and fit a covering door, slightly larger than the hole, to slide on runners over the aperture when ventilation is not needed.

Ventilation and Shading

Ventilation and shading are the main methods by which the temperature inside the greenhouse can be prevented from rising too high during hot weather. Preferably, both should be completely flexible and adjustable, and it is possible to have most systems automatically controlled.

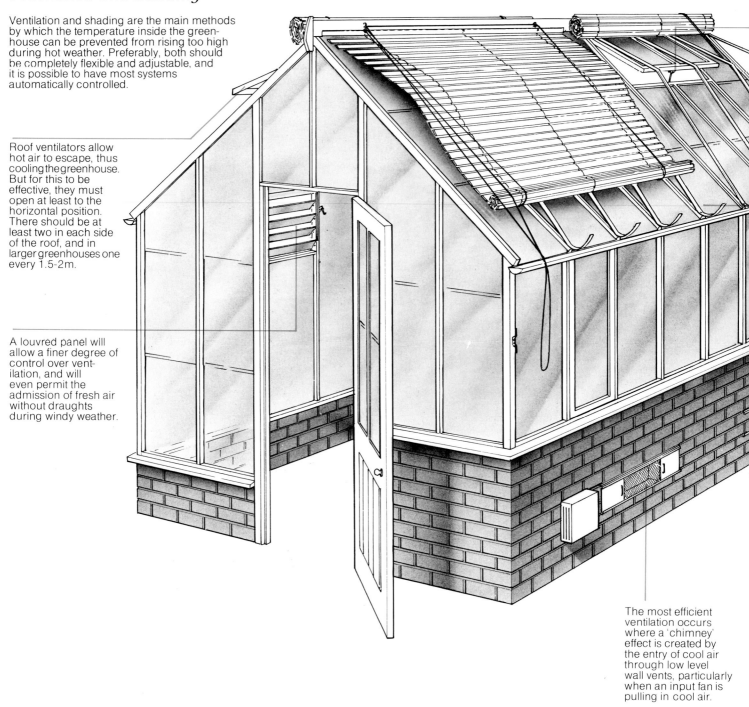

Roof ventilators allow hot air to escape, thus cooling the greenhouse. But for this to be effective, they must open at least to the horizontal position. There should be at least two in each side of the roof, and in larger greenhouses one every 1.5-2m.

A louvred panel will allow a finer degree of control over ventilation, and will even permit the admission of fresh air without draughts during windy weather.

The most efficient ventilation occurs where a 'chimney' effect is created by the entry of cool air through low level wall vents, particularly when an input fan is pulling in cool air.

Louvred panel ventilators

With glass-to-ground greenhouses, a different technique of ventilation is needed. Box ventilators would obviously be impractical in a glass wall, and instead a 'louvred panel' can be fitted in place of one or more of the panes of glass. The simple metal framework and specially toughened glass used in the construction of these louvres are obtained from most hardware stores, timber yards, builders' or horticultural merchants. When operated, the framework holding the pieces of glass turns on a centre pivot from vertical to horizontal. Depending upon the ventilation required, the louvre will remain in any position from completely open to nearly closed and, when absolutely closed, will remain locked in this position. Louvres give finer control of the amount of air admitted, and may even be opened slightly on the windward side of the greenhouse without harming the plants.

Roof ventilators

Greenhouses of yesteryear were frequently fitted with roof ventilators running the entire length of each side of the ridge. Undoubtedly this gave almost perfect control of the ventilation as one—or occasionally both—ventilator could be opened very slightly, even during inclement weather. Economics of modern times dictate that this type of ventilator is no longer a viable proposition, but even relatively small greenhouses should have at least three roof ventilators, two on the north-facing or leeward roof and one on the opposite side.

In larger greenhouses there should be at least one roof vent every 1.5m (5ft), alternating from north to south, as anything less will encourage the formation or 'still' areas within the greenhouse. Tests have shown that until a roof ventilator is approaching the horizontal position, very little hot air will escape; therefore, it is important to ensure that all ventilators in the roof are able to open beyond this critical stage.

Unsuitable ventilators

About the only place where plants growing on the staging do not need a ventilator is at staging level, yet most standard greenhouses—both glass-to-ground and plant houses—have ventilators fitted in this position. If these ventilators are open, the local humidity around the orchids will become far too low, and where this condition is prolonged the plants may become dehydrated, with the inevitable result of reduced growth. Therefore, any side ventilators are best permanently secured in the closed position!

An inexpensive device for automatically operating roof ventilators will remove one headache for the hobbyist orchid grower. Independent of electricity, these autovents can be pre-set to function when the desired temperature is reached.

Slatted roller blinds should be held clear of the glass on metal runners. This allows the roof vents to open correctly, and also creates a blanket of cool air between the glass and blind, so helping to maintain the correct greenhouse temperature.

Below: The cavity created by the wall vents should be covered with a fine mesh—perforated zinc is best—to exclude pests, such as bees or mice, which would wreak havoc inside the greenhouse.

Above: The filtered light provided by slatted blinds is ideal for a wide range of orchids. Used in conjunction with tiered staging, masdevallias can be grown in the extra shade created by the summer foliage of lycastes.

Right: Louvred panel ventilators are especially useful during cool weather, as they admit only small amounts of fresh air without draughts.

Extractor (exhaust) fans

In warmer climates, many greenhouses are ventilated, or cooled, by means of a large extractor fan fitted in one end of the greenhouse and louvred or open panels in the other. The fan is controlled by a thermostat, and comes into operation when the greenhouse temperature exceeds a preset level.

One of the drawbacks of this system is the rapid reduction in the atmospheric moisture. Moving air—especially *warm* moving air—takes moisture from any source, including plants. Even plants growing in a marsh will flag on a very hot windy day, and although, if temporary, this dehydration will not harm the plant, it must be compensated for (usually at night when temperatures cool naturally).

Warm air is capable of holding more moisture than cool air, and thus the oft-used term 'humidity' should more correctly be called 'relative humidity', the amount of moisture in the air being expressed as a percentage. For example, if the relative humidity of the air is 100 percent at 10°C (50°F) in the evening, during the day at a temperature of 26.7°C (80°F), the same *amount* of moisture may represent only 35 percent of the moisture the air is capable of holding at that temperature; therefore, the *relative* humidity is 35 percent, and plants will lose water to the atmosphere.

Where low relative humidity is a chronic problem it is advisable to install a 'wet-pad' in front of the louvred panel. (Fuller details of this method are given on page 84.)

It is possible to use a modified extraction system for ventilation in smaller greenhouses, and many amateur growers successfully use this as their sole method. A louvred panel, as already described, fitted to one end of the greenhouse, coupled with an extract/intake fan—preferably not less than 41cm (16in) in width—placed diagonally opposite, will prove adequate. The advantage of using a two-way fan is that moist night air, which is particularly advantageous during hot weather, may be drawn into the greenhouse.

Shading

One of the purposes of ventilation is to control excessively high temperatures, but to achieve the desired results it is usually necessary to also have some form of shading on the greenhouse during the hottest months, except when certain colours of orchids are in flower, particularly yellows and greens, as high light intensity may tarnish the blooms. The purpose of shading is not to reduce the light but to limit high temperatures. The best way to do this is to prevent the heat of the sun reaching the glass in the first instance, as once the outside of the glass becomes hot, this heat will pass through to the cooler interior of the greenhouse until the temperatures inside and outside the greenhouse are similar, the reverse problem to our heat retention during winter.

It will immediately be obvious that any form of interior shading—and several types are available specifically for this purpose—will be far less effective in controlling high temperatures than all forms of shading applied to the outside of the greenhouse. Indeed, in the small house, interior shading is almost wholly ineffective, and should therefore be avoided.

Painting

There are many methods of shading a greenhouse from the outside, and in many ways the depth of one's pocket is the limiting factor. The simplest method is to apply a coat or coats of 'paint' directly to the glass, either with a brush or through a coarse spray. Originally the material used was made from quick-lime and called a lime-wash, but over the years many proprietary brands have appeared.

Amongst others there is a green powder that must be mixed with hot water and applied immediately. This adheres to the glass very well, which is an advantage during summer storms, but less desirable in the autumn when it defies all but the most vigorous attempts at removal. A newer substance, white and—it is claimed —resistant to the heaviest rains, yet removable with a dry cloth when desired, has been used by many growers with moderate success. A point to remember when using paint shading to limit excessive temperature is that dark surfaces absorb and white surfaces reflect heat: a factor used to good advantage by people living in areas with extremes of temperature. It should also be remembered that to obtain good coverage, the glass should be clean and dry before the paint is applied.

Roller blinds

An equally proven but more effective method of shading is provided by lath roller blinds. These blinds are constructed from approximately 25mm x 4.5mm (1in x 0.2in) laths cut to the required length, and joined by simple clips. Cedar wood should preferably be used, and the clips manufactured from copper to give durability; less expensive materials are occasionally used. The clips fix the laths approximately 13mm (0.5in) apart, thus the sun moving over the greenhouse casts shadow and light alternately. The blinds can either be manually operated and open horizontally along the greenhouse, or raised and lowered vertically on the greenhouse roof using a system of ropes and pulleys. The advantage of blinds over

paint is mainly one of adaptability: on dull, sunless days the blinds can be rolled back—or up—so that the plants have the benefit of all available light. Similarly, the blinds may be removed each evening. The disadvantage is, of course, one of cost, but once the blinds are made—which is not difficult as all the components are readily available—they should last for many years. If the blind is designed to cover the entire roof, provision to open the roof ventilators by 'cut-out' sections in the blind should be made.

Shading clear of the glass

Both paint and roller blinds have one major fault; they are, to a greater or lesser extent, in direct contact with the glass and thus some of the heat will be transmitted into the greenhouse. Ideally, the shading material should be some

Above: There are many brands of greenhouse shading that may be painted on to the exterior of the glass. As light colours reflect the sun's rays, white shading is more effective at reducing the temperature of the glass, and thus the internal greenhouse temperature.

15-23cm (6-9in) above the glass in order to allow a good circulation of air which will assist in the reduction of temperature. This could be achieved by rolling the horizontal blinds on two or three runners fixed horizontally across the glazing bars, or preferably by keeping the vertical blinds on a metal framework well clear of the glass. This is not an inexpensive method but is highly effective.

Using this method of blinds with ropes and pulleys, it is possible to raise and lower the blinds automatically by means of a photoelectric cell. It is also possible in larger, commercial greenhouses to operate

Above: Greenhouse shading provided by slatted roller blinds, held well above the glass on metal runners, and controlled either by photo-electric cells that will activate the winding gear when the light intensity drops, or time switches (right) that will operate the blinds at a predetermined time.

internal blinds both by thermostat and photoelectric cell, with the shading being brought into position when either the light becomes too strong or the temperature too high. And perhaps the ultimate in automatic shading is provided by a form of glass that becomes translucent as the light intensity increases! Some may feel that this is taking one's hobby to extremes, and the provision of such lavish equipment is certainly not necessary in order to grow orchids successfully. But there are many useful gadgets that will be of great help in taking the chores out of greenhouse gardening.

SUPPLEMENTARY EQUIPMENT AND TECHNIQUES

The provision of extra equipment or 'gadgets' in an amateur's greenhouse is open to debate. It could be argued that a hobbyist chose to grow orchids as a means of relaxation, a way of returning to a more basic activity—the growing of plants—in an increasingly automated world. If this is the case, then 'automating' the greenhouse would obviously hinder this process.

Yet despite the large scale installation of time-saving equipment in both industry and commerce, most people seem to have less time than previously in which to indulge their hobbies. Thus, if by taking care of some of the daily routine chores, labour-saving gadgetry enables someone, otherwise unable, to grow orchids, then this is beneficial to the popularity of orchids and to potential orchid growers.

There are several small pieces of equipment available that will take the 'muscle' out of greenhouse culture, and the resulting decrease in required effort will enable partially disabled people or those who are no longer in their first flush of youth, to grow orchids successfully. Also of significance are the various aids which cut down the cost of growing orchids, and as the supply of winter heat is the largest single item of continual expense, any method of conserving heat is well worth considering.

Insulation

Although this subject does not specifically fall into the category of gadgets or even equipment, there are few orchid houses situated in the cooler, temperate areas of the world that do not have at least some degree of insulation. It is generally accepted that by raising the minimum night temperature by 2.7°C (5°F), ie from 10°-12.7°C (50°-55°F), the cost of heating is doubled. However, even a simple but efficient form of double glazing will save anything from 4°-5.5°C (8°-10°F), making it possible to reduce the heat input, and thus the cost, yet maintain existing minimum temperatures. Alternatively, the greenhouse can be transformed from a cool to an intermediate growing area without increasing the heating costs.

Double glazing

The major area of any greenhouse is obviously the glass, which is also the material with the greatest heat loss. Much of this loss can be prevented simply by lining the roof and walls of the greenhouse *completely* with a polyethylene skin. As with all double glazing systems, it is not the two surfaces—be they glass, polyethylene or acrylic—that prevent the heat from passing through to the outside, but the air trapped between them. As moving air has little insulative value, it is important that the air remains still. This can be achieved by ensuring that the seal

between the ridge bar and the polyethylene is as air tight as possible. In a wooden greenhouse it is comparatively easy to fix the polyethylene lining by means of 25mm (1in) wooden laths nailed along the ridge bar, stretching the polyethylene tightly down the roof before fixing to the glazing bars, again by using wooden laths. With metal-framed greenhouses it is more difficult, despite the availability of patent clips designed to assist the fixing of a lining. But help is at hand: some greenhouses are now produced with an inner channel on the glazing bars into which the polyethylene is fixed by means of a rubber grummet — a point well worth looking for when purchasing a new greenhouse. All folds and creases in the lining material should be straightened out before fixing, as any that remain will become a source of condensation, which drips onto the plants below.

From the eaves, the polyethylene should be continued down the side walls until below the staging level or, with a glass-to-ground greenhouse, completely to floor level. As polyethylene is easily obtainable in widths up to 4 m (13ft), it should be possible to line the roof and side walls of small greenhouses with only one piece; but where a joint is necessary, for instance when lining to floor level, a generous overlap should be allowed. The gap between outer glass and inner lining material should be at least 38-50mm (1.5-2in) as a smaller air space has a lower insulation factor, and there is a possible danger of the two surfaces touching and thus eliminating any insulatory effect. So that fresh air may be admitted on all favourable occasions, roof ventilators and those below the staging should be lined separately, cutting out the relevant areas in the main lining. Any outer doors—often neglected when a greenhouse is lined—should be similarly treated, or better still, a polyethylene curtain or 'second door' made to act as a windbreak when the outer door is opened.

Materials available

Some growers use a very thin grade of polyethylene which has to be replaced annually, or at the most every two years, whilst others prefer a thicker grade that is sufficiently tough to last five to eight years before deteriorating. Both methods have their advantages but where the greenhouse is relatively small, with not more 14m² (150sq ft) floor area, for example, and the quantity of plants to be moved is not too great, it is probably best to install the lining each autumn and to remove it late in the following spring. The principal advantages with this method are that the greenhouse is thoroughly cleaned at least twice a year, and this provides the opportunity to handle the orchids, which is the ideal way to spot and deal with potential trouble before it

Above: To eliminate the condensation that could occur during cold weather, the polyethylene lining should be stretched tightly. In a wooden greenhouse, 2.5cm (1in) laths are ideal for holding the lining permanently in position.

develops into anything too serious. Thus the installation and removal of a lining material provide at least two annual stimuli for necessary action.

In larger greenhouses, or where specific designs make lining a tedious and time-consuming job, it is preferable to use a more permanent material. A heavier grade of polyethylene has the advantage of being fairly tough and thus less likely to tear during installation or subsequent use. It will also retain its 'elasticity' for

several years, making it possible to wash off the accumulated dust and algae at regular intervals. A similar but superior material that will last almost indefinitely is acrylic sheeting, available from most hardware stores and builders' suppliers. This flat, clear material may be cut with either a sharp knife or a fine-toothed saw, to fit the required shape and size, and is held in place by laths or battens screwed to the glazing bars. Acrylic material is far tougher than polyethylene, and will take most normal wear without deteriorating. It will also remain clear—polyethylene discolours and becomes translucent after a few years—and is easily cleaned.

The ultimate in glasshouse insulation is provided by specially constructed double-skin glass units, hermetically sealed for life-long efficiency. However, not only are the units themselves extremely costly, but the greenhouse structure would need to be strengthened considerably in order to withstand the additional weight. This method of insulation, super-efficient though it undoubtedly is, can therefore be disregarded by most greenhouse owners.

The one problem frequently encountered with polyethylene-lined greenhouses is excessive condensation, particularly during prolonged cold weather when it is not possible to ventilate. Where the lining has been installed in such a way that folds and creases are almost non-existent, and the pitch of the roof is reasonably steep—35° or more, for example—this condensation will run down the polyethylene to the staging or floor without harming the plants. But where the greenhouse design renders this impossible, it is worth considering fixing the polyethylene as an *outer* skin; with this method internal condensation is minimal.

Installation of an outer polyethylene 'tent' is straightforward. Firstly, fix one end of the polyethylene to the outside of the wall or floor plate (whichever is applicable), then unroll the polyethylene over the top of the greenhouse and fix to the corresponding position on the opposite side. The ends can be dealt with separately. Apart from the lack of condensation, this method has several other advantages: the outer surface of a greenhouse is considerably less cluttered than the internal one, where various fitments have to be 'negotiated' by the lining, and, of course, the plants are not disturbed. Furthermore, the tent is very easily removed when warmer weather returns. Where this method has been successfully used for several years, negligible problems have been caused even by gale-force winds. The only drawback would seem to be the removal of the motivation to thoroughly clean the greenhouse interior.

When using a portable flueless oil or gas heater in a greenhouse that has been lined completely, it is imperative to make provision for adequate ventilation. A supply of air to the burner, coupled with a low-level vent through which the fumes may escape, is even more important where the lining renders the greenhouse almost a sealed unit.

Other areas of heat loss
Having taken great care to ensure a perfect lining within the greenhouse, it should not be forgotten that the glass will also need periodic attention, especially after winter gales. Before lining greenhouses became popular, even the smallest crack in the glass was immediately obvious. Even if all seems well, a regular inspection of the roof glass may prevent serious damage.

Many growers tend to forget that heat is also escaping—albeit at a slower rate—through the base walls and floor. In the conventional greenhouse that has some form of path and, usually, an earth floor covered with shingle or similar material, it is difficult, if not impossible, to provide effective insulation. But as the amounts of heat loss involved are not great, it is one of the least important areas to insulate.

In fact, it is only realistic where a greenhouse has been built on a concrete raft that incorporates a polyethylene damp-proof course about 25mm (1in) below the surface. A 13 or 19mm (0.5-0.75in) thick sheet of polystyrene positioned immediately below the damp-proof course should prevent some of the heat loss down through the floor. However, most growers prefer some form of earth floor through which excess water may drain, yet from which some humidity will rise.

Loss of heat through the basewalls of a greenhouse is another area often overlooked. Any solid wall will absorb heat from the inside of the greenhouse and pass it through to the cooler outside. Obviously, if the walls are constructed from 13mm (0.5in) thick match-boarding, there will be a greater heat loss than through a 23cm (9in) solid brick wall, but all non-insulated walls are a potential source of unnecessary expense. This expense could be reduced by fixing sheets of 13mm (0.5in) thick polystyrene to the inside surface of the greenhouse walls, or by constructing an interior false wall,

Above: An outer skin of polyethylene is easier to install and remove than an internal lining, and largely eliminates condensation.

after which the resulting cavity is fitted with any modern insulating material. A similar solution may be reached with an existing 35.5cm (14in) cavity wall, where the processes used for dwelling house insulation would be suitable. If building a new greenhouse, a 23cm (9in) building block is now on the market. This has a built-in 15.2cm (6in) deep cavity which, if filled with suitable material, will provide excellent insulation.

Establishing air circulation
These efforts to retain warmth within the greenhouse have, if functioning correctly, reduced the amount of natural air movement that was often synonymous with many of the draughty greenhouses of the 1950s. The post-war demand for greenhouses that were suitable for the average working man sometimes resulted in a rash of badly constructed greenhouses that within a few months were in need of major reinforcement. Plants will not thrive

if placed in a draughty position, yet conversely most plants like moving air around them. By studying the natural habitats of orchids, it has become increasingly clear that fresh air is nearly always in evidence—frequently in such quantity that their foliage and flowers are perpetually moving.

In temperate areas of the world, for many weeks or even months of the year, weather conditions make it impractical to open the ventilators. When these conditions prevail, growers are often advised to keep the greenhouse 'quiet' by barely maintaining the minimum temperature and only watering the plants sufficiently to prevent dehydration. This is fine for short periods, but any length of time under these conditions will certainly limit the plants' growth rate. Yet if surplus water is allowed to remain on the surface of either the plants or the greenhouse floor and staging when temperatures fall to their minimum or below, the atmosphere becomes dank and there is a real danger of fungal infection. Moving air would reduce this risk, but even if it were possible to open the ventilators it is

Above: In a small greenhouse, an oscillating fan used to circulate the air is ideal for maintaining a buoyant atmosphere.

Right: A small fan fixed at plant level will provide localized air movement for those orchids intolerant of stale conditions.

unlikely that the air within the greenhouse would move sufficiently to improve the situation significantly. It is now generally accepted that the modern greenhouse is incomplete without one or two fans that frequently run continuously. Various types are available to suit specific requirements.

The best method of moving the air within the greenhouse is to use an oscillating fan, which turns automatically back and forth through an angle of 180°. Most have three speed settings that may be adjusted to suit both the total greenhouse area and the prevailing conditions, and will give a buoyant atmosphere together with a more even temperature throughout the house. If more vigorous air movement is required by some plants—many high altitude South American genera such as *Odontoglossum* and *Masdevallia* seem to thrive in a 'gale'—these can be placed nearest to the fan where obviously the air movement is more brisk. Alternatively, a secondary smaller fan could be placed adjacent to this particular group of plants, thus giving localized 'mountain' conditions

for those that cannot tolerate any degree of stagnation.

The advantages of vigorously moving air are not, however, limited to the winter months when the heating system is operating and the ventilators have to remain closed. In warmer climates and during summer in temperate areas, it is often necessary to shade too heavily in order to prevent sun-scorch on the foliage. But in the wild, and in cultivation in tropical or equatorial regions, many orchids are exposed to almost full summer sun without burning. Here the air moving over the surface of the leaf takes off excess heat, and, of course, there is no layer of glass to accentuate the sun's heat. Therefore, a brisk movement of air over the plants within a greenhouse will reduce the risk of sun-scorch, with the result that more of the all important light can be admitted to the plants. Maintaining a buoyant atmosphere during the hottest of summer days is not easy. The air movement over the plants may not be sufficient and an additional fan positioned near a low-level ventilator would be of great help. By

pulling in fresh, cool air from near ground level on the shadier (north or east) side of the greenhouse, it is even possible with only light shading to maintain temperatures a few degrees below the temperature outside.

Maintaining a moist atmosphere

The maintenance of vigorous air movement, particularly where the ventilators are much in use, may result in a slight loss of humidity.

If water is sprayed around and beneath the plants and over the entire floor area, the percentage of moisture in the air will increase, thereby reducing the amount of water the plant needs to absorb through its root system. There are various methods of supplying this requirement, from the basic to a completely automated system which is equally suited to the amateur's small greenhouse as to large commercial nurseries.

Undoubtedly a hosepipe is still the most reliable method of creating humidity within the confines of a greenhouse. By

and large, this system does not break down, does not rely on a supply of electricity or the reliability of switches and controls. But its major weakness is the assumption that someone is available with the necessary time and enthusiasm to carry this out at least once daily, and frequently more often. It may be easy merely to saturate the floor of the greenhouse periodically, but there may be times when this is not possible.

In fact, the maintenance of atmospheric humidity when you are away for any length of time is probably one area where some degree of automation is called for. The simplest method is to remove a shallow layer of the soil from beneath the staging, and line the area with polyethylene, thus creating a broad but shallow trough

which can then be filled with shingle or, preferably, Lytag (or perlite). Fill the trough with water, not higher than 2.5-5cm (1-2in) below the level of the aggregate, and maintain the water level either by a drip-feed from a suitably placed header tank, or by topping-up by hand every three or four days. This method will not give a perfect result, but will prevent the atmosphere in the greenhouse from becoming excessively arid.

Another simple and more effective method, again independent of power supply, is provided by a length of flat, 3-section perforated hose fixed to the underside of the ridge board. This type of hose is normally used to provide a fine, drenching mist to seedbeds in the open garden, or similar areas needing careful but

thorough irrigation. Fix the hose with the holes downwards along the entire length of the ridge board, and turn on the tap just enough to obtain a steady drip through the perforations. If higher relative humidity is required, extra holes could be made in the hose. Although this method may sound unreliable, it has worked satisfactorily in at least one amateur grower's greenhouse for several years, even for a week to 10 days during his absence. One modification has been the installation of a short polyethylene curtain on either side of the hose, to prevent the water dripping onto plants nearest the centre path.

Both these methods, although reliable, have their limitations, as the quantity of moisture within the greenhouse will

Left: Interchangeable nozzles for standard watering lances are ideal for spraying orchids mounted on rafts or with aerial roots. Using this method, high level shelves can be reached effortlessly.

Above: Spray nozzles fixed into a pipeline below the staging can be either hand controlled or fully automatic. The jet is adjustable from a coarse spray to fine mist, and will cover an area of approximately 1.5m².

remain constant regardless of temperature and other factors. Thus, during very hot daytime conditions, the relative humidity may fall to less than 40 percent; conversely when night temperatures become low and the humidity is naturally higher, saturation point of 100 percent relative humidity may result.

The only alternative to using a hosepipe is is install some form of spray nozzle controlled through an electrically operated valve and humidistat, which is able to sense the quantity of moisture in the atmosphere (much as a thermostat senses temperature). If the relative humidity falls below the desired preset level, the humidistat opens the valve, which in turn operates the spray nozzles until the humidity reaches the correct

level, when the humidistat closes the valve. Alternatively, the system may be controlled by a time-clock, which opens the valve for, say, five minutes every hour; again, however, there is the risk of excessive humidity during cool conditions, and possibly inadequate atmospheric moisture—despite the adjustable spraying interval—on hot days.

Many different spray nozzles are available, from inexpensive plastic to a solid brass system in which the spray can be finely adjusted from coarse droplets to a fine mist. Similarly, the plumbing can be plastic hose using screwclips to seal the joints. But once again you get what you pay for! The water within a mains connected spray line is under mains pressure, and thus when the sprays are not operating

all joints must be capable of withstanding this pressure. In practice, there will be a weak spot, and within a few weeks the hoseline will split completely. For almost total reliability, use 15mm (0.5in) copper piping and compression fittings for all the joints. These fittings eliminate the need to use solder, as they can be tightened with a spanner.

By suspending the pipework below the staging, and having a spray nozzle about every 1.2m (4 ft) on either side of a central path, you can cover the whole greenhouse area. Although a fully automated humidity system may seem an unnecessary extravagance, it will give many years of reliable service and take at least one worry out of orchid growing when you are temporarily absent.

Labour-free watering

The automated humidity system will also provide labour-free watering of your plants. A pipeline, complete with the required number of spray nozzles, can be suspended from the glazing bars over the plants, and connected to the water supply through a humidistat or time-clock controlled valve or, preferably, direct to the tap for manual control.

The main disadvantage of this system for the amateur growing a very mixed collection, is that several orchids will always be flowering, and the blooms will not appreciate being saturated at regular intervals. But where a large number of similar plants are growing together in the same-sized pots, this system works extremely well. Similar criteria apply where a system of individual water pipes to each pot, radiating from a central supply line, is adopted. All automated watering depends upon every plant having the same water requirement, and all plant pots drying out at the same rate, which is obviously not applicable to most mixed orchid collections.

So how can the owner of such a collection take the effort and time out of watering? Fortunately, a reasonably priced method is available, and involves using a watering lance and a small, submersible electric water pump. Watering lances have a trigger control on the handle, and interchangeable heads from straight jet to fine spray. The submersible pump need not be large—one similar to that used for small garden fountains would

suffice—providing it has a maximum 'head' of not less than the height of your greenhouse. Anything less will not be sufficiently powerful to reach those plants on the high shelves. A suitable length of hosepipe connects the pump outlet to the watering lance, and by placing the pump in the nearest water tank, and connecting the lead to a convenient power point, an effortless and fully portable watering method has been installed, at little cost. One word of warning, however: do not leave the pump switched on for long periods without opening the valve on the watering lance, or back pressure may burn out the pump. More sophisticated—and hence considerably more expensive—electric water pumps have an on/off solenoid valve controlled by the water pressure, which turns off the pump when the lance valve is closed.

Despite the apparently complicated gadgetry involved with watering aids, it is very easy to install a basic pump/watering lance system that is more than adequate for even quite large collections.

For those who prefer the good old-fashioned watering can, there is again a choice. Discard any that have a short or wide spout; it is impossible to reach plants at the back of the staging with this type of can, and the wide spout will mean poor control of the water flow, with the

Below: An inexpensive electric water pump similar to those used in small garden fountains, connected through a length of hose from the tank to a watering lance, will be sufficiently powerful for most greenhouses.

inevitable washing-out of many smaller plants. Better quality watering cans have long slim outlets, and in addition to coarse and fine roses, an extension spout, even slimmer than the main one and usually curved downwards at the end, will enable those awkwardly placed plants to be watered with ease, without washing half the compost out of the pot.

Controlling pests

Pest control is another field in which gadgets have long been in use. In the early nineteenth century, growers used manually operated bellows on a 'horticultural vaporizer' in order to pump the insecticide (even at this time nicotine was recognized as an effective killer of most pests) into the greenhouse. Various forms of fumigating apparatus, often complicated, appeared at frequent intervals, and although most have now passed into history, at least one—Richard's Patent Fumigator—first available in 1925, is still in regular and frequent use in the UK today. It consists of a simple perforated metal cone, open at both ends, with a shallow saucer placed on top. The required amount of insecticide or fungicide is poured into the saucer, after which a small spirit lamp inside the metal cone is lit. This heats the chemical, which then vaporizes into the atmosphere to the detriment of the offending pest.

A modern version of this fumigator has been available for some years, but requires a supply of electricity. These vaporizing lamps, generally using crystals of the

chemicals that control most pests and diseases, are comprised of a cup-shaped metal unit into which a heat-resistant glass beaker containing the relevant chemical is placed. A thermostatically controlled heating element in the unit melts (where appropriate) and vaporizes the chemical into the atmosphere. The main advantages of this electric fumigator over the older but equally effective spirit lamp model, are cleanliness in operation and thermostatically controlled supply of heat to the fumigant.

Another electric fumigator, used for the rapid dispersal of insecticidal or fungicidal smoke within the greenhouse, has been available for several years. Designed on the lines of a hand-held hair dryer, a cartridge of chemically impregnated cardboard is placed in the nozzle of the unit, and hot air blown through the cartridge vaporizes the chemical into a smoke, which is then blown round the greenhouse.

Many pesticides are also available in liquid or powder form, the latter often in puffer packs ready for immediate use. Liquids should be diluted with the appropriate amount of water and, sometimes, soft soap (to act as a 'spreader'), and applied with a simple syringe or pressure sprayer.

Obviously when handling or using potentially dangerous chemicals, you must observe certain precautions for your own and your plants' safety. These, together with other general guidelines for the successful culture of your orchids, will be discussed in following pages.

Above and Below: Fumigation is best carried out on warm evenings so that the greenhouse can remain closed all night and allow the insecticide to take effect. But ventilate the greenhouse well the next morning. Electrically operated fumigators (above) can be used to control most insect pests and fungal diseases, but take care that plants are not directly above the unit during operation. Below: By blowing hot air through an impregnated cardboard cartridge, this hand-held fumigator fills the greenhouse with insecticidal smoke.

HOW TO GROW ORCHIDS

Advice on the culture of any plant is always extremely difficult to offer: there are so many contributing factors to be taken into account, and no two growers will put the same interpretation on results. There are no hard and fast rules by which to abide, and no scientific or mathematical formulae that will ensure successful culture. Instead, various suggestions based on practical experience can be made in the hope that understanding an orchid's basic requirements will at least point the unsure grower in the right direction.

Successful cultivation of any group of plants depends upon the correct balance of the various aspects of culture, and is as important with orchids as any hardy garden plant. Before starting to grow a plant, a knowledge of its natural environment is helpful. For example, the area and altitude at which a particular species grows, and thus the temperature it enjoys; how far it is subjected to seasonal droughts (interpreted in cultivation by 'resting' the plant) or monsoon periods; or whether it revels in full sunshine, or requires at least partial shade. When dealing with a group of plants so widely distributed as orchids, coming as they do from almost every conceivable location or ecological niche, a knowledge of this natural environment is even more critical.

Temperature categories

It would be impossible to replicate exactly these presumably ideal conditions for every different species or genus growing in most amateurs' orchid collections. Almost all orchids are extremely resilient, and have proved very adaptable to 'foreign' conditions.

Basically, orchids can be divided into three main temperature categories: warm, ie needing a minimum night temperature of 15.5°C (60°F), intermediate, slightly cooler at 13°C (55°F), and cool, where the minimum night temperature may be allowed to fall to around 10°C (50°F). Obviously, different orchids prefer different temperatures, and it will be found that many artificial microclimates exist within the confines of any greenhouse. Areas nearest the heating pipes will naturally be slightly warmer and less moist than those not directly affected by heating apparatus, even when an air-circulating fan is in operation. Conversely, any plants positioned near the door must be tolerant of the slightly lower temperatures that will inevitably occur at frequent intervals.

Making the most of
your greenhouse

The majority of amateur growers have but one greenhouse in which to grow their frequently mixed collections, and usually this greenhouse is heated only to maintain a minimum temperature of 10 to 12°C (50°-54°F). In this case only

orchids in the 'cool' category are generally recommended. Yet warmer areas do exist within such greenhouses, and by finding these and incorporating a high-level shelf, it is possible to grow a much wider range of genera. Many of the South American Laeliinae, such as *Cattleya, Brassavola* and *Laelia,* would appreciate the slightly warmer and less humid conditions obtainable on a shelf. Their leathery leaves and stout pseudobulbs would also benefit from the extra light and, providing the temperature does not fall below 12°C (54°F), these normally intermediate species will produce their flamboyant blooms in a cool house.

From this it could be deduced that greenhouses should be divided vertically to obtain the various temperature differentials, and certainly more effective use could be made of the natural convection within most greenhouses. But *physical* horizontal divisions would not only prevent heat from rising, and thus defeat the advantages of convection, but would also prove impractical. Therefore, if you need an area for growing warmth-loving orchids within a cool house, it will be necessary to curtain off the warmest part of the greenhouse, thereby retaining more of the heat within this confined space. This area could be either a permanent structure, in which case the curtain should be similar in construction to the greenhouse, or a short-term winter home for less cold-tolerant orchids, when a polyethylene curtain would suffice. In either case, a means of access and provision for ventila-

Left: Although a few of the species will thrive in the cool greenhouse, most paphiopedilums require intermediate temperatures. Because of this, and their compact growth and long-lasting flowers, they make ideal pot plants for the home.

Right: A modern version of the Wardian case, heated by an air-warming cable, will provide a small area for growing warmth-loving orchids in a cool greenhouse.

Below: Dendrobiums such as this species, *D. victoriae reginae,* are best grown in a warm greenhouse, though a cool resting period may be needed to produce the flowers.

tion must be provided. To further boost the temperature within this area, a secondary supply of heat could be introduced by means of a small electric fan heater, or a length of space-heating cable (as used in many propagating cases).

Orchids for the warm or intermediate house

The warmest part of any greenhouse is the top third, yet very few orchid growers utilize this area except to 'rest' certain (mainly deciduous) orchids during the winter months. Small greenhouses of less than 3m (10ft) in width, are unlikely to have sufficient headroom for a high-level shelf over part of the central path, although it is seldom impossible to arrange some form of two-tier staging, especially where

the standard bench height of 84 cm (2ft 9in) can be lowered to accommodate a second layer of plants above it. Temperatures at this higher level will remain 3 to 4 °C (5-8°F) above the floor-level temperature, thus enabling some intermediate house orchids to be successfully grown in what is ostensibly a cool house. A similar situation pertains in a greenhouse normally maintained at intermediate temperatures — certain warm-growing orchids will thrive on the high-level shelves.

There are two main drawbacks to growing plants on these high shelves, both of which are accentuated during the summer months. As a result of their position near to the glass, any plants growing on these shelves will receive a great deal more light than those at the lower level.

Furthermore, as temperatures are higher the relative humidity in the upper areas will be lower, therefore those plants growing on high-level shelves or staging will dry out rapidly and consequently may need watering more frequently. Although this area may sound an inhospitable home for plants, many orchids positively enjoy the conditions, particularly during late summer and autumn when it is important to ripen the maturing growths and pseudobulbs.

Dendrobiums

Dendrobiums are not the easiest of orchids to flower really well, but if the developing pseudobulb is fully ripened during late summer by exposure to full light and air — a high shelf near the roof ventilators providing these conditions perfectly — there is a greater chance of successfully bringing these beautiful orchids into flower. The fleshy leaved species, such as *D. lingueforme* and *D. teretifolium,* which come mainly from Australia where they grow exposed to almost full sun in what are regularly drought conditions, are especially well suited to 'life at the top'; indeed these dendrobiums are unlikely to flower under northern temperate conditions unless they receive all available light, especially during the winter months.

Paphiopedilums and Phalaenopsis

A wider range of temperatures will enable the grower to satisfy that natural urge to diversify, and areas where a minimum 15.5°C (60°F) can be maintained will be perfect for the warmer-growing paphiopedilums and phalaenopsis. Both genera require fairly shady and humid conditions during the summer months — as will the majority of the warm-growing angraecoids from the African continent.

Suitable partners for these three groups, but more sun-loving and thus candidates for the high shelf, are many of the vandaceous orchids from Southeast Asia. Plants in this group have either strap-leaved or terete (pencil-shaped) foliage, with several intermediate types. Hybridizers have created other intermediate types by crossing terete with strap-leaved vandas, producing semiterete and quarter-terete forms; but the higher the percentage of terete 'blood', the more light the orchid will demand in order to flower. Indeed, terete vandas are not good subjects for small greenhouses in northern temperate zones. Not only do they require strong light all the time—a commodity that is sadly lacking during winter months—but the majority also have a climbing habit with the leaves spaced well apart on a tall stem. Many aerial roots, so necessary to climbing orchids in their natural environment, are also produced, making conventional pot culture impossible.

Oncidiums

Not all light-loving, warm-growing orchids have such embarrassing habits. Oncidiums are normally thought of as cool-growing companions to their cousins the odontoglossums, but there are several species and an increasing number of hybrids that make ideal subjects for a shelf in the warm house. (However, only a small group of oncidiums [equitant oncidiums] will thrive in these conditions; most species should be grown in the cool house.)

These have thick, almost terete or 'squared' leaves not more than 8-10cm (3-4 in) long, which grow closely together to form a tuft of foliage. The comparatively sparse root system is intolerant of wet conditions, as the fine roots like to dry out rapidly after watering. This environment can be supplied by using very small pots, just large enough to accommodate the plant, and ensuring that the compost is both free draining and durable, in order to avoid frequent repotting. A very open compost, such as a chunky, large-grade bark, will mean daily watering during hotter weather, particularly as these miniature-growing orchids like good light conditions and not too much humidity.

However, there is nothing miniature about the sprays of brightly coloured flowers produced by these particular oncidiums, derived mostly from the species *Oncidium desertorum, pulchellum* and *variegatum*—a reward well worth the extra effort required to grow these orchids. In the wild these plants enjoy strong light, little rainfall and occasionally almost desert conditions; they come from several of the West Indian islands.

Orchids for the cool house

The provision of high temperatures will not ensure success with all orchids.

ORCHIDS FOR DIFFERENT TEMPERATURES

Warm Growing	Intermediate Growing	Cool Growing
Aerides fieldingii	Bifrenaria harrisoniae	Ada aurantiaca
Angraecum sesquipedale	Brassia verrucosa	Coelogyne cristata
Angraecum veitchii	Brassolaeliocattleya Norman's Bay	Cymbidium devonianum
Ansellia africana	Cattleya Bow Bells	Cattleya aurantiaca
Calanthe vestita	Cattleya bowringiana	Cymbidium Pearl Balkis
Chysis bractescens	Dendrochilum glumaceum	Cymbidium Peter Pan
Dendrobium phalaenopsis	Epidendrum cochliatum	Cymbidium Vieux Rose
Phalaenopsis aphrodite	Epidendrum ibaguense	Dendrobium nobile
Phalaenopsis equestris	Gomesa crispa	Dendrochilum glumaceum
Phalaenopsis lueddemanniana	Lycaste aromatica	Gomesa crispa
Phalaenopsis Party Dress	Maxillaria luteo-alba	Laelia anceps
Phalaenopsis sanderiana	Miltonia clowesii	Masdevallia coccinea
Phalaenopsis Temple Cloud	Paphiopedilum callosum	Masdevallia simula
Phalaenopsis Zada	Paphiopedilum fairieanum	Maxillaria tenuifolia
Potinaria Sunrise	Stanhopea wardii	Odontioda Memtor
Rhynchostylis gigantea	Trichopilia suavis	Odontoglossum crispum
Sobralia macrantha	Vanda coerulea	Odontoglossum grande
Thunia marshalliana	Vuylstekeara Cambria	Pleione formosana
Vanda sanderana	Wilsonaria Lyoth	Vuylstekeara Cambria
Vanda tricolor suavis	Zygopetalum intermedium	Zygopetalum intermedium

Left: Cymbidiums are ideal for the greenhouse in which winter night temperatures are maintained to 10°C. But they also need cool summer nights to flower successfully.

Right: The compact growth and tall flower spikes of *Odontocidium* Thwaitesii make it a popular orchid for the cool greenhouse.

Although many of those classified as cool-growing will grow in warm temperatures, they will almost certainly not flower without a low night temperature—preferably down to or below 10°C (50°F)—during mid-summer, which is needed to initiate flower buds. In tropical and subtropical areas of the world, where nocturnal temperatures seldom drop sufficiently, it is almost impossible to grow such genera as *Cymbidium, Odontoglossum,* most *Masdevallia* and many cool-growing species derived from high altitudes.

Knowledge of the altitude as well as the country of origin of many species is the pointer to successful cultivation of the hybrids derived from these species. One example may be seen in Thailand, where the traditional area for commercial orchid growing is around the capital, Bangkok, once a coastal city. Cattleyas, the warmer-growing *Dendrobium phalaenopsis* hybrids and superlatively vanda hybrids and intergenerics grow in abundance on every verandah and front garden. The constant heat and high humidity are ideal for these orchids, but impossible for the cooler-growing genera so widely known in temperate zones. Yet on a visit to Chiang Mai, a hill town some 800km (500 miles) north of Bangkok, cymbidium hybrids were observed growing well and flowering abundantly. Although daytime temperatures of 30-32°C (86-99°F) are common in Chiang Mai, at night the temperature often falls to 11-13°C (52-55°F) and bud initiation is therefore possible.

Amateur growers of cymbidiums who are experiencing problems with the production of ample flowers may like to apply the 'Thai' solution to their own situation. Where cymbidiums are grown in a greenhouse without other orchids, the problem of obtaining good flower production—every mature cymbidium pseudobulb is capable of producing at least two spikes—does not exist, as the entire cultural regime can be directed toward the cymbidiums' requirements. But, as in the majority of amateurs' collections, where cymbidiums are just one of 20 or 30 genera, the provision of light, warmth and ventilation must be dictated by the requirements of the majority.

Orchids outside

To obtain as low as possible summer night temperatures (especially desired by cymbidiums), it is advantageous to create a 'summer quarters' area outside the greenhouse where the cymbidiums will

live happily from summer to early autumn.

Indeed, in temperate areas that do not suffer from frosts during the winter, many commercial cymbidium growers house their plants all year round in 'shade houses'. These consist of a tubular metal framework covered by Sarlon cloth, a fine mesh material that provides both the necessary shade in summer and protects the blooms from heavy rain during the cooler winter months. Shade houses also provide partial protection from strong winds. This will not only prevent any possible physical damage to young or semimature growths, but will also assist in the maintenance of a humid atmosphere around the plants, and reduce rapid drying out of the compost.

Alternatively, some growers place their cool-growing orchids on benches in the dappled shade provided by, for example, a large apple tree. However, many fruit trees, unless regularly sprayed, become infested with red spider mite and aphids during the summer and autumn months,

and great care must be taken to ensure that the orchids do not become similarly affected. This is particularly important immediately before the orchids are returned to the greenhouse where, in the artificially extended 'summer' provided by the additional warmth, a few stray insects or even eggs could rapidly result in potentially dangerous colonies.

An added bonus of moving at least part of the collection outside for the summer months is the extra—albeit temporary—space created in the greenhouse. The temptation to fill this space with additional orchids should be resisted, unless autumnal accommodation problems can be solved in another way! Instead, use this extra area to space out the orchids remaining in the greenhouse. In this way they will be able to take full advantage of the all-important light and air during the growing season; and, being in full view, will also receive the correct amounts of water and food. However conscientious the grower, crowded conditions are not conducive to perfect culture. During late summer, it is desirable to clean the greenhouse thoroughly before the onset of winter weather, and to ensure that the structure is in good repair—two tasks that are carried out more easily in a partially empty greenhouse.

Orchid resting periods

So far we have dealt solely with the conditions that are desirable for the growth of orchids, but of almost equal importance to the successful flowering of a well grown plant is that part of culture known as 'resting'. The question of when and how to rest an orchid causes much confusion among amateur growers, and even more experienced growers cannot offer precise guidelines on the subject. In most cases, resting a plant is merely co-operating with the orchid's natural desire to slow down its rate of growth during winter months. This is usually less critical with hybrid orchids than with species which, in their natural environment, would adapt their growth pattern in order to survive a seasonal period of drought. In extreme cases, all foliage is shed in order to reduce the plant's moisture requirement, and severe shrivelling of the pseudo-bulbs is occasionally evident.

Requirements of deciduous orchids

In areas where this seasonal drought is severe, it is normal for average temperatures to be lower than those during the wet season, thus extreme desiccation of the orchid is uncommon. But it is not only the orchid that adapts to the changing season: the tree on which it grows, having provided shelter from the hot sun, also becomes deciduous, thereby exposing the mature pseudobulbs and growths to all available light. Not all orchids receive this treatment in the wild, as some grow in evergreen forests or in areas with little seasonal fluctuation in temperature, but careful observation of each individual orchid will greatly assist in deciding the degree of rest required.

With orchids that naturally become completely deciduous during winter and early spring—most pleiones, calanthes, *nobile*-type dendrobiums and catasetums, for example—the supply of water should be gradually reduced as the foliage begins to turn yellow during early autumn. Simultaneously, the amount of light and air given to the plant should be increased. This can be achieved by reducing the shading or by moving the orchid to a brighter position in the greenhouse. Where possible, it would also be advantageous to reduce the temperature slightly.

Another indication that the orchid is approaching a natural period of rest is a reduction or even a complete stop in root activity. When this occurs the velamen (the greenish-white outer layer of absorbent cells) grows partially or completely

Above: The bluish venation of the leaves indicates that this plant is in need of water. But do not saturate the compost when the plant is at rest, as the roots may be killed.

Below: The end of the resting period is heralded by the appearance of a new shoot at the base of the previous year's pseudobulb.

over the normally bright green root tips. This is the plant's way of saying that winter is approaching, and the velamen covers the very tender root tip as a form of protection from both the elements and possible physical damage.

With negligible root activity and partial or complete loss of leaves, the moisture requirement of the plant is very small. Unless severe shrivelling of the pseudobulbs is noticed, all watering should be withheld until new growth is apparent with the onset of brighter, warmer conditions the following spring. An occasional overhead spray will prevent excessive desiccation of the plant during its resting period, but this light spray should be applied infrequently, for example, during the occasional spells of brighter winter weather.

Requirements of evergreen orchids

Not only deciduous orchids require a rest; evergreen types also undergo a period of reduced activity, usually coinciding

Above and Right: Many cattleyas produce their flower buds in autumn just before their resting period. Late winter sunshine encourages the buds to develop within the sheath (right), and in a few weeks they will grow through the top to produce a flamboyant display.

with the duller days of winter. With an orchid that discards its foliage—providing this is for natural reasons—and thus loses little water, the moisture requirement is obviously minimal. However, with orchids that retain their foliage for several seasons, the grower must be more critically observant; taking careful note of the root tip activity. The foliage also offers subtle guidelines: if the leaves become lank, or in extreme cases slightly desiccated, the plant has been left too long without water. But just before this stage, the leaves of many genera take on a bluish tint, an indication that water should be applied before dehydration of the tissue causes permanent damage.

Duration of rest

The duration of rest may vary from a few weeks to several months, but the plant will indicate when normal culture should be resumed by recommencing growth. In sympodial orchids, a new shoot will start to grow from the base of the current

pseudobulb, and this resurgence of activity will frequently coincide with the development of the overwintered flower buds that have remained wholly or partially dormant during the resting period. Spring-flowering cattleyas that produced a flower sheath the previous autumn will send up their flower buds within the sheath; in dendrobiums, the nodes of the pseudobulbs will start to swell and produce flower buds. When this occurs some moisture will be required, but do not try to hurry the orchid into growth by applying too much water before the new shoot is growing vigorously.

As with all arbitrary rules, there are exceptions. The tropical species from the Philippines, *Dendrochilum glumaceum,* which produces its long sprays of sweetly scented, creamy white flowers in early spring, completes its new growths by midsummer, and then has a lengthy period of very reduced activity until early winter, when the new shoots — from the centre of which the flower spikes emerge — start

into growth. The angraecums, aerangis and other members of the subtribe Sarcanthinae, when grown in northern temperate areas, undergo a short rest period during late summer. As these African species are evergreen monopodial orchids, this lessening of activity is indicated by the root tips, which stop growing for approximately three to four weeks. During this period, water should not be withheld completely as these orchids are without pseudobulbs and cannot store much moisture. But this reduction in water, coupled with almost full exposure to light and an abundance of fresh air, appears to stimulate the production of flower spikes, which appear from the leaf axils simultaneously with the resurgence of root activity.

Survival of terrestrial orchids
Whereas tropical orchids enter a period of rest in order to survive a dry season that is unfavourable for growth, the problem facing terrestrial European and northern hemisphere orchids is not one of

drought, but freezing temperatures. As with other temperate perennial plants, these hardy orchids protect themselves from the severe cold of winter by dying down to the surface of the soil. Many of these orchids possess a tuberous or thickened root system underground that stores the food manufactured by the plant during one growing season. With the return of warmer weather the following spring, this food is used to produce a new shoot, which in time will manufacture its own tubers to replace the by now exhausted ones from the previous season. Potatoes and dahlias have similar patterns of growth and survival, except that they are not frost hardy.

However, the problems of growing these hardy terrestrial orchids need not concern us, as apart from their essential mycorrhizal fungus associations, which make garden culture difficult, nearly all temperate orchids are protected plants, and therefore it is illegal to collect them.

Composts and Potting

As with all other aspects of plant culture, selection of the correct medium in which to grow an orchid is an important part of its environment. Successful cultivation depends upon each part of this environment being as near the ideal as possible, therefore it is necessary to ascertain what an orchid needs from the compost around its roots.

Basic requirements of a compost

Most orchids grown commercially or in amateurs' collections are derived from the tropics. Many are epiphytes, their roots growing exposed to the atmosphere, and even the terrestrial orchids, which live on the ground, do not send their roots down into the soil in the manner of most ground-dwelling plants. Instead, they spread out horizontally in the aerated upper layer of humus on the forest floor, and therefore the most important constituent of the medium around the orchid roots is air.

In tropical areas, where rainfall—although often seasonal—is usually very heavy, orchids are not commonly found in places that remain waterlogged. Despite the frequent, often daily, falls of rain, both epiphytic orchids and those growing in the loose surface of the ground do not remain wet for long once the rain has stopped. A second prerequisite of the compost, therefore, will be perfect drainage —a quality that will almost certainly be present if there is an abundance of air.

Yet orchid roots also require reasonably firm anchorage as they like to be in close contact with the surface on or in which they are growing. Anyone who has grown vandas or phalaenopsis will have experienced the adventitious roots that adhere very firmly to any solid surface within reach. Even the finer roots of oncidiums and odontoglossums, for instance, will become attached to the inner surface of the pot or to the drainage material, particularly potsherd or polystyrene. In most cases the root adheres so firmly that it will break when removed.

Despite these requirements, orchids appreciate a reasonably retentive compost, except for a few species that revel in mainly dry conditions. If the compost dries out too quickly, within hours after each watering, most orchids are unable to absorb sufficient moisture for steady growth. Where this situation persists, the plant grows on a stop-go basis, which results at the end of the growing season in smaller growths and/or pseudobulbs that are unlikely to flower satisfactorily.

Coupled with a retentive compost is a supply of nutrient to the plant. Less emphasis than previously is now placed on

Right: Orchids will grow well in pots, pans, baskets or on rafts, and a mixed collection will make a varied and attractive display in greenhouse or sun lounge.

the compost's ability to release nutrient to the plant over a long period, better results being obtained by regularly adding feed to the watering schedule. Obviously the compost should be reasonably water-retentive, otherwise the nutrient will not remain in the pot.

The perfect compost will be free-draining yet retentive, and provide good physical support to the orchid. If this sounds contradictory, remember that similar qualities are sought by the grower of hardy plants in the selection of the most suitable soil. But above all, an abundance of air in the compost is essential, as very few plants will thrive where the medium around their roots is airless. In the open ground the texture of the soil is improved by incorporating extra humus or by applying lime. Such processes allow more air to enter the soil, with the result that better growth is achieved. Orchids, however, require far more air around their roots than most other plants.

A brief review of composts over the past two centuries may reveal how present-day mixtures have evolved.

Evolution of composts

When tropical orchids were first introduced into Europe during the first half of the eighteenth century, very little was known about their cultural requirements. Mistakenly thinking that all orchids needed an abundance of heat and moisture, early growers placed their newly imported plants in a mixture of rotted wood and leaves, then plunged the pots in beds of sawdust placed over the heating pipes or the brick flues of coal fires. Although the excessively high temperatures and humidity did little to encourage the orchids to thrive, it was the almost completely airless conditions—particularly around the roots—that were primarily responsible for the hundreds of thousands of orchids that perished, mainly in England, during the first 100 years of importation.

Success was not achieved until the middle nineteenth century, when it was realized that light and air were important to the orchid's well-being. By this time a peat-based compost was being used, with reasonably satisfactory results, but 'hard potting' was still practised, and hence very little air remained in the compost. As suitable peat became scarce, growers—by now armed with a greater knowledge of the orchid's natural environments—searched for an alternative material. Fibrous roots of ferns, *Polypodium vulgare* in Europe, and *Osmunda gracilis* and *O. regalis* in the United States, when finely chopped and mixed with sphagnum moss, provided the alternative that was to remain the standard compost for over half a century, and which is still used by some growers today.

Modern composts

Apart from diminishing resources, with the inevitable large increase in cost, osmunda/sphagnum compost has several big drawbacks. It decomposes rapidly when subjected to modern inorganic fertilizers, and preparation of the mixture, which involves cleaning the osmunda, gathering and cleaning the sphagnum moss, then cutting it into approximately 2.5cm (1in) lengths, is very time-consuming. Additionally, it may take many months or even seasons to become proficient at potting with this compost, whereas anyone can successfully pot an orchid when using a modern potting material. Thus, although a peat-based compost is still favoured by some growers, one based on shredded pine bark or redwood bark is now widely used. It is difficult to be precise about the various constituents of composts, but the following two mixtures have proved satisfactory with a wide range of genera in many parts of the world.

Bark-based compost
10 parts medium grade pine bark
5 parts fine grade pine bark
1½ parts perlag
¼ part granulated 0.6cm (0.25in) charcoal

Peat-based compost
2 parts sphagnum moss peat
1 part horticultural sand
1 part perlite

Charcoal
Perlag   Fine grade pine bark
Medium grade pine bark
Polystyrene chunks
for pot drainage

Horticultural sand
Perlite
Sphagnum moss peat
Polystyrene chunks
for pot drainage

Above: Bark-based compost

Above: Peat-based compost

Composts and Potting

Added to this should be approximately 85g (3oz) of Dolomite lime per 36 litres (1 bushel) of mixture to reduce the acidity of the compost (bringing the pH up to around 5.5-6.0). Some genera, notably paphiopedilums, require a slightly more alkaline compost, with a pH up to 6.5. Medium-grade bark is generally about the size of a finger nail, with an average particle size of around 1.3cm (0.5in), whilst fine-grade is approximately one third of this size. Perlag and perlite are both thermally processed volcanic rock, highly absorbent and light in weight. Neither breaks down under bacterial action nor do they absorb or release measurable amounts of nutrient. Both are widely used in horticulture. The possible advantages of perlag over perlite are superior strength and greater absorption. This results in a more evenly moist compost throughout the pot, regardless of size, and hence less frequent watering.

One word of warning: although it is possible to aerate a peat-based compost by the addition of shredded bark, do not be tempted to increase the density of a bark mixture by adding peat. The finer particles of peat will be washed through the upper layers of a bark compost by the action of normal watering, until the lower half of the pot becomes clogged with wet peat and drainage is seriously impaired.

If a closer bark compost is needed, for instance when potting young seedlings, increase the quantity of fine bark whilst simultaneously reducing the medium bark content until the two ratios are reversed (10 parts fine: 5 parts medium).

In some parts of the world, alternative materials are used with great success. It is obviously more economical to use locally available materials—one South African orchidist living near a fruit cannery used to grow cattleyas on peach stones. The rough outer surface of a peach stone would hold only a limited amount of moisture, but would be an ideal material to which the roots of epiphytic orchids could adhere. Also in Africa, and presumably Asia, rice husks are used to aerate composts in place of grit or sand. But the greatest economy is practised by many growers of vandaceous plants in Southeast Asia: the orchids— *Vanda, Arachnis, Renanthera* and other monopodial genera —are tied into teak baskets without *any* medium around their roots, which, in the very humid conditions, rapidly grow round and through the baskets. Repotting merely involves fixing the small initial basket into a larger basket.

Orchids in baskets

Growing orchids in wooden baskets is not confined to the Far East. Once the theory of fresh air around an orchid's

Right: While smaller-growing orchids can be successfully cultivated in pots, larger plants may fair better in wooden baskets.

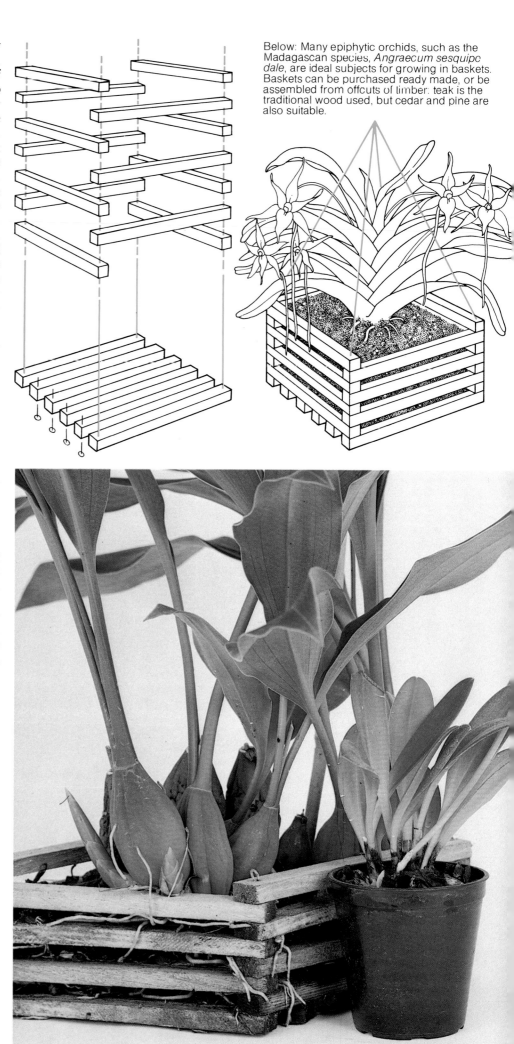

Below: Many epiphytic orchids, such as the Madagascan species, *Angraecum sesquipedale*, are ideal subjects for growing in baskets. Baskets can be purchased ready made, or be assembled from offcuts of timber: teak is the traditional wood used, but cedar and pine are also suitable.

roots became accepted practice, growers in nineteenth century Europe and the United States adopted baskets for the successful culture of many genera, even the terrestrial paphiopedilums (or cypripediums as they were then called).

Baskets are best made from strips of approximately 1.3 x 1.3cm (0.5 x 0.5in) teak (cedar being a modern alternative); the size of the basket can easily be varied by altering the length of the strip. Small holes are drilled through both ends of each strip, and a strong wire threaded through the holes. The sides of the basket need not exceed 7.5cm (3in) in depth, thus using three or four strips of wood with an equal space between each strip. Similar strips are tacked across the base, again leaving a space between each piece.

There is no doubt that some very fine orchids were grown in these containers. The fibre/moss compost of the day, coupled with an abundance of cheap labour needed to maintain many of the large collections, was admirably suited to basket culture. But as modern peat or bark-based composts came into use and with skilled horticultural workers both scarce and relatively expensive, it became impractical to use baskets unless essential. Some genera, for instance *Stanhopea* and *Coryanthes,* produce pendulous flower spikes that would languish in the compost if grown in pots. Indeed, stanhopeas could not be brought into bloom in Europe until, in about 1820, one was accidentally dropped, breaking the pot and thereby exposing the frustrated flower spikes!

However, modern composts do not

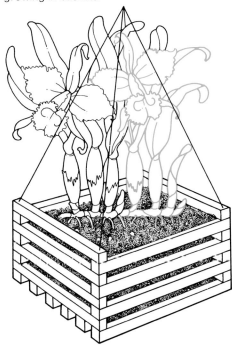

Below: Positioning a sympodial orchid diagonally in the basket makes maximum use of the growing area and allows the plant to remain undisturbed for two or three years. The long rhizomes of some cattleyas make pot culture difficult and bulbophyllums are happier growing in baskets.

lend themselves easily to being used in basket culture, and it will be necessary either to line the basket before use, or to reduce the size of the spaces between the slots in the basket's sides and base by inserting additional pieces of wood. If lining the basket is preferred, use either fresh sphagnum moss or strips and offcuts of polypropylene mesh.

Once the basket is prepared, position the orchid so that there is ample space for the next two years' growth; for this reason diagonal placing is often preferred. Then merely fill the basket with compost, ensuring that the spaces under the rhizome and between the roots are firmly packed, but not compressed, as this will assist in steadying the orchid until the new roots become active.

Top heavy orchids may need to be secured initially with fishing line, from one side of the basket, around the rhizome, and across to the other side of the basket. When finished, the orchid plant should not sway in the breeze, and the rhizome should lie just on the surface of the compost, with all available space in front of the leading pseudobulb(s) or new growth(s).

Orchids in pots

During the early part of this century a special orchid pot was developed, with large holes around the sides and in the base. In those days, clay flower pots were made by hand, and it was not difficult to obtain pots of almost any design or size. These pots were unglazed, leaving a rough, permeable surface through which, it is said, the plant's roots could 'breathe'. So firmly did the orchid roots adhere to this rough surface that the only practical way to repot the plant was to smash the pot, a perfectly acceptable method where labour and materials are both available and inexpensive.

The demise of the local pottery — a trend fortunately now reversed—in the 1930s, coupled again with a changing compost, meant that by the middle of this century most pot plants, including orchids, were being grown in factory produced, semi-glazed clay pots with just a small drainage hole in the centre of the base.

With the advent of plastics, clay pots became increasingly scarce. However, the major disadvantage of conventional plastic pots is that they become brittle and useless after a few years. They have now been superseded by pots made of polypropylene, which has many advantages over both clay and plastic. Polypropylene pots are light, flexible, seldom break or crack in storage or when dropped, and are readily available in a great variety of sizes and shapes, including square pots. There is even a mesh or basket pot for those orchids requiring drier conditions around their roots, and another with very large drainage holes through which pendulous spikes of coryanthes, stanhopeas and, for instance, *Cymbidium devonianum,* can easily emerge. Polypropylene is not a permeable material, there is no evaporation of moisture through the pot sides and thus no accumulation of

Left: There is a pot to suit every orchid. Available in polypropylene or clay they come in all shapes and sizes. Mesh pots make good substitutes for wooden baskets.

Composts and Potting

salts on the inner surface of the pot. It also has good insulation qualities, thus the roots are less subject to the fluctuations in temperature that frequently occur where clay pots are used.

Mesh pots, also made from polypropylene, are suitable for some vandas, phalaenopsis, and several of the smaller cool-growing species that prefer a reasonably fine retentive compost, but produce pendulous or horizontal flower spikes, thus making both basket and conventional pot culture impractical. *Masdevallia bella* is a typical example. The standard potting procedure is followed when using mesh pots but 'crocking' the pot bottom with drainage material is not necessary.

Orchids on trees or rafts

Adaptable as orchids generally are, there are some species that, because of either their straggling, strictly epiphytic habit of growth or their insistence on having their roots fully exposed to the atmosphere, are not comfortable when pot culture is attempted. These orchids may be contained in a variety of ways: by tying them to blocks of tree-fern fibre or pieces of cork bark, or even by arranging a small 'tree' within the greenhouse to which all such orchids could be attached.

In the tropics this method can easily be practised in the open garden where spraying or watering several times daily, if necessary, will not interfere with the growth of neighbouring plants. However, this may be difficult under glass, so all plants mounted on blocks should be grouped in one place.

Many of the monopodial angraecoid orchids, from mainland Africa or Madagascar, are particularly well suited to mounting on rafts of tree fern or cork bark—none more so than *Cyrtorchis arcuata*, a beautifully scented, white-flowered species from East Africa. This orchid, when grown in a pot or pan, seems to produce its roots horizontally, and any attempt at training these roots towards their intended home merely results in their breaking. However, if you grow this species as a true epiphyte—which it is in the wild—the roots will very rapidly cling to the surface of the raft provided.

Mounting these plants is simplicity itself. First, select a piece of tree fern the dimensions of which match the size of the plant. Although it would be wasteful of space to use a large raft for a compact, slow-growing species, conversely you should not need to reraft the orchid for at least two or three years, so allow room for future growth. Both tree-fern fibre blocks and rafts and cork bark pieces are readily available in a wide variety of sizes

Right: Many orchids—especially those with long, aerial roots—will thrive on rafts of bark suspended from the greenhouse roof.

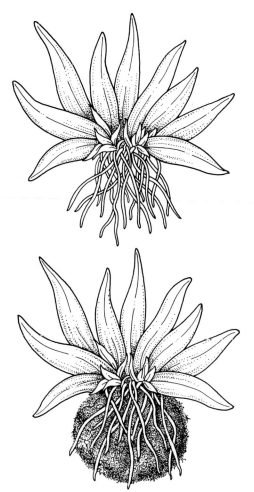

Below: To cultivate orchids on rafts, place a pad of osmunda fibre and/or sphagnum moss between the raft and the orchid, then secure the plant with fine wire or nylon fishing line.

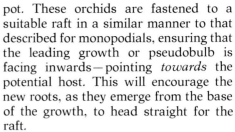

Above and Below: A tree branch 'planted' in the greenhouse makes a good home for orchids with long, climbing rhizomes. The pendulous flower spikes of *Coelogyne massangeana* (below) are displayed to full advantage when the plant is grown in this way.

and shapes, making correct selection easy. Having chosen a suitable raft, merely fasten the orchid on top with fishing line or plastic-covered wire. Some growers place a pad of osmunda fibre and/or spagnum moss between the orchid and the raft, as this helps to retain some moisture around the plant until the new roots emerge.

Sympodial pseudobulbous orchids are also suitable candidates for growing on rafts. Some have a lengthy rhizome between each pseudobulb, while others possess a rhizome that grows upwards at an angle of approximately 45°, thus the orchid rapidly 'climbs out' of a normal pot. These orchids are fastened to a suitable raft in a similar manner to that described for monopodials, ensuring that the leading growth or pseudobulb is facing inwards — pointing *towards* the potential host. This will encourage the new roots, as they emerge from the base of the growth, to head straight for the raft.

However aesthetically pleasing it is to grow plants in this 'natural' manner in the greenhouse, there are certain disadvantages. The main one is maintaining sufficient moisture around the plant for steady growth. This will entail spraying at least once daily, which will be difficult when the plants are taken into the house whilst in flower. A compromise solution for these undisciplinable orchids is to plant them in baskets. The monopodials will still have a hard surface to which their roots may adhere, yet there will be some compost around them. For those orchids with elongated rhizomes, most baskets will squeeze into a long diamond shape to allow extra forward space when required.

Repotting Orchids

The most advantageous time to repot an orchid is when the new growth is approximately 5cm (2in) high, just before the new roots emerge. In most cases this will be during early spring and will coincide with the orchid's resurgence of activity as the day length increases. Plants may also be repotted in early autumn, when the heat of the summer has diminished, but there is still time for the orchid's root system to re-establish before the onset of winter. It is obviously not possible to repot every orchid at these times, and in practice any period except midsummer — when plants need their entire root system intact in order to grow well — and midwinter — when most orchids are at least partially dormant — has proved satisfactory.

How to repot

Orchids scheduled for repotting should be allowed to dry out slightly beforehand, as this will loosen the compost around the roots. To remove an orchid from its pot prior to repotting, place one hand over the top of the pot with the orchid plant between the fingers. Invert the pot and then sharply tap the top on the edge of the potting bench or table. If the plant is reluctant to leave the pot, some gentle persuasion may be needed. Here another advantage of polypropylene pots becomes evident; being pliable, they can be squeezed, thus encouraging the plant's removal. As the plant is removed, much of the old compost will fall away. Unless you are potting-on seedlings or young plants to slightly larger pots, all old compost should be removed, thus exposing the root system for scrutiny. On an old plant,

Composts and Potting

or one that has not been repotted for several years, part of the root system will be dead. Cut these decaying roots back to healthy tissue, and shorten any overlong roots that could easily by broken during potting.

Place the orchid in a pot just large enough to accommodate its root system and allow for approximately two years growth. Orchids prefer to be slightly underpotted rather than be planted in too large a pot. For forward growing orchids, such as cattleyas, odontoglossums and lycastes, the oldest pseudobulb should be placed against one side of the pot, with all available space in front of the new growth. Other types which usually grow on all sides—paphiopedilums and masdevallias are but two examples—should be placed in the centre of the pot, as should monopodial orchids.

Holding the orchid so that the base of the growth is approximately 2.5cm (1in) below the pot edge, place a handful of drainage material into the pot, working it through the root system until about 1.3 to 2.5cm (0.5-1in) of material covers the bottom of the pot. Polystyrene or large-grade perlag are preferred for this purpose, but pea-grit or large-grade pine or red-wood bark may also be used. Then fill the pot with the chosen compost—which should be moist—tapping the pot on the bench and steadily working the compost under the rhizome and between the roots.

Gentle pressure round the surface of the compost will steady the orchid in its new pot, although tall pseudobulbs may need staking until the new root system is underway. Any orchid scheduled for propagation is obviously best divided during a repotting session.

Potting-on
This procedure is sometimes used when

Above: When growing orchids with pendulous flower spikes in pots, watch for the emergence of the young spike. In *Cymbidium devonianum*, the spike grows downwards from the base of the pseudobulbs and may bury itself in the compost. Planting the orchid high up in the pots—slightly above the level of the rim—(Above right) allows the spike to grow freely down over the side of the pot.

Right: This plant is well overdue for repotting—the new roots should be in compost. The new growths can be cut from the parent plant and potted up in fresh compost.

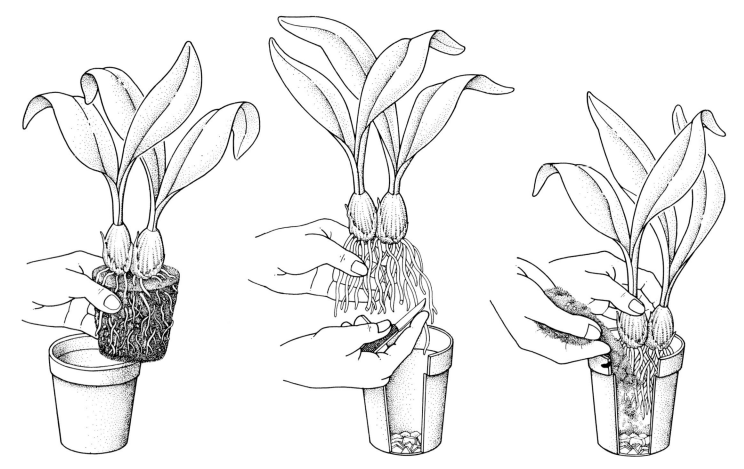

Above: To remove the plant from its pot, invert the pot, holding the orchid between your fingers, and tap the pot rim sharply on the bench.

Above: Remove all the old compost, cut away dead roots and trim back any overlong roots that might be damaged during repotting.

Above: Position the orchid so that the base of the growth is about 2.5cm (1in) below the pot rim. Fill in around the plant with compost.

the compost in which a young plant is growing is still sound, but the orchid's root system has outgrown the pot. The plants should be watered the day before, as this will help to keep the root ball intact when the plant is knocked out of its pot. Select a pot one or possibly two sizes larger, depending upon the size and vigour of the root system, and place crocks and a little compost in the base of the pot sufficient to bring the level of the old compost to just below the rim of the pot. After positioning the plant in its new pot, simply fill in the space around the sides with fresh material. A few gentle taps on the bench, coupled with light pressure around the edges of the compost, will settle the orchid into its larger pot.

Rehabilitating repotted orchids

Preventing dehydration is the biggest problem when repotting. Orchids, with their water-storing pseudobulbs and fleshy roots, are better equipped than most plants to withstand this temporary set-back, but a few simple precautions will greatly assist the process of re-establishment. After repotting or potting-on, the plant should be watered thoroughly to settle in the new compost. After this, the pots should be kept slightly drier than usual to allow any damaged or cut root surfaces to form a callus, and to encourage the roots to look for moisture in the fresh compost.

To compensate for this reduction of water to the orchid's roots, the atmospheric humidity should be maintained at a higher level than previously. Indeed, freshly potted orchids—especially those in baskets or mounted on tree fern—benefit from a light overhead spray each morning, and a second misting during the early evening if the day has been warm. If the weather becomes very bright and hot, repotted orchids will need additional shading, although those merely potted-on will not need this extra care.

After approximately three to four weeks, it should be possible to revert to a normal cultural routine as the new roots grow into the fresh compost. The interval between each repotting may vary from a few months to two or three years. Young seedlings benefit by being moved to a slightly larger pot with fresh compost every few months, whereas adult plants are best left undisturbed for several seasons.

However, if the compost has become too decomposed (broken down), or the plant's roots are not happy, a complete repot at the earliest opportunity is often the only solution. Thus it makes good sense to ensure that all the compost used is fresh and in good condition, so that mature orchids may thrive in the same pot for at least two years.

Increasing Your Collection

Apart from achieving new growth there are two main reasons for dividing an orchid plant. First, it may have become unmanageably large so that it no longer fits easily into a container of convenient size. Second, some part of the plant (usually the centre, though occasionally the back section) may have become diseased and/or, by reason of age, defoliated. In monopodial orchids, for example, the lower, older leaves drop, leaving an ugly bare stem.

Every plant is an individual and needs different treatment, but there are two basic techniques, one for monopodial and the other for sympodial growth.

Monopodials — simple division

The main direction of growth in monopodial orchids is from the top of the plant, though some orchids in this group (notably the smaller angraecoids) do produce growth from the base. In general terms, any monopodial orchid that has grown taller than 75cm (30in) becomes an embarrassment to many amateur growers' greenhouses. In places such as Singapore, Hawaii and the West Indies, where they are grown as garden plants or in cut-flower nurseries, these orchids grow to several metres tall. Under greenhouse conditions in temperate areas, however, it is likely that many monopodial orchids approaching 1m (39in) in height will already have lost some of their lower leaves, exposing the woody stem. Aerial roots will have developed on at least the lower two thirds of the plant and to propagate new growth the stem should be cut through immediately below one of these roots, preferably leaving three or four pairs of leaves on the lower section. These leaves will act as a 'sap drawer' (rather like the two or three leaves that should be left beyond the upper truss on a tomato plant), allowing this part of the plant to photosynthesize.

The top part of the plant, removed with its own root system already growing, should be potted into a suitable container, remembering that monopodial orchids in particular like an abundance of fresh air around their roots.

Within six to eight weeks during spring or early summer one or more dormant buds, or 'eyes', situated in the leaf axils of the lower section will have started into growth. These can either be left to develop on the parent, or, when each new growth has initiated its own small root system (which may take several months), they can be removed and potted separately. Exceptionally, the old and by now very woody lower section will produce further new growth, but for all practical purposes it is not worth retaining.

Monopodials — nature's way

On certain monopodial orchids, notably species of *Phalaenopsis* and *Vanda*, plantlets called 'keikis' (a Hawaiian word meaning babies) develop on the flower spikes. (Keikis also develop on some sympodial orchids, such as dendrobiums.) As soon as a keiki possesses an independent root system it is possible to remove it

Vegetative Propagation of Monopodial Orchids

The photographs on these two pages show how a typical monopodial orchid can be divided into three healthy plants. Although all growers like to see their greenhouses full of plants, the temptation to divide plants unnecessarily should be resisted. If divisions of orchids are too small, all their energies will go towards building up plant strength and they will seldom, if ever, produce flowers.

Basic rules

Only propagate vigorous, free-flowering stock; there is little merit in producing additional stock of orchids that were unsatisfactory to begin with.

If it appears that the plant being divided is infected by a virus, heat sterilize the cutting tools by passing the blades through a flame.

When there are signs of fungus or rot in the plant, all cut surfaces should be liberally dusted with captan or a similar fungicide to control the infection.

1 This plant of *Vanda cristata* has become too tall and is an ideal candidate for propagation by division. The top section can be removed by cutting through the stem and the keiki growing in the centre can also be removed and grown into a new plant.

2 When cutting through the stem to remove the top section, ensure that the cut is made cleanly, and immediately below one or more new roots. Any damaged tissue should be trimmed off.

3 The keiki growing on the end of a previous flower spike has developed its own root system and can be used as the starting point for a new plant. To remove it, cut through the flower spike immediately behind the young plantlet.

from the parent plant and pot it up.

A good example of keiki production is shown by the plant of *Vanda cristata* illustrated on this page. A young growth appeared on the end of a short flower spike in early summer, but did not develop a root system until the following spring. While attached to the parent plant the keiki gained all its nourishment through the old flower spike, which remained green. As soon as the keiki produced a healthy root system it was removed from the parent plant and potted up.

Species from the *Phalaenopsis lued-demanniana* group, which originate in the Philippines, will frequently produce young plantlets from the ends or nodes of flower spikes. Unlike dendrobiums, this is not at the expense of flower production; keikis and flowers often appear together.

Right: Phalaenopsis commonly produce keikis, both in the wild and in cultivation, and one parent plant may give rise to many plantlets. This *Phalaenopsis lueddemanniana* keiki has produced an excellent root system and is itself in flower; it is at the ideal stage for removal and potting up.

4 Both the top section of the plant and the keiki should be potted up in coarse bark chips. Most monopodial orchids thrive in baskets because these containers allow ample air circulation for the roots. The polypropylene baskets shown here are pliable and are able to accommodate awkward roots.

5 A vandaceous orchid three months after removal of the top section. Already three new growths can be seen developing in the uppermost leaf axils. The older leaves are turning yellow.

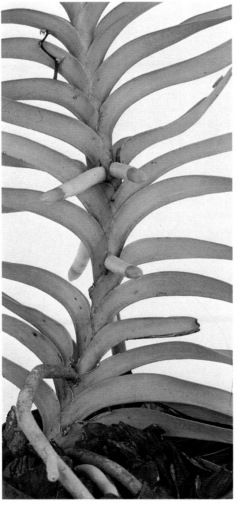

6 The top section six months after division. Removal from the older, lower section has stimulated activity in the younger tissues and healthy new roots produced since the division are able to grow straight into fresh compost. A new stem can be seen growing from near the base of the original one.

7 The top section, now re-established after division, grows vigorously into a sturdy and healthy new plant.

Sympodials — when to divide

During routine cleaning and checking of the orchids you will be able to assess which ones are scheduled for repotting, and it is at this time, prior to the start of the new growth on the leading pseudobulb, that vegetative propagation should be planned.

At the base of all pseudobulbs there are several dormant growing buds, often referred to as 'eyes'. Unless the pseudobulb is very old or the base has become damaged or diseased, these eyes can be stimulated into growth if given the correct conditions. Any sympodial orchid that has more than two or three pseudobulbs behind the leading growth, is sufficiently large to be divided. If you cut through the rhizome between two pseudobulbs some months before repotting time, then it is likely that a new growth will have already started when you remove the orchid from its pot preparatory to repotting. Thus you are well on the way to a second plant.

Deciduous orchids, such as *Thunia, Pleione, Calanthe* and *Cycnoches,* that need to be kept dry during the winter, can be divided before the resting period begins. When the leaves have died back, remove the orchids from their pots, clean off all the compost and dead foliage and/or roots, divide the pseudobulbs singly and then place them in trays. They should be kept in a light airy position, such as a shelf above the staging; until the new growths appear from the base of the pseudobulbs with the onset of spring, when the pseudobulbs can be potted up.

Sympodial orchids without pseudobulbs are equally responsive to this method of propagation, provided the old back growths that have flowered once have retained their foliage. Whereas it is possible to regenerate growth from an old pseudobulb that may have been leafless for two or three years, for all practical purposes any once-flowered growths of, for example, paphiopedilums or masdevallias that have lost their leaves are dead. To compensate for this, the foliage of many pseudobulbless sympodial orchids is more persistent and will remain in good condition for several years after the growth has flowered.

Sympodials — how to divide

The technique for both sympodial types is similar. Orchids that have become too large and are scheduled for division should have the initial cuts through the rhizome made during mid- to late winter, when the plant is least active. Many large plants will have developed naturally into three or four divisions, or leads, merely linked by the common rhizome to the central, frequently leafless, pseudobulbs or old growths. By gently pushing two pseudobulbs apart at a point where the plant will divide, you can cut through the rhizome with a sharp knife or secateurs if there is space. (The rhizome will be growing just below the surface of the compost.) Take care not to cut through any new roots, or to damage the dormant eyes that will subsequently produce the new growth.

If the orchid is particularly rare or valuable, or is a vigorous grower, each

---

Vegetative Propagation of Sympodial Orchids

Sympodial orchids may or may not have pseudobulbs, but both types can be readily divided provided that the plant is large enough. Before starting assess the situation with regard to both plant size and available growing space. There is no point in pulling a plant into many small pieces as they not only clutter the greenhouse but also — at least for those pieces that manage to survive — will take many years to reach a flowering stage. When splitting a plant try not to destroy its character, and where possible use only healthy and well established plants. The photographs on these two pages illustrate the method used to divide a sympodial orchid with pseudobulbs. The technique for those without pseudobulbs is similar, but only the back stems with leaves should be used: those that have lost their leaves are probably dead or dying. However, most orchids of this type retain foliage on the back stems for many years. Cleanliness is important, always sterilize the blade before each cut is made.

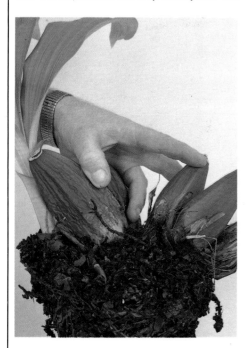

1 During winter assess which plants are ready for splitting and decide where the divisions are to be made. Using a heat-sterilized knife cut through the rhizome at these points. Treat the cut surfaces with fungicide and leave the plant until repotting time. Then, when the plant is removed from its pot, it can be easily split.

2 Carefully remove the growing medium and then trim back all the old dead roots. Whenever possible ensure that each division of the plant has at least two pseudobulbs. Although single pseudobulbs will survive, they will often take many years to grow to a stage where they produce a plant that flowers.

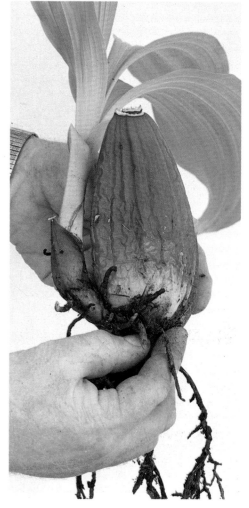

3 Carefully continue trimming the old roots almost back to the base of the pseudobulb. Take your time and be sure not to remove or damage the few new actively growing roots or dormant buds at the base of the pseudobulb. Hopefully, the earlier cutting of the rhizome will have encouraged some of these buds to start growing.

Where to Divide Sympodial Orchids

1 A line of 6 bulbs can be split to give two plants.

2 Try to ensure that each division has three bulbs.

3 and **4** The terminal parts of both these plants

can be split from the older bulbs as indicated.

5 This plant can be left as it is or split up as shown.

6 This plant should not be split until it has increased.

pseudobulb or growth behind the principal division can be separated by cutting through the rhizome between every back bulb. This method is less likely to succeed with pseudobulbless orchids, and it must be accepted that a new plant starting from a single pseudobulb will probably need to be grown for several years before it produces a flower. Thus, this practice

should only be used with plants of particular merit or those that cannot be obtained from any other source.

Apart from being careful not to damage the plant whilst cutting through the rhizome, two other precautions will help to ensure success. The cut surfaces should be dusted with orthocide—a puffer pack is ideal—to prevent any fungal infection

entering the plant. Similarly, to prevent the spread of any virus that may be present, heat sterilize the cutting tools—by passing the blades through a flame—after dealing with each plant. After cutting through the rhizome in one or more places, the plant should remain intact in its pot until normal repotting time some months later.

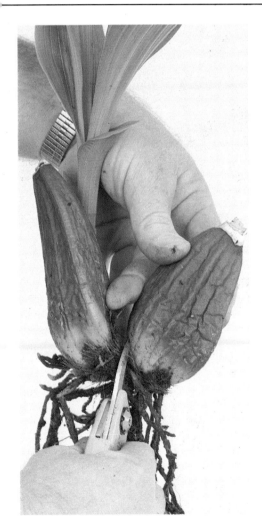

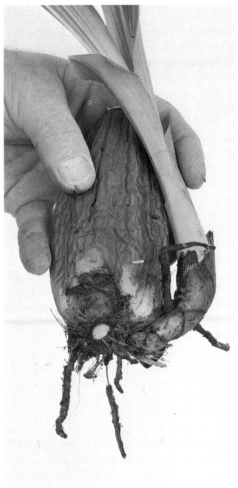

4 The more vigorously growing plants or those from which a large stock is required can be further split into single pseudobulbs, but this should not become a standard practice. Those sympodials without pseudobulbs should never be divided into single stems as their chances of survival are minimal; always split them into twos or threes as a minimum.

5 The cut face of the rhizome is a site liable to fungal infection and consequent rot. It is important to treat it as soon as it is cut with a liberal dusting of fungicide. This pseudobulb with its actively growing bud is now ready for potting up; it should soon form a healthy and thriving plant.

6 The actively growing part of the parent plant should now be repotted allowing sufficient space for several new pseudobulbs to grow. The removed back bulbs are then potted up. Try to provide a moist atmosphere with little temperature fluctuation. Do not plant the back bulbs too deeply otherwise the shoot may rot before reaching the surface.

Watering and Feeding

When and how to water orchids are questions most frequently asked by first-time buyers, and watering is always the most difficult aspect of culture about which to offer advice. More plants are killed by drowning than any other single cause.

As far as water quality is concerned, orchids can generally be watered safely with ordinary tap water. However, *never* use water that has been through an artificial softener.

Watering from the top

There are many good reasons for not watering orchids from the base of the pot. Most orchid composts, even those based on peat, are of an extremely open nature and thus have a poor capillary action. As a result it is possible for an orchid growing in these composts to stand in at least 2.5cm (1in) of water for more than a month with the top half of the compost remaining dry. If this occurs the roots in the waterlogged lower half of the pot will die through lack of air, whilst those nearer the surface will perish due to lack of moisture—and even orchids cannot thrive for too long without the support of a healthy root system! For similar reasons, orchids have not yet adapted to growing on capillary beds or by hydroculture—methods practised with the majority of houseplants in modern commercial nurseries.

Having accepted that orchids enjoy overhead watering, it is important that water should not be allowed to remain in new growths when they first appear each spring. Different genera tolerate this to varying extents, cattleyas possibly being the toughest. With the exception of several of the bifoliate species, such as *Cattleya bowringiana* and its hybrids, their new growths do not develop an open leaf until the growth is several centimetres high and sufficiently hard to withstand overhead watering. At the other end of the scale, the genus *Lycaste* and its related group start production of their relatively soft, pleated leaves with the emergence of a funnel-shaped growth that is potentially very susceptible to rotting, if water gets inside the growth. Dendrobiums also produce very tender new growths which should be allowed to grow to several centimetres in height, thus hardening the base, before much water is splashed around the pot. Indeed, it is best to avoid all new growths when watering, as there is nothing more frustrating than to see a promising new growth turn to a brown soggy mass as a result of careless watering.

Other areas to keep clear of water are the leaf axils of vandaceous monopodial orchids and, in particular, the crowns of phalaenopsis, which can easily trap water. Paphiopedilums do not seem to suffer problems from water remaining in the new growth, but the flower buds, produced in late summer from within these almost mature growths, will certainly rot if water remains trapped around the bud for long. All watering problems are accentuated by low temperatures, where evaporation is slower, and orchids in a cool house or where night temperature falls below 10°C (50°F) need special care.

How often to water

The interval between each watering depends on several factors—chiefly experience and growing conditions. As a general rule, small pots will dry out faster than large ones, and plastic pots hold more water than clay. Plants will need watering more frequently in hot sunny weather, or if surrounded by dry air, and a large plant will require more water than a small one.

To check whether a plant is in need of watering, if you have a small collection it is not too difficult or time-consuming to lift each plant in turn: those that feel heavy are obviously wet whilst the lighter ones are in need of a drink. You will soon find out which plants dry out more rapidly than others, and after a few weeks you can gradually dispense with the procedure. But even experienced growers will sometimes use this method, particularly with large pots, where the correct moisture content can be difficult to maintain.

Even if the compost at the top of the pot feels dry the bottom may be wet. You can check this by examining the compost through the drainage holes, or by lifting the pot as above.

Very few orchids enjoy their roots being surrounded by constantly moist conditions. In nature these roots are frequently saturated by tropical rain but they often dry out almost completely before the next downpour. To simulate these conditions in the artificial environ-

Below: Be careful to keep water away from paphiopedilum flower buds, as they may rot and spoil your hopes of flowers the next spring.

ment of a greenhouse, it is necessary to allow the compost in the pots to become partially dry between waterings. Orchids with pseudobulbs are capable of withstanding near drought conditions for short periods, and whilst too little water is not being advocated, this would be far preferable to overwatering. Overwatering means giving the plant water too *frequently*— not giving too much water at each watering. Thus, when water is needed, ensure that it washes completely through the pot and does not merely moisten the top level of compost.

In the greenhouse, plants near the edge of the staging will often dry out more quickly than those in the centre, owing to the greater movement of air. This occurs particularly during cold weather when any heating pipes below the staging will be in use. The same will happen when plants are grown in the proximity of a fan, especially if this is a fan heater, and, therefore, all plants should be at least 2m

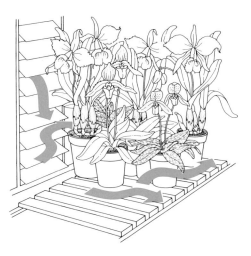

Above: Orchids in the direct path of a fan or near a ventilator or louvred panel, where the air flow is greatest, will need more frequent watering. When the heating system is in use, plants at the edges of the staging will become dry more rapidly than those in the middle not directly affected by warm air.

(6.5ft) away from this type of heating device.

Orchids with an abundance of foliage will obviously lose more moisture through transpiration, and will need watering more frequently than smaller growing varieties. On the other hand, as small pots contain less compost, they will hold a lower reserve of moisture, and therefore need watering relatively frequently. The most frequent watering will be needed by large plants growing in a comparatively small pot, especially when the root system has filled this pot and the plant is growing vigorously.

During the main growing season, from late spring until early autumn, orchids that are in good health and growing vigorously will probably need watering twice or three times a week, depending upon the prevailing weather and greenhouse atmosphere. Plants grown in the house, where the atmosphere is drier, may require watering once a day.

At the other end of the spectrum, the interval between waterings should be increased to a week or even longer in the depths of winter in temperate conditions. Many growers of cool-house plants, such as odontoglossums, most dendrobiums, some laelias and encyclias, do not apply water to the pots during the winter, particularly with the species that are partially or completely resting. Instead, the plants are sprayed overhead during periods of brighter winter weather, to prevent desiccation and to counteract the drying effect of the heating system.

Although it is impossible to give an arbitrary rule on when to water, the following is a helpful guideline: if you are not sure whether or not an orchid needs water during the growing season, apply water, but, if in doubt during the winter months, delay watering until the next watering session.

Reducing water loss

A high humidity around a plant will obviously reduce its rate of water loss through transpiration, thus also reducing the amount of water the plant needs to absorb through its root system in order to thrive. Although orchids enjoy a moist atmosphere more than most other plants, the relative humidity in the greenhouse should be kept in balance with all the other factors, such as temperature and light, and like them should fluctuate during any 24-hour period. Just as it is undesirable to maintain any plants on a 24-hour daylength or at constantly even temperature, it would also be a disadvantage if the humidity were to remain too even.

Left: Automatic watering systems perform a dual function of keeping the greenhouse atmosphere buoyant and the compost moist. They are ideal for young plants, but not for orchids in flower as water may spoil the petals.

Overhead spraying

During spells of warm summer weather, when the plants may have been subjected to temperatures in excess of 32°C (90°F) during the early afternoon, together with a relative humidity of 30 percent or below, it is a positive advantage to spray water over the plants, between the pots, and beneath the staging etc, during the evening. Like having a cool shower after a hot day in the office, the orchids perceptibly recover from the heat of the day. If the air becomes too dry at temperatures much lower than this, the shading/ventilation/moisture retention balance is probably incorrect.

Overhead spraying of plants under glass, whether to increase humidity or to water those orchids growing on rafts, should be restricted either to early morning before the greenhouse temperature becomes too high, or to the evening when the sun's heat is diminishing. There are two reasons for this, both connected with the temperature of the orchid's foliage. When water is applied by overhead spray, it is inevitable that some will remain in the form of droplets for a considerable time. These areas of water will act as a magnifying glass to the sun's rays, thus increasing the chance of burning the foliage. The other problem arises from the effect of cold water on warm foliage. Some orchids, notably phalaenopsis and its allied genera, are particularly sensitive to this and, where the water is more than 11°C (20°F) colder than the foliage, the plant tissue may be damaged. Such tissue then becomes more susceptible to fungal infection. Therefore, it is advisable not to apply cold water to warm foliage.

Misting the greenhouse

One way of overcoming these problems on exceptionally hot, windy days when the air is in danger of becoming extremely dry, is to briefly apply a *very* fine water mist into the greenhouse atmosphere. This is best done early in the morning with a special nozzle attached to the hose-pipe. With this method only a very small amount of water is spread onto the foliage, which can dry before the sun's heat causes burning. However, in very bright and hot conditions, avoid even this small amount of overhead water.

Additional devices for the small greenhouse

As with other aspects of culture, the smaller the greenhouse area, the more difficult it will be to maintain reasonable humidity during hot weather. To overcome this problem, additional shading, more efficient ventilation, including low-level apertures, air-circulating fans and more moisture-retentive material on the staging and greenhouse floor, may be necessary. Where normally cooler growing orchids are being cultivated in tropical and sub-

Above: To maintain a bouyant atmosphere on very hot days is difficult, but spraying water beneath the staging and between the pots will assist the cooling process.

tropical areas, some form of air conditioning may be necessary. Systems are available commercially, or the domestic refrigerator could be adapted to supply cool air for the greenhouse.

An alternative method, widely used in the United States, South Africa and Australia, is the adoption of a 'wet-pad' system. This consists of large panels of moisture-retentive material (fibreglass would be suitable), set in vertical wiremesh containers across one end of the greenhouse, with a large extractor fan on the opposite end wall. The fibreglass panel is kept perpetually saturated and the extractor fan pulls in fresh air through open louvres positioned behind the panel. As the air passes through the saturated fibreglass, it is cooled and moistened, thus improving the greenhouse atmosphere. The system may be operated manually, or controlled automatically by the use of thermostats and humidistats. To function correctly, no other ventilators should be open, as no air should be allowed to enter the greenhouse except through the wet-pad.

Feeding orchids

Orchids cannot live entirely on fresh air, and like other plants need moderate amounts of food in order to thrive. In the wild, much of this is provided in the form of gases given off by the decaying matter on the forest floor below—a method that has been adapted successfully by some growers of monopodial orchids in tropical and equatorial regions. The myth that orchids do not require feeding probably arose from the days of sphagnum moss/osmunda fibre compost, as most fertilizers have a harmful effect on the moss and subsequently the whole compost. Modern composts do not provide much food by themselves and even where a base fertilizer is included in the compost recipe this is generally exhausted after about eight to ten weeks.

Orchids do not require a special feed, although liquid fertilizer is preferable as all plants are able to absorb this more

rapidly. During the active growing period, from spring to late summer, a high nitrogen feed will encourage rapid growth. To aid the ripening of this growth and to help initiate the flowers, a more balanced fertilizer should be used during the autumn until growth virtually stops during the winter, when little food is needed.

Root feeding

Most compound fertilizers, which include

Below: Applying a fine mist of water into the greenhouse atmosphere first thing in the morning ensures the correct humidity around the plants as day temperatures increase.

nearly all commercially available liquid or solid feeds, have a three-part formula stated on the packet. This gives the ratio of nitrogen (N) to phosphate (P) and potassium (K); thus when growers talk of a 'high nitrogen' feed, the NPK ratio would be 25:15:15 or similar. A 'balanced' feed would be 10:10:10. Minute quantities of other elements are also included, the most important of which is magnesium. A shortage of magnesium in the plant can lead to a chlorotic effect, where parts of the leaves may turn yellow, by breakdown of some cells, which will be attacked by a secondary fungal infection. If you are using a bark-based compost, Dolomite lime watered into the compost every four to six months will also supply the required amount of magnesium.

As a general rule orchids require less feed than most other plants, but it should be given little and often. You will get the best results by applying one of the standard liquid feeds at half to two-thirds strength in three out of every four waterings during the growing season, reducing these applications to one in three during the winter. In warmer climates where the light intensity is good for most of the year orchids may require feeding more often, say at most waterings during the growing season.

Foliar feeding
In recent years, foliar feeding has become more widespread. With this method the fertilizer is diluted in water and then sprayed overhead, either in the early morning or preferably during warm summer evenings. As this form of nutrient is absorbed by the plant through its leaves or aerial roots, spraying in the evening allows a greater time for absorption before the feed is evaporated by the sun's heat.

PESTS AND DISEASES

Orchids are not attacked by many pests, although even the best cultivated plants will be liable to damage from time to time. Prevention is better than cure, and therefore a regular monthly spraying with a systemic insecticide should keep most plants clean. Against this must be weighed the undesirability of spreading potentially harmful chemicals into the atmosphere. Whenever chemicals are used to kill insect pests, remember that most chemicals cannot differentiate between the insects and you—so it is most important to follow the manufacturers' instructions and take all necessary precautions.

Red spider mite

Undoubtedly the most difficult insect pest to eradicate, and consequently the one most commonly seen is the red spider mite (*Tetranychus urticae*). These minute, sap-sucking pests are normally greenish yellow—rather than red—wingless and thrive in warm, dry conditions. They feed on the undersides of leaves, and although they will attack any orchids, the soft-leaved genera such as *Lycaste, Calanthe* and *Catasetum* seem particularly susceptible. Cymbidiums, too, are a favourite diet, especially in smaller greenhouses where at times the temperature may be too high and relative humidity low. With a casual approach to control, this provides an ideal environment for rapid multiplication of the pest.

Plants should be inspected regularly for red spider mite, which is just visible to the naked eye. Any leaf showing a slight whitish mottling on the underside is probably under attack. In severe infestations the leaves will turn yellow and a fine gossamer web can be seen on the underside. Although humid conditions will discourage red spider mite, a regular monthly spraying—using a systemic insecticide alternated with malathion—should be an effective control. Where active colonies have built up, three or four applications at 8 to 10 day intervals should eradicate each generation, as most chemical controls will not kill the eggs.

Alternative methods of control are fumigation, using azobenzene or Naled; or greenhouse aerosols containing malathion. Biological control is also possible using predatory mites, usually available from the local Agricultural Development Advisory Service or the Department of Agriculture, but their introduction would preclude the subsequent use of any chemical control as this would obviously affect both predator and prey.

False spider mite

In recent years, phalaenopsis have frequently been attacked by a false spider mite (*Brevipalpus russulus*), which causes pitting on the upper surface of the leaves. If left unchecked, secondary fungal infection is probable, with the inevitable de-

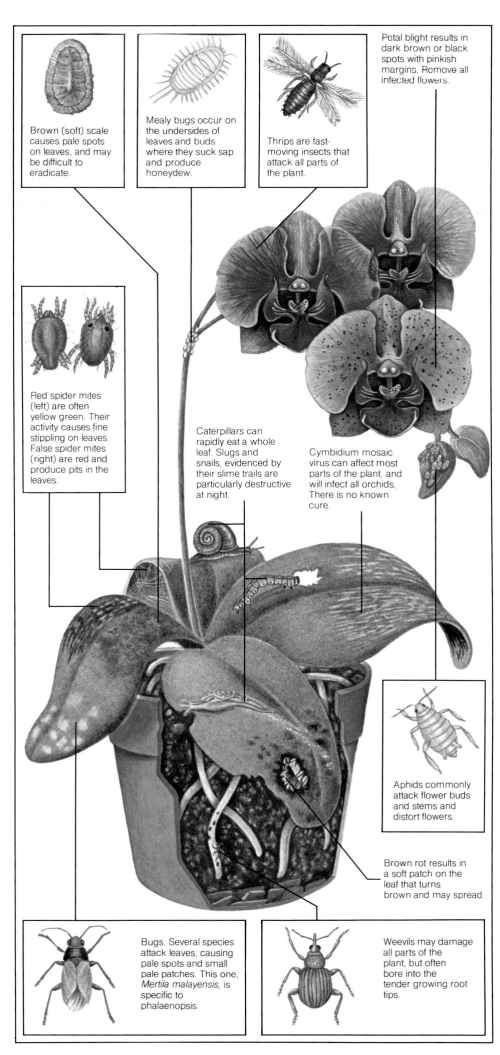

Brown (soft) scale causes pale spots on leaves, and may be difficult to eradicate.

Mealy bugs occur on the undersides of leaves and buds where they suck sap and produce honeydew.

Thrips are fast-moving insects that attack all parts of the plant.

Petal blight results in dark brown or black spots with pinkish margins. Remove all infected flowers.

Red spider mites (left) are often yellow green. Their activity causes fine stippling on leaves. False spider mites (right) are red and produce pits in the leaves.

Caterpillars can rapidly eat a whole leaf. Slugs and snails, evidenced by their slime trails are particularly destructive at night.

Cymbidium mosaic virus can affect most parts of the plant, and will infect all orchids. There is no known cure.

Aphids commonly attack flower buds and stems and distort flowers.

Brown rot results in a soft patch on the leaf that turns brown and may spread.

Bugs. Several species attack leaves, causing pale spots and small pale patches. This one, *Mertila malayensis*, is specific to phalaenopsis.

Weevils may damage all parts of the plant, but often bore into the tender growing root tips.

Above: The results of attack by false spider mite show clearly on the upper surfaces of these leaves of *Phalaenopsis,* the only genus to be severely affected by this pest.

Below: Colonies of scale insects may build up in the greenhouse if scrupulous hygiene is not observed. Although they are simple to eradicate, their damage leaves a permanent scar.

foliation of the plant. The treatment recommended above should achieve effective control.

Aphids

Similar treatment should also control the common aphids, although Lindane and liquid derris will be equally effective and will help to avoid a resistance to any one particular chemical building up in these pests. Although many forms of greenfly may appear in the greenhouse, the orchid aphid, *Cerataphis lataniae,* is most commonly found. The pale green aphids are particularly fond of tender young growths and flower spikes, the developing flower bud being especially attractive. Where these buds are attacked, the flower —if it opens at all—will be mottled and distorted.

Mealy bugs and scale insects

These two relatively common pests are more difficult to eradicate because of their protective outer covering. Both the mealy bug (*Pseudococcus longispinus*) and the scale (*Diaspis boisduvalii* or *Coccus hesperidum*; the latter often known as the soft scale), are sap-sucking insects, which feed by puncturing the surface of the leaf. They are clearly visible to the naked eye, being 3.2mm (0.125in) or more in diameter. Mealy bugs are covered with a waxy, whitish substance and frequently hide in the leaf axils of plants. Dendrobiums, especially *nobile* soft cane types, are particularly vulnerable to attack. Scale insects, as the name indicates, are protected by a dome-shaped hard shell, which is resistant to most chemical sprays. Systemic insecticide, which makes the plant toxic to sap-sucking pests, will control both these pests if applied two or three times at intervals of 10 to 14 days. Where only a small number of orchids is involved and infestations are minor, methylated spirit applied with a small paintbrush will clean up the plants.

Slugs and snails

The warm, humid conditions of the greenhouse encourage slugs and snails. Few greenhouses are completely clear of these two invaders, but if cleanliness around the plants and under the staging is normal practice, there will be fewer hiding and breeding places for these mainly nocturnal feeders.

Metaldehyde is the traditional method of control, but liquid and pellet-form slug killers are also currently in use. The liquid has the advantage of treating the compost as well, thus poisoning one of the favourite hiding places. Bait in the form of an upturned potato or grapefruit skin, or even an orchid bloom, is also effective but relies on daily inspection and the disposal of any pests attracted to the bait.

Other pests

Although the pests listed above are the most frequently encountered, thrips, weevils and caterpillars may also cause damage. They can all be brought into an orchid collection inadvertently on new plants, and will inevitably enter through the open ventilators and doors of the greenhouse during summer months. Control is important, as apart from weakening the orchids and spoiling flowers, all these pests are responsible for the spreading of virus diseases. Regular examination of the plants will enable any problems to be handled at an early stage, and a moist yet buoyant atmosphere will discourage them.

Bacterial and fungal diseases

Whereas pests will damage healthy tissue, the main access to the plant for fungal and bacterial diseases is through damaged areas. Therefore, if you experience either of these two problems, dust every cut surface with orthocide powder as a matter of routine. This chemical has proved effective in controlling most forms of 'rots', including 'damping off' problems, in orchids, as in all other plants.

The spores of fungi and bacteria are present in all atmospheres, but will thrive especially where air circulation is poor and the relative humidity high. They will also multiply rapidly where decaying matter is left lying about in the greenhouse — yet another reason for maintaining a high level of cleanliness around the plants.

Many diseases could attack your plants, but where good hygiene is practised and the orchids are carefully observed, all problems will be minimized. Rapid action to eliminate the disease is essential, as all fungi and bacteria spread extremely quickly where conditions are to their liking.

Brown spot

This disease, caused by the bacterium *Pseudomonas cattleyae,* occurs particularly in phalaenopsis and paphiopedilums. An early sign of infection is a soft watery area on the surface of the leaf, which, if left alone, will rapidly turn brown and spread. It is essential to cut out the infected area with a clean, sharp knife, after which the cut surfaces should be dusted with orthocide. Where large numbers of plants are affected, they should be heavily sprayed with a solution of natriphene. Alternatively, all infected plants could be soaked in natriphene or Physan for approximately one hour. Many fungicides and bactericides are available, and those suitable for other greenhouse plants would be ideal for orchids.

Petal blight

This disease is caused by the fungus *Sclerotinia fuckeliana,* and is common on

early autumn flowers of phalaenopsis and cattleyas. At first a few small circular spots may appear on any part of the flower. The spots are usually dark brown or black, and on close examination, have a slight pinkish margin. To treat the disease, first remove all infected flowers immediately you notice them, and then ensure that the night-time humidity is not too high. In temperate areas it will probably be necessary to supply a little artificial heat during autumn to prevent the problem spreading.

Virus diseases

Virus has become the 'dirty word' of orchid growers during the past 20 years, and whilst the potential dangers of a virus disease should not be minimized, do

Left: Pseudobulb ruptures are invariably caused by small snails and slugs that eat into and eventually hollow out the bulb.

Below: The symptoms of mosaic virus infection show clearly as pale blotches on the petals of this cymbidium.

not assume that every malformed flower or marked leaf is caused by a virus. In fact many plants that appear healthy may have some form of virus infection, and it is therefore essential that insect pests which spread viruses should be controlled. Many growers sterilize their cutting tools between use on each plant. Although this may seem fastidious, it is certainly advisable to isolate any plant about which you are suspicious.

Symptoms will vary according to the genus attacked and the virus, and plants that are not growing well will show more extreme signs of the disease at an earlier stage. With some genera, notably cattleyas, virus symptoms first become obvious in the flowers, which although they will open normally and appear healthy, will develop colour breaks— irregular stripes or blotches of different colours—in either the petals or sepals after about a week. Isolate suspect plants so that subsequent flowers can be examined for any malformation, which, if present,

will almost certainly confirm virus infection. Most orchid nurserymen will advise you if in doubt, but for a more certain diagnosis it will be necessary to have the suspect plant tested. Many commercial tissue laboratories will offer this service.

The only cure for infected plants, be they orchids or others, is to burn them. Hence the importance of thorough pest control and clean conditions within your collection.

Cymbidium mosaic virus

This virus is misnamed, as it will attack almost all orchids. Typical symptoms are chlorotic, or discoloured, areas on the leaf as a result of the breakdown of cells, these marks becoming darker and sunken as the disease advances. The marking often becomes regular, sometimes forming a diamond-shaped pattern on the leaf. On cattleyas and phalaenopsis virus infection often shows up initially as purplish markings, but these too become brown after a few weeks.

HELPFUL HINTS

The following advice provides a quick reference to the essential points about orchid cultivation, and is a guide round the pitfalls that occasionally beset the grower.

Plan carefully

Do not be in too great a hurry to start your orchid collection. Evaluate the conditions available before deciding on your first purchases, and preferably visit a few orchid shows and nurseries. Most commercial orchid growers are pleased to welcome newcomers and advise you on the varieties most suitable for your environment, with no obligation to buy plants. The local nursery can also provide you with information about the nearest orchid society, where you will be able to make contact with interested hobbyists. This is extremely valuable, as most of them will have started growing orchids in a similar way, and will therefore be able to offer advice from a comparable level. Remember, however, that there is no *one* correct way to grow orchids.

Time spent planning is recouped many times over, and only when you are certain that a particular orchid will thrive in your situation is it wise to purchase. Buy mature plants initially, from an obviously clean nursery. Lower priced young plants or seedlings may seem a more attractive proposition, but it is important to the success of the venture to have at least some flowers during the first season. Imported species may also be less expensive than those reared at a nursery, but establishing an orchid newly imported from the jungle takes both time and skill, and is best not attempted by the complete novice. Above all, avoid so-called cheap offers in the non-orchid popular press, and those orchids that have been languishing for generations in someone's conservatory. Experience has shown that the former are frequently extremely poor in quality and the latter are probably infested with every possible ailment.

Cultural requirements

Specially constructed orchid houses are not essential; any greenhouse that is satisfactory for the culture of other plants will be adequate for orchids. All electrical installations should be fitted by a competent engineer and kept away from damp areas, preferably well above staging height.

Temperatures

The day temperature should be at least 5.5°C (10°F) higher than the night temperature during winter, and as much as 14-16.5°C (25-30°F) higher in summer. Low nocturnal temperatures—down

to 10°C (50°F)—are needed to initiate the flower buds in many genera.

Ventilation

Ventilation, especially from below staging height, should be used at most times except during foggy or extremely cold weather. It is essential to provide adequate ventilation—both high and low level—if a flueless burner is being used to supply heat in the greenhouse. Ventilators should be covered with gauze or fine mesh netting in order to keep out insects and other pests. Field mice are particularly attracted to a warm greenhouse, where they will rapidly demolish the orchid pollens, and anything else that tastes sweet.

Shading

Shading is used to help control the temperature, not necessarily to reduce the light, and therefore all shading

material should be applied to the outside of the greenhouse. Internal shading will not reduce the temperature, and in certain circumstances can even increase it by limiting the air circulation.

Insulation

Polyethylene lining installed to insulate the greenhouse in winter is also useful during the summer months. It will assist in retaining humidity, and recent experience has shown that the temperature in uninsulated greenhouses rises more rapidly and remains higher than in insulated greenhouses.

Repotting

Repotting is best completed when the new growth is developing, but try to avoid mid-winter and periods of very hot weather. Plants in bud or flower, or carrying a seed capsule, also prefer not to be repotted. But if a plant looks sick at

Right: To obtain the best display of flowers, try not to turn a plant when the buds are developing, or the flowers may open facing different directions.

any time, examine the roots and compost because a repot may be the answer.

Avoid having a variety of composts in one greenhouse, as this will lead to cultural problems. All orchids, as they join the collection, should be repotted into your chosen standard mixture at the earliest opportunity. Do not keep diseased plants or runts. If the care and attention often lavished on these ailing orchids were redirected towards the thriving plants, the whole collection would benefit.

Water
Rain water is not necessary, though it may be desirable. In city or industrial areas the rain water may be severely polluted. Mains water is not harmful, but *do not* use water that has been softened by means of a conventional salt softener. The sodium in softened water will slowly kill your plants. Some means of water storage, such as a tank fed from the greenhouse roof gutters, is desirable, in case of a temporary drought or water shortage.

Provided the compost is sound, orchids need frequent waterings during the growing season, but far less during the winter. If you are in doubt, orchids are best kept relatively dry. Do not spray or water overhead when the foliage is warm, or when the sun is shining on the plants as the foliage may become burned.

Feeding
Apply liquid fertilizer only in balance with other cultural requirements, such as light and warmth. Do not try to 'push' plants when growing conditions are poor, or when a plant is sick. Feeding is no panacea, and will not compensate for cultural deficiencies.

Plant hygiene
Cleanliness in the culture of plants is essential. Apart from the aesthetic considerations, many weeds make excellent hosts to insect pests and they should not be allowed to grow in the greenhouse. If you wish to cultivate plants under the staging, most fibrous rooted begonias, such as *Begonia rex* and its varieties, also saintpaulias and impatiens, make excellent groundcover plants. Ensure that they too do not become pest-infected, by regularly attending to them.

All new acquisitions, from whatever source, should be thoroughly inspected for insect pests or fungal diseases, which must be dealt with immediately to prevent the problem spreading. Regular spraying with insecticide is advisable, particularly in spring and early summer. Flower buds and new growths are especially suscept-

ible to attack by aphids. It is not a good idea, however, to attempt preventive spraying against fungal attack. There is some evidence to support the belief that more than two applications of systemic fungicide in any one season could restrict the growth of some genera. Therefore use a fungicide only after the disease has appeared, or better still, ensure that the problem is minimized by thoroughly clean culture.

Flower spikes and buds are a delicacy to snails and slugs, and only early preventive action will avoid damage. Apply slug killer just before the spikes are expected, and a 'collar' of cotton wool on the developing spike will prevent these pests from reaching the flowers.

Flower spikes
Some genera or species produce flowers sequentially from the same spike, occa-sionally over two or even three seasons. Therefore, the flower spike should not be removed—providing the plant is in good health—while it is still green. *Oncidium papilio, Onc. krameranum* and *Paphiopedilum glaucophyllum* produce flowers sequentially, and *Phalaenopsis lueddemanniana, P. violacea, P. cornucervi, Masdevallia tovarensis* and many others will produce flowers in the correct season from spikes several years old, in addition to the current ones.

Be consistent
Above all, do not change your cultural regime after hearing or reading about new techniques. Plants need time to adjust and cannot possibly thrive if the environment is radically changed three or four times each year. It is best to sieve out any cultural advice applicable to your situation, and accept that there are many different routes to success.

Right: During their early development, buds are most susceptible to chemical spray damage. Be careful when applying chemicals, as damaged buds may produce scarred flowers (left).

USING ORCHIDS IN FLOWER

With reasonable care, mature orchid plants will produce flowers regularly in their correct season. Species usually flower once each year at approximately the same period, and although within a single species there will be clones flowering at slightly different periods, each clone will generally come into bloom at a similar time each year. Hybrids are more variable in their flowering habits, many odontoglossums producing flower spikes at 10 to 11 month intervals, whilst phalaenopsis that are in good health will often produce two flower spikes each year. Cymbidiums, paphiopedilums and many other genera are usually more regular in their habits, and it is not unusual to see the same plants in flower on the showbench on identical dates year after year.

Training flower spikes

Orchid flowers do not appear in perfect condition on the showbench by accident or good fortune. Nearly all flower spikes need some form of training in order to present the flowers at their best, and in many cases this preparation should start when the spikes are only a few centimetres high. It is best to place a suitable cane next to each flower spike when it first appears. Marking the spike in this way helps to prevent accidental damage, which can so easily occur during routine watering or handling of the orchid, and the cane provides a suitable support to which the spike may be tied at regular intervals as it develops.

Select a cane of suitable size and strength to support the fully open spike of flowers, and push it into the compost next to the flower spike. Be sure to keep it clear of the base of the plant, where young growths could be damaged, and away from the side of the pot where the majority of the active roots will be found. For cymbidiums, which produce sturdy, heavy flower spikes, a bamboo cane approximately 1.2m (4 ft) long and 1.2cm (0.5in) in diameter should be adequate, while for the more slender spikes on odontoglossums and phalaenopsis, a split cane, 61-91cm (2-3ft) long will be sufficient. If one end of the cane is sharpened to a blunt point it will be easier to push it vertically into the compost.

Make the first tie when the spike is approximately 10-15cm (4-6in) long, using either raffia or a soft green string available from horticultural shops. Young spikes are extremely brittle, and any that are growing horizontally should be gradually trained to the vertical position over a period of several weeks. This would obviously not apply to species such as *Cymbidium devonianum*, *Coelogyne massangeana* and *flaccida*, and *Odontoglossum citrosmum*, which produce naturally pendulous spikes. In general, species orchids with their daintier flowers and lighter spikes will need far less support than their hybrid cousins. But try to keep all canes and ties to the minimum so that they remain unobtrusive. Approximately three ties should be sufficient for each spike, the top one positioned just above the first flower on the spike, after which the spike should be allowed to arch naturally, and the cane cut back to just above the top tie. In paphiopedilums, the one tie should be positioned just beneath the solitary flower, or, with multi-flowered species, immediately below the top flower.

Orchids in the home

Many orchids that normally grow best in the greenhouse environment can safely be brought into the home when in flower,

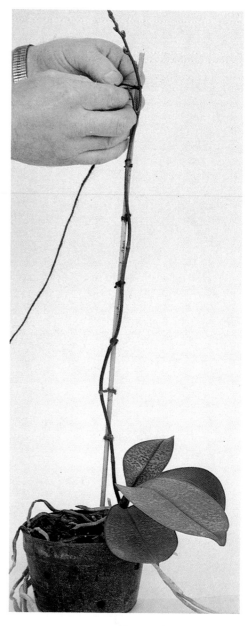

Below and Right: When training flower spikes use soft string; make the first tie near the base and work towards the apex.

Right: Since flowers of the cattleya hybrids are too heavy to be supported by their own stems, they should be tied to the supporting cane.

if a few simple precautions are taken. After all, there is little point in growing orchids merely to decorate the greenhouse!

Try to provide some local humidity around the plant by standing the pot in moist pebbles or similar material. Although these could be put in a saucer, a more aesthetically pleasing effect is obtained if some form of pot-holder or jardinière is used. The space between the plant pot and the outer container can then be filled completely with moisture-retaining material, which will help to keep the root system cool and moist. Even better, is a trough or similar container—the old fashioned, lined wine coolers are ideal—in which several orchids can be grouped with a few ferns or other foliage plants to form a pleasing display. This has the added advantage that several plants growing together will create their own microclimate.

Some areas within the home are unsuitable for orchids. Mantleshelves above hot fires or shelves over radiators may look perfect for the smaller plants, but the rising heat will rapidly cause the plant to dehydrate beyond the point of no return. Areas that are too light, such as a sunny windowsill—and even vandas do not like direct sun through glass—or too dark, excessively draughty or where the temperature fluctuates too frequently, such as a busy hallway, are all harmful to the plants. East or west facing windows are suitable, but if the curtains are drawn across on a cold winter's evening, be sure to bring all the plants into the comfort of the room.

To compensate for the lower humidity indoors, orchids will probably need watering more frequently than in the greenhouse. Plants should be watered thoroughly and it is best to take them to the kitchen or bathroom to avoid spoiling furnishings. Providing that their stay indoors does not exceed three to four weeks, feeding should not be necessary. Similarly, any plants showing symptoms of pests or diseases should be returned immediately to the greenhouse where the trouble can be dealt with.

Orchids in vases

When the last flower on a spike has been open for two or three weeks, the plant will benefit if the spike is cut. This allows the plant to put all its energies into growth, thus ensuring even more flowers for next season. The cut flowers too will last nearly as long off the plant as on, particularly if not placed in the unsuitable areas already described. But do not cut the spike before the terminal flower has been open for at least 8 to 10 days, and as with all cut flowers, orchids will last longer if regularly given fresh water. In the smaller 'specimen' vases, which are ideal for the dainty sprays of many species or a single paphiopedilum flower, the water level drops very quickly and will need daily topping-up. Every few days it is advisable to renew all the water, at the same time cutting a thin slice off the bottom of each spike or flower stem, at a slant, to allow the greatest possible area of stem to absorb the water. Do not crush the stem as often advocated; this merely blocks the capillary passages in the stem and restricts the flow of water, thus shortening the life of the flower.

Corsages and bouquets

Orchid flowers are ideal for buttonholes, corsages or wedding bouquets. What could be more appropriate than white phalaenopsis and dendrobiums mixed with stephanotis and silver foliage to

Above: Flowering orchids make fine house plants, and are even more attractive when the flower pots are pleasingly disguised.

Below: A delightful corsage—the green of the fern contrasts beautifully with the delicate pink of the phalaenopsis flowers.

Above: The components required to make a corsage: plants, wire and ribbon. Left: First wire the main bloom, and then the other foliage components as shown.

Above and Left: All wires should be covered in green florists' tape as shown (left).

Above and Left: Having brought all the wires of the individual parts together, arrange the foliage to complement the main bloom. Twist the wires together, trim them, and finally tape the 'stem'.

adorn the bridal gown? On a very limited scale, the local florist would probably be happy to purchase good quality, fresh orchid flowers, but although this may provide some funds for the purchase of new plants, orchid growing as a hobby should not be thought of as a paying concern.

To make a single corsage you will need two or three orchid flowers, depending upon size, together with a few small leaves of fern, thin copper wire, florist's tape, and, if desired, a short length of ribbon. To increase durability, all plant material should be stood in deep water overnight before making up the corsage or bouquet. Wire the stem of each flower to increase its length and ensure its correct positioning. Then cover each stem with florist's tape (usually dark green), and arrange the flowers and fern leaves together so that the flowers are just touching and the foliage forms a background. Next, twist the wires from the stems together and round all the stems to hold everything in place. Finally, trim back this central wire 'stem' to within approximately 5cm (2in) of the flowers, and, if you wish, tie the ribbon in a bow around it. If you put the completed corsage into a plastic box and place it in a domestic refrigerator, it will keep perfectly for two or three days.

A similar technique can be used for bouquet making, although instead of single flowers it is preferable to leave the

Right: It is not only the flowers that win an exhibitor a prize, but attention to detail, such as cleaning the foliage.

whole spike intact, allowing the natural presentation of the flowers to predominate.

Exhibiting orchids

For many, the ultimate accolade for their orchids is to gain a prize at an orchid show. But win or lose, there is much to learn and enjoy by exhibiting, and a certain satisfaction in knowing that your orchids have helped in making the show a success. Preparations for exhibiting are not too dissimilar to the normal cultural routine followed by all enthusiastic growers; plants should be maintained in a pest- and disease-free condition, weeds should never be allowed to grow in the pots, and flower spikes always benefit by being trained properly. Extra attention to these details, coupled with a thorough cleaning of the plant and pot, may make the difference between 'just another exhibit' and a 'polished performer'.

Preparing for the show

Dead bracts around the base of pseudo-bulbs should be split vertically and then each half removed by gently pulling sideways, taking care not to damage any new growths that may be hidden in the base. Any leaves which have died back or have brown tips should be trimmed back in a natural contour, after which the foliage should be sponged with clean water. Before wiping both sides of the leaf with a clean sponge or cloth, hold the base of the leaf to prevent it pulling out. The centre leaves on semi-mature growths of cymbidiums and odontoglossums are particularly vulnerable and, as all foliage is needed for the plant to grow well, care should be taken not to lose any needlessly. Finally, clean the pot and label the plant clearly according to the show schedule.

To transport the plants to the exhibition hall, place the pots in boxes and pack tightly with paper. Where several plants are to travel in the same box, ensure that all the flowers are held apart from each other and any other surface. With large arching spikes it is advisable to insert a second cane into the compost at an angle, so that the end of the spike may be tied to it and held steady.

When staging the plants, ensure that you have complied with the show regulations, and, if in doubt, consult the show secretary, who is there to help make certain that all plants are exhibited to their full potential.

Orchid societies

In all parts of the world there are now orchid societies established to bring together people of similar interests. Many function under the umbrella of a national council, whilst others flourish equally well on an independent basis. There are many advantages to membership, not least the facility to purchase orchid 'accessories' at competitive prices. Regular meetings are held, so the grower is kept informed about current events in the orchid world. Speakers from the commercial sector will frequently attend such meetings, and orchid forums regularly discuss cultural and other questions—basic or more advanced—to the benefit of all. Visits to nurseries and private orchid collections are a normal part of a society programme, as are social events.

But above all, membership of a society offers the opportunity to take a broader view of your hobby, something that is certain to be of benefit to you and your orchids.

Below: A superb display of orchids—the culmination of much painstaking work and effort. Critical attention to culture and detailed preparation have made this a collection to be envied, and as such an inspiration to all other growers.

BREEDING AND TISSUE CULTURE

Since the first manmade orchid hybrids flowered over a century ago, orchidists have been transferring the pollen from one orchid to the stigma of another in the hope of combining the best features of each parent into the resulting seedlings. The process got off to a fine start as *Paphiopedilum* Harrisianum, which first flowered in 1869, is still much used today as a cut flower, and grown by many hobbyists.

Whether it was by chance or inspiration that John Dominy, the chief grower on the famous Veitch nursery at Exeter, crossed *Paphiopedilum barbatum* with *Paphiopedilum villosum,* the results were far reaching. The strong colour of the pod parent, *barbatum* (the plant fertilized) combined with the vigour and tremendous texture of the pollen parent, *villosum* (the plant contributing the pollen) to give richly coloured long-lasting flowers produced on tall stems from a plant that grows and flowers more freely than either of its parents. Appropriately, this first paphiopedilum hybrid was named in honour of Dr John Harris, the Exeter surgeon who had suggested to Dominy the feasibility of pollination—a technique that had previously eluded orchid growers.

The success of hybridization

Once it became certain that orchids would hybridize, many collected plants originally thought to be species were re-examined, and the first natural hybrids were classified.

Even today, some growers ask why, with the vast numbers and diversity found in species and naturally occurring hybrids, do we breed more orchids. There are, of course, many reasons, and possibly the commercial cut flower aspect is of prime importance. To fulfil the requirements of a good cut flower, orchid flowers must be freely produced from compact plants, be well spaced on tall spikes (or, if produced singly as in paphiopedilums, have long stems), be easily packed into boxes (thus arching sprays are less popular than upright spikes) and be sufficiently tough in texture to withstand long journeys, yet still last for weeks in the customer's home. Modern tastes also demand large, rounded flowers.

Unfortunately, not many species or primary hybrids satisfy all these criteria. Thus orchid breeders have sought to combine, for example, the strong colour or lip markings of an otherwise insignificant orchid with the spike habit and flower shape of a more vigorously growing one. Very few of the resulting seedlings will have all the desirable features, but by carefully selecting the best plants for subsequent breeding, hybridizers have succeeded in producing, over many generations, orchids that have most of the good characteristics.

This process of selection is limitless, as new varieties are constantly being demanded by an expanding market. To satisfy the whims of growers in warm climates who wish to cultivate high altitude—thus, cool growing—orchids, there has also been some breeding for temperature tolerance. The cool growing

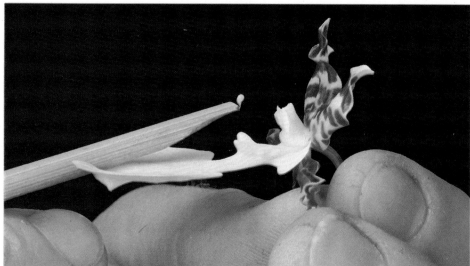

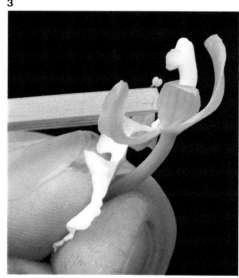

Hand Pollination of Orchids

From the orchids man has artificially produced many more hybrids than from any other group of commonly cultivated plants. The naturally occurring species and hybrids rely upon insects for transfer of pollen from one flower to the stigma of another. Those insects are attracted by a variety of lures, such as scent, colour and nectar. Some orchids have evolved very highly specialized techniques to ensure that the pollinia are deposited on the correct part of the insect, so that when visiting subsequent flowers the pollen mass is brought into contact with the glutinous receptive surface of the stigma. For synthetic hybrids, however, man has to undertake the pollinating role of these insects.

The plant produced from artificial pollination usually takes many years to reach a flower-

1 First of all decide which plant is to be the pollen parent and which the pod parent. The latter should always be the stronger grower of the two. The pollen masses are found on the column beneath the apex of the cap, except in *Paphiopedilum* and allied genera where there is no cap and they are on either side of the column.

2 Place a small pointed piece of wood, such as a matchstick, under the pollen cap and lift upwards; the cap will fall away leaving the pollinia stuck to the end of the piece of wood. Check that the pollen mass is a clear yellow colour (yellow-brown for *Paphiopedilum* and allied genera) and not infected with mildew.

3 Remove the pollinia of the flower chosen for the pod parent in the same way and either discard or use it for further crosses. Next transfer the pollinia removed from the pollen parent to the pod parent flower.

odontoglossums, for instance, have been bred with the warmer growing Brazilian miltonias to produce flowers that resemble those of odontoglossums, and plants that will tolerate the higher temperatures of tropical areas. *Odontonia* Purple Ace is an example of one of the more successful hybrids.

A more recent reason for breeding is aimed at conservation. By selecting two clones of the same species and crossing one with the other—thus producing a species under cultivation—it is hoped that those species especially endangered in their country of origin will be available to the general public, and even to repopulate depleted colonies in the wild. Luckily, many of these nursery-raised species seem to grow better than their jungle-collected cousins that have to adapt to an unnatural environment.

The commercial orchid industry is reacting swiftly to fill the void created by the Endangered Species Act, which controls the international movement of all orchids—hybrids and species—in an attempt to prevent threatened species from becoming extinct. But while accepting the ideals behind the legislation, far more effort is required from the countries concerned if some species are not to become extinct. Agricultural and mining interests are having a far greater effect on depletion than the relatively small amount of commercial collecting now taking place, and blame for the extinction of species orchids should not be laid solely at the door of orchid growers.

The art of breeding

After successful pollination, in most cases the pollinated flower rapidly wilts and loses much of its colour. Paphiopedilums are a notable exception to this rule, but in all orchids the ovary behind the flower begins to swell and the seed pod, or capsule, develops. This process continues until the capsule is ripe and the seed is ready for harvesting. The time taken to ripen varies even within one genus, from 4 to 14 months, and rather than relying on arbitrary ripening dates, it is best to keep an eye on the individual capsule. The capsules should be removed when the end starts to turn yellow or brown and becomes a little crisp, but before it splits longitudinally.

Seed raising

The seed should be sown immediately, and there are many specialist seed-raising laboratories that offer a good service. Orchid seed is extremely small and needs to be sown in flasks of a chemical agar under sterile conditions. Any bacteria that enter the flask will rapidly spread and ruin the valuable seed. For those hobbyist growers able to supply the necessary sterile conditions, various proprietary brands of sowing medium are available, mostly based on the formula worked out by Professor Lewis Knudson at Cornell University in 1922. For the most detailed information on the subject, see *The Orchids: A Scientific Survey* edited by Carl Withner of the Brooklyn Botanic Garden.

Most orchid seed begins to germinate

---

ing size, and it is only then that the merit of the new hybrid can be fully assessed. Thus the parent plants should always be chosen from good healthy stock and between them possess all the characters desired in the offspring. Unfortunately, there is no way to ensure that the resulting hybrids will display all the desired characters; it is just a matter of chance.

The photographs on these two pages clearly illustrate the technique for artificially pollinating orchids—having a steady hand is certainly an advantage. After the seed has ripened it is usually sown on nutrient agar gel where it may take several weeks before any signs of germination are visible. With patience and good cultivation techniques (as well as some luck) any orchid grower should be able to produce new and improved hybrids himself.

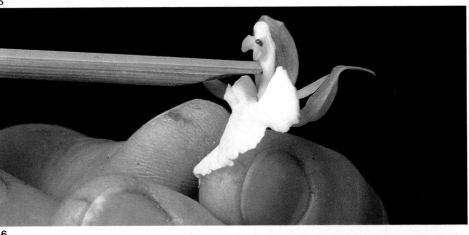

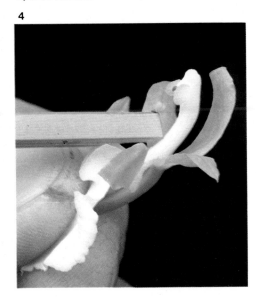

4 Introduce the pollinia of the pollen parent into the flower of the female parent, taking care not to damage the flower. Although it is best to have both parents flowering at the same time it is possible to store the pollinia of some orchids for a few months in the dry atmosphere of a sealed and labelled test-tube containing silica-gel.

5 Push the pollinia up on to the stigma—just behind the site from where the pod parent's pollinia was removed. In *Paphiopedilum* and associated genera a 'window' has to be cut in the pouch so that the pollen masses can be placed on the stigma.

6 Once the pollinia has stuck to the glutinous surface of the stigma, the wooden stick can be removed. Finally, label the flower with all the relevant details of the hybridization, such as parents and date of pollination. If pollination has been successful the flower will collapse soon afterwards and the seed pod will swell.

pot, then refill to within 2cm (0.75in) of the top.

If the roots are decayed or the compost is sour, remove all the compost and trim back the roots. Any leafless pseudobulbs can be removed by cutting the short rhizome at the base of the bulb with a sterilized knife.

It is often advisable to split plants into divisions of two bulbs with leaves. The repotting procedure is the same as outlined except that more drainage material may be needed in the bottom of the pot. Do not use too large a pot for these divisions—a pot that has room for a year's development is adequate.

Seedlings require more frequent potting than mature plants, but take care not to use too large a pot. Not more than one year's growth should be allowed for, otherwise there is a possibility of the compost becoming sour.

Propagation and division
Plants should be divided during the early spring or directly after flowering. First clean the plant as outlined above, then decide where the plant is to be split. Normally two-leaved bulbs with a new growth make up a division, and cuts should be made with a sterilized knife between the bulbs to sever the short rhizome connecting them. Once all the cuts have been made the plant can be pulled apart. The potting procedure outlined for plants with decayed roots or sour compost should then be followed. You can also increase your stock by removing the leafless pseudobulbs and potting them individually in small pots, which should then be placed in a warm shaded position in the greenhouse. Alternatively, the pot and the bulb could be placed in a polyethylene bag which should then be sealed and hung up in the greenhouse. After a few weeks new growths will develop on most of the bulbs. The polyethylene bag can then be removed and the plants grown on as normal.

The mass propagation technique used by the major cymbidium growers throughout the world is known as meristem tissue culture and is outlined on page 98.

Watering and feeding
Watering is always a difficult subject to offer advice upon, but the golden rule is to allow the compost to become partially dry and then give a thorough watering from the top of the pot, ensuring that the compost is thoroughly saturated. Plants usually require more frequent watering during their active growing season in spring, summer and early autumn, than during the late autumn and winter months.

Newly potted plants in a peat-based compost containing a fertilizer should be given a very thorough watering directly they have been repotted ensuring that the compost is thoroughly wetted. Then they

should be allowed to become partially dry and watered as outlined above.

Although the use of fertilizers was frowned upon by the early orchid growers, they are certainly necessary with today's compost. A balanced fertilizer should be given during the late spring and summer months, and a high potassium feed used during the autumn. This feed should be given at about half the manufacturer's recommended strength and carried out at fortnightly intervals.

Pests and diseases
Although cymbidiums are not troubled by many insect pests, the red spider mite causes considerable problems if not controlled. The pest can normally be controlled by one of the recommended proprietary insecticides, such as azobenzine, which will specifically eliminate red spider mite.

Aphids will sometimes attack the flowers and flower buds, but they can be dealt with quickly by spraying with malathion. Scale insects can be more troublesome but a double strength spray of malathion normally kills them.

Slugs and snails occasionally attack the flower spikes and a pellet of metaldehyde and bran placed between the spike and the bulb at an early stage will ensure that no damage is done.

Providing you obtain good clean stock from a reliable source, disease should not present much of a problem. The worst situation would be a plant infected with virus; if you have such a plant it must be destroyed for fear of the problem spreading to other stock.

Fungal and bacterial diseases are not common and will normally only occur where the plants are in a poor condition or if the environment in which the plants are grown is unsuitable.

Looking for flower spikes
Spike hunting is always an exciting time whether you have a large or small collection, as it is then you can speculate on the colourful display for the coming winter and spring months.

It is often difficult for the beginner to distinguish between a flower spike and a new growth. The new growth is invariably broader at the base and flatter than the flower spike. The flower spike tends to be rounder and if *gentle* pressure is applied some 'give' will be detected. Once the flower spike has been located it should be marked with a bamboo cane and tied as it develops.

A word of warning about cymbidiums in flower. The cymbidium is such a generous plant that it will often flower for up to three months. But during this time it is using up most of its resources, so that it is beneficial to remove flower spikes after they have been open for six weeks. This will give the plant an opportunity to

produce new growth for the following year's flowering. You can, of course, still enjoy the cut flowers indoors.

Species and hybrids
In the early 1900s several interesting species were discovered in Burma and Indo-China, including *Cym. parishii, insigne* and *erythrostylum*. This group had white to rose-pink flowers and were to be important in the cymbidiums' future development. The earlier discovered species included *Cym. hookeranum (grandiflorum), lowianum, traceyanum, giganteum, i'ansonnii* and *schroderi,* although the last three were not much used in hybridization. The numerous flowers of these species are generally borne on large spikes and tend to be green or brown with some intermediate shades. *Cym. hookeranum* and *lowianum* have been very important in the production of the green-flowered hybrids.

The species *Cym. eburneum* and *insigne* are primarily responsible for the production of the white and pink-flowered hybrids. The autumn to winter flowering types originated from the species *Cym. erythrostylum, hookeranum* and *traceyanum. Cym. traceyanum* is also responsible for imparting some of its yellow colour to the modern yellow hybrids. Although not much used in breeding, *Cym. i'ansonnii* provided the starting point of many of the modern deep pink and red types. Similarly, *Cym. parishii* has had quite an impact on past and present hybrids, often producing varieties with beautiful well marked lips. Such famous cymbidiums as Miretta, Promona and Kittiwake have *parishii* in their backgrounds, and several of their clones have the most outstanding red lips.

When considering cymbidium breeding, mention should be made of H.G. Alexander who began hybridizing cymbidiums in 1907 and was responsible for many fine cymbidium hybrids, the most famous of which is *Cym.* Alexanderi 'Westonbirt' (FCC/RHS) (*Cym.* Eburneo-lowianum × *Cym. insigne.*) This cymbidium has exerted its influence on hybridization from the start and is still important today.

It is interesting to note that most of today's best modern hybrids have the common parents of Alexanderi at some point in their pedigree. This is true of the finest whites, pinks, yellows and greens, and for most of the very finest autumn and winter flowering types.

Cym. Pauwelsii (*Cym. insigne* × *Cym. lowianum*), another hybrid which was to play an important part in hybridization, made its appearance at the same time as Alexanderi. This plant contributed fine qualities of vigorous growth and very large flower spikes to its progeny. The most important hybrid it produced was Babylon (*Cym.* Olympus × *Cym.* Pauwelsii) which, in turn, became the parent of many of the best coloured varieties.

At present, work on cymbidium hybridizing is being carried out in several countries. There are many breeders in Australia, the United States, Holland and England. Some do this on a small scale, while others have vast planned breeding programmes covering the whole colour range and different times of flowering.

Autumn to winter flowering hybrids
The finest autumn to winter flowering cymbidiums will undoubtedly be produced from a combination of the best *Cym. erythrostylum* line crossed with the Lucy Moor lines. This line should produce good quality pastel shades and some fine yellows. For the pink red types *Cym.* Lilliana will be of great importance, and some progeny that have already flowered have shown great promise.

Winter to spring flowering hybrids
The winter to spring flowering types will continue to improve with the use of such parents as *Cym.* Pearl Balkis and Dingwall for whites, and Loch Lomond, York Meradith and the old favourite, Baltic, for greens. For red and orange flowers the most important parent is probably Hamsey 'The Globe'. Some of the Hamsey progeny have already flowered and will be very useful breeding plants for future generations.

A shining star of the future is *Cym.* Howick 'Cooksbridge' (AM/RHS). The clone has very large white flowers of full shape with a very heavy deep crimson banded lip.

The yellow-flowered group remains a problem but Many Waters 'Stonehurst' (AM/RHS) seems to be a possible parent together with Cariga 'Tetra Canary' (AM/RHS). It is important not to forget that some of the autumn to winter flowering cymbidiums are very fine yellows and the best of these crossed with the good winter to spring flowering yellows should produce some very worthwhile results.

Late spring flowering hybrids
There are several fine hybrids available for use in breeding for late spring flowering plants. The most exciting of these is *Cym.* Caithness 'Cooksbridge' (FCC/RHS). This clone has massive light green flowers of perfect shape with a broad attractive lip. The first seedlings have produced some of the finest flowers seen to date. Other interesting parents to look out for are Dingwall 'Lewes' and the old Prince Charles 'Exbury'.

Pure coloured hybrids
An interesting development in recent years has been the appearance of the so-called pure coloured cymbidiums. These plants do not produce red pigment and therefore only three colours are available—white, yellow and green, all without

the normal red lip markings. Instead, the markings on the lip are yellow. This line of breeding has been developed from *Cym. lowianum* var. *concolor,* and by crossing and back crossing a fine strain has been built up, although there is still considerable room for improvement.

Most of the work on this type of cymbidium has been carried out in Australia, although recently some very interesting clones have been produced in the United States and England. Recommended hybrids are Sleeping Gold 'Tetragold' (AM/RHS), Pharaoh and several clones of Highland Surprise.

Future trends
In the future novelty type breeding should prove very interesting. This would involve selection for flamboyant colour combinations, such as occur in hybrids like Mavourneen 'Jester' (AM/RHS). Breeding from this clone will hopefully result in plants with beautiful white sepals, red lips and red petals or yellow sepals and a similar combination.

Miniature cymbidiums
The most important miniature *Cymbidium* species used in breeding are *Cym. devonianum, ensifolium, pumilum* and *tigrinum.*

The *devonianum* hybrids are characterized by arching and sometimes pendulous spikes and flowers of green, yellow, bronze or some intermediate shades, many of which have bold lip markings. Some outstanding hybrids from this line of breeding include Touchstone, Miniatures Delight and Bulbarrow (*Cym. devonianum* × *Cym.* Western Rose). The Bulbarrow hybrids have very bold lip markings.

The two most important breeding characteristics of *Cym. ensifolium* are its season of flowering (late summer and autumn) and its fragrance. The progeny from *ensifolium* tend to have inherited the best characteristics of the species. The fragrance of the flowers is striking and can be detected immediately you enter the house. Such fine hybrids as Peter Pan (*Cym. ensifolium* × *Cym.* Miretta) and Ensikhan (*Cym. ensifolium* × *Cym.* Nam Khan) can be recommended.

One of the most important miniature hybrid groups are those bred from *Cym. pumilum.* The most charming plants are found in this group, and the make ideal pot plants, even in the small home. Some outstanding recent hybrids include Lerwick, Stonehaven, Strathavon, Nip × Kurun and Nip × Clarissa: these lovely plants have inherited the best *pumilum* characteristics and have a wide range of flower colours.

Some fine examples of *Cym. tigrinum* breeding are Wood Nymph (*tigrinum* × Sea Foam), Tiger Cub (*tigrinum* × Esmerella) and Tiger Tail (*tigrinum* × Alex-

anderi). All these hybrids flower in spring (derived from *tigrinum*), and are dwarf, compact plants with short broad leaves and small pseudobulbs. The colour range is rather limited, being mainly green or yellow, but there are some beautiful plants amongst them. Recently improved hybrids have been obtained as a result of breeding from Wood Nymph crossed with a selected standard (non-miniature) cymbidium, Western Rose. These plants

are compact growers, late spring flowering, and range in colour from bronze, yellow and green to pastel pink.

Starting a collection

Assuming that you have the necessary facilities, before starting a collection it would be wise to approach one of the commercial growers who specializes in cymbidiums. If you choose well, it is possible to have plants in flower for more than six months of the year—indeed all year round if you grow hybrids bred from *Cym. ensifolium.* Provided you have room to accommodate them, all cymbidiums make good houseplants.

Do not be afraid to seek the experts' advice on starting a collection and on all aspects of orchid culture. Most of the varieties illustrated here are readily available, but they vary in price according to the size of plant and considered quality of the flower. Do not buy very expensive plants at first. However, you must be sure that the stock is good and robust, for it would be a waste of time and money to start with weaklings.

Below: Because cymbidiums tolerate cool conditions, they make ideal plants for garden rooms and conservatories. Being tall, with flower spikes bearing many blooms, the standard cymbidiums make an impressive display in this large ornamental garden.

Cymbidium Species

Cymbidium devonianum

○Cool ✿Late spring

Above: This miniature species originates from the Himalayas and has been used often in miniature breeding. The flower spikes are pendent, and its progeny tend to have arching spikes. The flowers, which normally open in late spring and early summer, are basically green speckled with red, while the triangular lip is pink spotted with crimson.

Photo x 1

Cymbidium eburneum

○Cool ✿Winter/Spring

Right: Discovered in the 1830s by the botanical explorer William Griffiths, this species is native to the Khasia hills in northern India. It is a compact grower with narrow pseudobulbs, and leaves that can grow to more than 61cm (24in) in length. The erect flower spike arises higher up on the bulb than in most cymbidiums, and several spikes are often carried at the same time. The plant is often erratic in its flowering, producing from one to three, 7.5cm (3in) flowers to each spike. The flowers, which open in winter and early spring, are white to ivory in colour, with a deep yellow band in the middle of the lip, flanked by two yellow keels. Very prominent in hybridization, *eburneum* was one of the parents of the first hybrid cymbidium to be raised in cultivation—Eburneolowianum—which was registered by Veitch in 1889. Whilst it is an important species in breeding, the plant is not a vigorous grower and is a shy bloomer.

Photo x 1

Cymbidium giganteum
○Cool ✿Autumn/Winter

Left: This species was first collected in Nepal in 1821. The name *giganteum* refers to the size of the plant and not the flowers. The leaves, which grow up to 76cm (30in) long, spring from stout pseudobulbs. From 5 to 15 yellow-green flowers, each 7.5-10cm (3-4in) across, are carried on strong spikes. This species is little used in hybridization because of the dull colour and relatively poor quality of its flowers.
Photo x 1

Cymbidium lowianum
○Cool ✿Late Spring

Below: This species was discovered in 1887 in upper Burma, and was also found in Thailand. Its influence is present in almost all of our modern hybrids. The plant, which flowers in late spring, normally carries very large arching sprays of green flowers, up to 10cm (4in) across, with a V-shaped red mark on the lip.
Photo X 1/3

Cymbidium traceyanum
○Cool ✿Autumn/Winter

Below: A very interesting and flamboyant species imported in great quantities from Thailand at the beginning of the century. The number collected in the early years resulted in the virtual disappearance of the plant from its natural habitat. The species is autumn to winter flowering and produces long arching sprays of 10-13cm (4-5in) flowers. The petals are green, heavily striped with dark red, and the white lip is spotted with red. It has been important as a base species for producing spring flowering types and is also in the background of some yellow hybrids.
Photo X 1/4

Cymbidium Hybrids

CYMBIDIUM
Angelica 'Advent' (AM/RHS)
○*Cool* ✿*Autumn/Winter*
Below: This superb autumn to winter
flowering yellow hybrid (*Cym.* Lucy Moor
× *Cym.* Lucense) is fast becoming a very
famous breeding plant and is being used
by cymbidium hybridists throughout the
world. Up to 14 large flowers.
13cm (5in) across, are carried on
upright spikes. The petals and sepals are
pale yellow and the cream-coloured lip is
lightly spotted with dark red. the spotting
becoming dense in the throat. This very
attractive cymbidium deserves a place in
every collection.
Photo x ¼

CYMBIDIUM
Ayres Rock 'Cooksbridge Velvet'
○*Cool* ✿*Winter/Spring*
Above: This is one of a new generation of
cymbidiums in which the colour range has
been extended even further towards the
deeper pinks. The interesting breeding of
this hybrid (Hamsey × Rodkobb) points
the way for the future. The plant
illustrated is only a seedling, but should
give upright spikes of up to 12 flowers
when mature. The flowers, 11cm
(4.25in) across, are crimson tinged with
white and the lip is a rich dark crimson,
boldly edged with white. The plant
flowers in winter and spring.
Photo x ½

CYMBIDIUM
Baltic (AM/RHS)
○*Cool* ✿*Winter/Spring*
Left: A cross between *Cym.* Riga and
Cym. Midas, this is one of the most
famous breeding plants in the green
colour range, and has been responsible
for numerous fine hybrids which have
gained awards throughout the world.
Raised by the famous Dell Park
Collection, it will continue to be important
for many years to come. The plant is
small growing, producing arching spikes
of bright green flowers with crimson
markings on the cream lip. The flowers
are 11cm (4.25in) across and open in
the winter and early spring.
Photo x ⅔

CYMBIDIUM
Cariga 'Tetra Canary' (AM/RHS)
○*Cool* ✿*Winter-Spring*
Below: This hybrid variety is a mutation of the original *Cym.* Cariga 'Canary' (AM/RHS) (*Cym.* Carlos × *Cym.* Riga), which arose during the tissue culture processes. It is a great improvement on the original, having much rounder greenish-yellow flowers, and a larger lip with heavier crimson and white markings. The plant is free growing and flowers freely from winter to early spring giving up to 12, 11.5cm (4.5in) flowers on semi-arching spikes.
Photo x ½

CYMBIDIUM
Dingwall 'Lewes'
○*Cool* ✿*Late spring*
Right: This hybrid is the result of a cross between *Cym.* Pearl Easter and *Cym.* Merlin. Pearl Easter is a superb parent for producing flowers with clear white sepals and petals and the combination with Merlin has produced some very fine late spring flowering whites (the flowering season being derived from Merlin). This plant is free flowering and bears up to 12 large (13cm [5in]) flowers on an upright spike. The petals and sepals are white the lip is marked with red.
Photo x ½

CYMBIDIUM
Fort George 'Lewes' (AM/RHS)
○*Cool* ✿*Winter/Spring*
Below: One of the finest. free flowering green-coloured cymbidiums in the world. often giving two spikes per bulb with up to 14 flowers per spike on an upright stem. The flowers. which open in the early spring. are up to 12.5cm (4.75in) in diameter. The bringing together of two of the most famous green-flowered parents (*Cym.* Baltic × *Cym.* York Meradith) has produced an excellent result.
Photo x ½

CYMBIDIUM
Gymer 'Cooksbridge'
○*Cool* ✿*Late spring*
Right: This cross between *Cym.* Dorama and *Cym.* Cariga. has produced a late spring flowering hybrid with yellow flowers with deep crimson lips. The flowers can be up to 13cm (5in) in diameter and are carried on upright spikes of up to 24 flowers. The plant is very free flowering. sometimes producing up to three spikes per bulb, and has certainly inherited the very best properties from both its parents.
Photo X 1

CYMBIDIUM
Mavourneen 'Jester' (AM/RHS)
○*Cool* ✿*Winter/Spring*
Below: Cymbidiums with lip markings on the petals and sepals (peloric cymbidiums) are very rare. This plant clearly shows the characteristic lip colour and shape taken on by the petals. It is fortunate that the mutation occurred in this particular variety (*Cym.* Sussex Moor × *Cym.* Miretta) because it is in itself a very fine flower. This clone has already been used for breeding but to date none of the seedlings carried the peloric characteristics. although some very fine varieties were produced. The back cross with Sussex Moor has now been made and the results are awaited with anticipation. The plant flowers in winter and early spring. and the flowers are 11cm (4.25in) across.
Photo X ²/₃

CYMBIDIUM
Mavourneen 'Tetra Cooksbridge'
○*Cool* ❀*Winter/Spring*
Left: The original plant of Mavourneen 'Cooksbridge' (AM/RHS) was a very fine clone, but this mutation is far superior, having rounder flowers of heavier substance. This plant has erect flower spikes, and blooms during the winter and early spring. The flowers, 11cm (4.25in) across, are moss-green, lightly flushed with pink, and the large lip is rose-pink lightly spotted with dark red.
Photo X ⅔

CYMBIDIUM
Ngaire × Clarissa
○*Cool* ❀*Winter/Spring*
Above: Although there is a quest for flowers of a pure colour, such is the diversity of the cymbidium that some outstanding multicoloured flowers have also been produced by the hybridist. This plant has 11cm (4.25in) flowers carried on erect spikes and blooms during the winter to spring. The petals and sepals are white flushed with rose-pink, and the lip is boldly marked with red.
Photo X ¼

CYMBIDIUM
Pearl Balkis 'Fiona'
○*Cool* ❀*Winter/Spring*
Left: A very beautiful white cymbidium, the result of combining two very famous large-flowered cymbidiums (Pearl Easter × Balkis). Up to 14 flowers, 13cm (5in) across, are carried on upright spikes. The contrasting lip is pale rose-pink spotted with crimson. This is a very fine winter to spring flowering variety.
Photo X ⅔

CYMBIDIUM
Rievaulx 'Cooksbridge' (AM/RHS)
○*Cool* ✤*Late spring*
Right: This cross between *Cym*. Rio Rita
and one of the world's most famous
large-flowered cymbidium parents, *Cym*.
Vieux Rose, produced this outstanding
deep pink hybrid. The featured plant is
free growing and flowering, producing
up to 20 large flowers, 11.5cm (4.5in)
across, on a semi-arching spike. The
plant flowers in late spring.
Photo X 1

CYMBIDIUM
Rincon 'Clarisse' (AM/RHS)
○*Cool* ✤*Autumn*
Below: This American plant *Cym*. Pearl
× *Cym*. Windsor is famous as a parent
for producing high quality early autumn
flowering cymbidiums. It imparts its good
shape, colour and well marked lips to
most of its progeny. The 9cm (3.75in)
flowers are white, striped with light pink,
and the cream lip is boldly marked with
crimson. The shape of the flower is
primarily inherited from the species *Cym*.
erythrostylum in its background. A worthwhile plant, parent and grandparent of
fine progeny.
Photo X 1

CYMBIDIUM
Sparkle 'Ruby Lips'
○*Cool* ✿*Spring*

Right: The cross between Vieux Rose and Defiant that produced Sparkle was remarkable for the consistent quality of the progeny. The range of colours obtained includes pink, yellow, orange and green. This particular example has moss green flowers, 11cm (4.25in) across, which are lightly marked with red, and a deep crimson lip. The arching spike can bear up to 20 flowers at a time. The plant is free growing and flowers easily.

Photo X ½

CYMBIDIUM
Stanley Fouraker × Highlander
○*Cool* ✿*Autumn/Winter*

Above: An interesting combination of the *Cym. erythrostylum* and *Cym. traceyanum* x *hookeranum* lines of breeding, which has resulted in flowers of good size and shape, in lovely pastel shades with attractive lip markings. This plant, which has white flowers and a pretty pink-spotted lip, flowers in autumn and early winter and carries its blooms on upright spikes. The flowers are 10cm (4in) in diameter.

Photo X ½

CYMBIDIUM
Vieux Rose × Loch Lomond
○*Cool* ✿*Winter/Spring*

Right: This hybrid is an interesting combination between a pink flowered and a green flowered cymbidium. Most of the progeny from this cross have green-bronze flowers, though a few pinks are also found. The flowers of this hybrid are pale green, while the large lip is whitish-green, spotted with crimson and yellow in the throat. The spike habit tends to be semi- to fully arching, and the flowers, which are 12.5cm (4.75in) across, open from winter to early spring.

Photo X 1

Miniature Cymbidiums

CYMBIDIUM
Annan 'Cooksbridge' (AM/RHS)
○*Cool* ❀*Spring*
Right: This cymbidium of miniature background (*Cym*. Camelot × *Cym*. Berwick) has some of the deepest, richest coloured flowers seen in the genus. The plant tends to be a little larger than others from this line of breeding but the uniqueness of the 7cm (2.75in) deep crimson flowers more than compensates for the slightly large plant. The upright spikes are normally in full flower in spring.
Photo x ¾

CYMBIDIUM
Bulbarrow 'Our Midge'
○*Cool* ❀*Late spring*
Above: The Bulbarrow hybrids have rightly gained a reputation throughout the world. The crossing of the standard Western Rose with the miniature species, *Cym. devonianum,* resulted in some excellent clones, most of which have flowers with very fine lips of striking colours.
'Our Midge' bears spikes of up to 20 flowers in late spring. The 2.5-4cm (1-1.5in) flowers are soft rose-red with deep crimson lips.
Photo x ⅓

CYMBIDIUM
Lerwick
○*Cool* ❀*Autumn-Spring*
Left: This cross between *Cym*. Putana and *Cym*. Sussex Moor was exceptional for producing fine quality white and pastel shades in the flowers. The plant illustrated, which has pale green flowers and a white lip marked with red, is a typical variety. The plants are very free growing and flower easily from autumn to spring.
Photo x ¼

CYMBIDIUM
Nip × Kurun
○*Cool* ❀*Autumn/Winter*
Right: This very fine autumn to winter flowering second generation *Cym*. *pumilum* hybrid has inherited the very best qualities from its parents. It is free growing and often produces two flower spikes per pseudobulb. The 6cm (2.5in) flowers are brownish-pink with a crimson-spotted white lip. As many as 16 flowers may be carried at a time on an upright spike.
Photo x ¼

CYMBIDIUM
Peter Pan 'Greensleeves'
○*Cool* ❀*Autumn*
Below: A fine example of *ensifolium* breeding with the clone inheriting the best characteristics from both parents (*Cym. ensifolium* × *Cym.* Miretta). From *ensifolium* the plant has inherited its autumn flowering habit together with a beautiful fragrance, while Miretta has greatly enhanced the quality of the flower. The petals and sepals are soft green, while the lip is heavily marked and edged with deep crimson. The flowers are a little over 7.5cm (3in) across.
Photo x ²/₃

CYMBIDIUM
Stonehaven 'Cooksbridge'
○*Cool* ❀*Autumn/Winter*
Below: This second generation *Cym. pumilum* hybrid (*Cym.* Putana × *Cym.* Cariga) is a very good quality, medium sized plant that produces fine strong spikes with up to 25, 7cm (2.75in) flowers. Opening in autumn and early winter, the flowers are cream coloured and the lip is pale yellow, edged with dark red. The plant is very free flowering and easy to grow. Such plants are becoming increasingly popular as high class pot plants for the home.
Photo x ¼

CYMBIDIUM
Strathavon
○*Cool* ❀*Winter/Spring*
Above: For the medium to deep pink shades the cross of Strathavon (*Cym.* Putana × *Cym.* Berwick) produced some excellent progeny and several clones gained awards from the Royal Horticultural Society in Britain. Up to 18 flowers, 7cm (2.75in) across, are carried on upright spikes, and are normally in full bloom during the winter and early spring.
Photo x ²/₃

CYMBIDIUM
Touchstone 'Janis'
○*Cool* ❀*Winter/Spring*
Right: This miniature variety is another fine example of *Cym. devonianum* breeding (*devonianum* × Mission Bay). The plants from this crossing tend to be small, free growing and produce beautiful arching sprays of flowers during the winter and early spring. The flowers are bronze with contrasting deep crimson lips and are 2.5-4cm (1-1.5in) across.
Photo x ¼

CYMBIDIUM
Wood Nymph × Western Rose
○*Cool* ❀*Late spring*
Right: Most of the smaller growing cymbidiums tend to flower during the autumn and winter, but this cross between a large-flowered, standard cymbidium and a *Cym. tigrinum* hybrid has produced a late spring flowering miniature. The cross produced a range of colours with attractive lip markings. This particular example is characteristic of the range, having yellow-green petals flushed with light red, and a large cream lip, marked with deep crimson and edged with pink. The flowers are 7.5cm (3in) in diameter.
Photo x ¼

DENDROBIUMS

The beautiful and varied genus *Dendrobium* has always been held in high esteem by orchid growers throughout the world, and is one of the finest groups from the Old World. There are an estimated 1,600 species of dendrobiums, making them the second largest genus in the orchid family, the first place being taken by the strange and intriguing genus *Bulbophyllum*. They are the most important members of the subtribe Dendrobinae, which they share with related species in the smaller and lesser-known genus *Epigenium*.

Dendrobiums in the wild

The genus *Dendrobium* was founded in 1800 by the famous botanist Olof Swartz from a mere half dozen species, which were all that were known at that time. The name is derived from *dendron*, a tree, and *bios*, life—tree life: a good description for these epiphytic plants that exist by clinging to the branches and trunks of host trees. In this situation they thrive on the humidity rising from the jungle floor and on the meagre nourishment obtainable from old leaves and other debris collected in the branches of the trees.

Like other epiphytic orchids, dendrobiums have become beautifully adapted to their aerial existence. They store food and water in swollen stems, or pseudobulbs, that enable the plant to survive through the dry season. In dendrobiums these bulbs have become elongated into canes, often resembling bamboo, leading to the popular name of 'bamboo orchids'. These canes range from a few centimetres to a metre or more in length, the longer canes hanging down from the tree. A mass of aerial roots extends from the base of the plant, often forming a thick mat.

Many of the plants are deciduous, shedding their leaves after one season's growth and remaining dormant throughout the dry season. At the start of the rains they burst forth with new growth and flower buds. The buds appear along the whole length of the bulb on some types and from the upper nodes only on others. It is nearly always the previous year's growth which flowers. At flowering time the completely bare plant, looking like a cluster of dead canes, becomes transformed into a most beautiful display. In some varieties each of the previous season's canes is festooned with delicate and brightly coloured flowers; in others heavy bunches of flowers hang from the nodes of the canes, which become bowed under their weight; other varieties produce large heads of flowers from the upper portions of their canes.

The petals and sepals of dendrobium flowers are of equal size. The colours to be found in the genus are white (often suffused with pink or mauve), golden

yellow and subtle shades of pink, cream and brown; the rounded lip carries a colour which contrasts with the rest of the flower. In many, a delicate fragrance adds to their appeal.

As may be expected from such a vast group of plants, their global range is extensive. They can be found throughout the Himalayas and southern India, through Malaysia and on into China and Japan, and also in parts in northern Australia. They inhabit every type of environment from hot lowland jungles to the snowline of the Himalayas, often in exposed areas provided these enjoy continuous sunshine.

Dendrobiums in cultivation

For ease of culture, dendrobiums can be loosely divided into two main types: the soft-caned, or nobile, type and the hard-caned, or phalaenopsis, type. The former generally require cooler conditions and are therefore more widely grown by amateurs; the phalaenopsis type require more heat to succeed well. Both thrive on plenty of light and humidity.

Dendrobiums enjoy immense popularity wherever orchids are grown. Many of the original native species that delighted our forefathers, and which were grown into huge specimen clumps, are today becoming increasingly rare in cultivation as measures are taken in their countries of origin to protect those which remain. Those species which are still obtainable are distinctive and beautiful and are preferred to the hybrids which have been developed.

Dendrobiums were among the first orchids to be hybridized, a practice which began towards the end of the nineteenth century. In those early days of hybrid orchids, every conceivable cross was made and each new variety was hailed as a botanical wonder. But as the production of hybrids became commonplace, hun-

dreds were obtained from relatively few parents and the results became similar in appearance and of minimal value. Eventually, little progress was made with hybrids from the nobile types, but among phalaenopsis dendrobiums hybridizing has produced some extremely beautiful varieties highly valued for cutting. These are grown in tens of thousands in the warm climates of Malaysia and Thailand.

The seasonal pattern of growth

Dendrobiums start their new growth in the spring, following their resting period. The new growth usually coincides with the formation of the buds along the length or from the top of the previous season's canes. From this time on, the plants, which have remained dry for the duration of the winter months, can be watered regularly. It is advisable to flood the surface of the compost two or three times to ensure that the moisture penetrates throughout the pot.

During the summer months the aim should be to keep the compost continually moist, to ensure a continuous steady rate of growth. Old canes which may have shrivelled slightly during the resting period will quickly become plump again, and the new roots will take up sufficient water for the plant's needs. In addition, they may be lightly sprayed with water several times a day during bright sunny spells. Where the plants are being grown indoors, making spraying difficult, they will benefit from having their leaves sponged over just as often.

During the summer growing season, dendrobiums should be given artificial feed in a liquid form. Any phosphate or nitrate based liquid food is suitable for orchids, but bearing in mind that they are generally weak feeders, and a weak solution is called for. Apply this either to the pot or as a foliar feed sprayed over the plant. This feeding can be given at every third or fourth watering throughout the summer until the slight yellowing of foliage indicates the end of the plant's growth for the season.

Dendrobiums usually complete their annual growth by the autumn months, when the terminal leaf can be seen at the top of the completed cane. When this has been achieved, gradually reduce the watering and feeding to nil over a period of about four weeks. At this time of the year the plants should receive as much light as possible. To ensure flowering in the following spring it is important that the bulbs are sufficiently hardened and ripened by exposing the mature canes to full light. The deciduous varieties will react immediately to the shortening days and cooler temperatures by shedding their leaves, which turn yellow before dropping off. The evergreen types do not show the changing seasons so drastically, and may lose one or two leaves from the oldest canes only. Nevertheless, they too need full light and dry conditions until their reawakening in the spring.

In a greenhouse both deciduous and evergreen varieties should be placed on a shelf for the winter, in a position close to the glass where they can receive full light and be kept partially or completely dry, according to their needs. Indoors it is more difficult to provide the necessary light, but placing the plants in a large, south-facing window of a cool room should suffice. They should not be so close to the glass as to risk damage by frosts on cold winter nights. They can be left in this position until new growth begins in the early spring months.

Temperatures for growth

Dendrobiums have a fast growing season followed by a long resting period. During the summer the cool-growing varieties require a minimum night temperature of 12°C (55°F) with a daytime rise of up to 25°C (80°F), this varying from day to day according to the immediate weather. The warmer-growing types should be kept nearer to 18°C (65°F) at night, again with a considerable rise during the day, which can exceed the cool house temperature for a few hours during the hottest part of the day.

The higher the temperature, the higher should be the humidity, combined with frequent overhead spraying of the foliage. During the late autumn months the plants should be moved to their winter quarters. For the cool-growing types, a winter night temperature of 10°C (50°F) will suit them well, with a daytime rise to at least 16°C (60°F). The warmer growing varieties will require a night time temperature of 16°C (60°F) with a correspondingly higher daytime temperature.

Ventilation

Ventilation is an important aspect of orchid culture, and this is particularly so with dendrobiums, which flourish in a humid but buoyant atmosphere. Regular damping of the surroundings will create a high humidity and this should be maintained throughout the summer months. If the humidity falls significantly when ventilators are opened the remedy is not to allow the ventilators to remain closed, but rather to open them fully on hot sunny days, and to spray extra water round the plants, underneath the staging, and on the paths, until the greenhouse is running with water. In such an environment the ventilators can be brought into full use.

During the summer there will be periods when the ventilators can be left open both day and night, while at other times it will be necessary to close them at night. During the winter the ventilators should be opened on every occasion when this can be done without causing a drastic

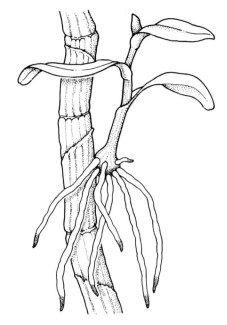

Above: Most dendrobiums propagate themselves by producing young plants from their older canes. When these have sufficient roots they can be removed from the parent plant and potted up on their own.

drop in the inside greenhouse temperature. It will sometimes happen that the ventilators are opened for no more than half an hour before being closed again for the remainder of the day, but this will have been sufficient to freshen the air inside the greenhouse and prevent a stagnant atmosphere, which is detrimental to all orchids.

Potting and composts

Repotting of dendrobiums should always be done during the spring months at the start of the growing season. The ideal time is when the new growth can just be seen at the base of the leading cane, and before the new roots appear. This can sometimes be difficult if the plant is flowering at the same time, and in this case the repotting should be completed immediately after the plant has flowered. Dendrobiums have a fine root system, and they like to be potted in as small a pot as possible. Overpotting can lead to overwatering, resulting in the loss of roots and, in extreme cases, loss of the plant. Plastic pots are quite suitable for dendrobiums, although they can sometimes become extremely top heavy. An alternative method of culture is to grow them on blocks of wood. Dendrobiums are especially suited to this growing method, and they very quickly establish themselves and produce an abundance of aerial roots.

The compost for dendrobiums should be open and well drained. An excellent potting medium is pine bark, and this is usually available from orchid nurseries in various forms. A good, chunky material and not powdered bark should be used. To this can be added a small percentage of sphagnum peat, which will assist in

holding moisture in an otherwise very dry compost. A further small percentage of charcoal can also be incorporated to keep the compost sweet. In this basic mixture dendrobiums will grow and thrive.

Vegetative propagation

Most dendrobiums will occasionally produce young plants from a node along the cane. The nobile type are particularly prone to this. These young plants can be removed from the cane when they have roots about 2.5cm (1in) long and one completed bulb. They can be potted up separately and grown on to flowering size. If you require propagations on a more regular basis, remove the older leafless canes (leaving at least four on the main plant) and cut these into pieces about 5cm (2in) long, severing the cane in between the divisions left by the leaves after they were shed. Put the pieces into a community pot with the division on a level with the compost and within a few weeks these will be showing a new growth which in turn can be potted singly when large enough.

Pests and diseases

Provided the greenhouse is kept comparatively free from pests, dendrobiums will remain in a clean and healthy state. Few pests, and even fewer diseases, will attack them. Apart from the general annoyance of slugs and snails, which may enter the greenhouse at any time and must be continually watched for, there may be an unwelcome visit from red spider mite. This pest will attack the undersides of the soft-caned dendrobiums, producing silvery white patches on the undersides of the leaves, particularly the younger ones. The mite is extremely small and difficult to see with the naked eye. It can do considerable harm by sucking the sap of the plant, and if allowed to remain unchecked it will quickly build up into large colonies. Any well-tried insecticide can be used against red spider mite, but the treatment may have to be repeated several times.

Species and hybrids

Of all the many species grown throughout the world, the following short list features a few of the most popular varieties noted for their beauty and ease of culture. All of them are suitable for a beginner provided their particular temperature requirements are catered for. These species are usually obtainable as imported plants from their country of origin, or they may have been raised in the nursery where purchased.

The brief selection of hybrids represents the different *Dendrobium* types that are grown. Although suited to different climates throughout the world, they can be grown together provided different sections of the greenhouse are allotted to suit their particular needs.

Dendrobium Species

Dendrobium aureum
○*Cool* ✿*Winter*

Right: This widely distributed species is found throughout India and in the Philippine Islands. The Indian variety is in general cultivation: the Philippino variety may be offered under the name of *D. hetero-carpum*. The type produces stoutish bulbs of medium length and is deciduous in winter, when it needs a definite rest. The flowers appear during the earliest months of the year, making it one of the first dendrobiums to flower. The blooms, up to 5cm (2in) across, are creamy yellow with a buff brown lip covered in short hairs. A very pleasant fragrance adds to the great appeal of this free-flowering, cool-growing species.
Photo X 1

Dendrobium fimbriatum
var. *oculatum*
○*Cool* ✿*Summer*

Below: An extremely beautiful cool-growing, Indian dendrobium, this species produces bunches of bright, buttercup yellow flowers during the early summer months. The flowers, 5cm (2in) across, are striking and the beautifully fimbriated lip carries a rich maroon blotch in the throat. The canes are tall and slender and the flowers appear from nodes on the uppermost portion of the older canes. It is an evergreen plant that sheds part of its foliage in the autumn, after which it should be allowed an almost completely dry rest. Water should be given sparingly if the canes begin to shrivel.
Photo X ¾

Dendrobium chrysotoxum
◑*Intermediate* ✿*Spring*

Above: This is one of the showiest of the intermediate range of dendrobiums. The plant is widely distributed throughout southern China, the Himalayas and into Burma and Thailand. It produces stout club-shaped bulbs which carry dark, glossy green foliage from their upper portions. The nodes appear close to the top of the previous season's bulbs, the old bulbs often flowering over several years. The blooms are 5cm (2in) across, and a rich golden yellow, with the well-rounded lip a deeper orange, sometimes with a maroon disc. The highly fragrant flowers last well and are carried in many-flowered, pendent sprays. The plant requires a decided rest during the winter, when it must be given full sun to encourage blooming the following spring.

The species is somewhat variable and is synonymous with *D. suavissimum*, which was at one time considered to be a separate species or a distinct variety of the type.
Photo X ¼

Dendrobium densiflorum
○*Cool* ✿*Summer*

Right: Once plentiful, this delightful species is becoming increasingly difficult to obtain. The flowers, up to 5cm (2in) across, are carried in large pendent trusses from nodes at the top half of the club-shaped bulbs. They develop at great speed during the spring months and last for up to ten days in perfection. Their colour is a brilliant golden yellow, the lip similarly coloured and very striking. The plant likes to be grown in the cool greenhouse with a decided rest in the winter. It is an evergreen variety from India which produces stout bulbs that grow to a considerable length.
Photo X ¼

Dendrobium infundibulum
○*Cool* ✿*Spring*

Below: This very fine and distinct species produces large, white flowers, 10cm (4in) across, of a soft papery texture. One to three flowers are produced from each node at the apex of the completed bulb. Well-grown plants produce huge heads of long-lasting flowers, the lip stained with bright yellow in the throat. *D. infundibulum* is an evergreen variety and enjoys cool house conditions. In its native India it grows at considerable altitudes. The stems and the sheaths around the young buds are covered in short, protective black hairs.
Photo X 1¼

Dendrobium lituiflorum
◑*Intermediate* ✿*Spring*

Left: Originating from India, this elegant species produces long, slender canes which become deciduous during the winter months. The flowers, 5cm (2in) across, appear the following spring along the entire length of the newest canes. Usually occurring in pairs, they vary in colour from almost white to rich amethyst purple, paling towards the centre. The lip is trumpet-shaped with a purple margin. The plant is seen at its best when grown in the intermediate house on bark slabs and allowed to assume a pendent habit. In this way it can also be hung closer to the glass during the winter to gain maximum light. This free-flowering species will produce several new growths in one season and can be grown into a specimen plant within a few years.
Photo X 2

Dendrobium nobile
○*Cool* ✿*Spring*

Below: Perhaps the most popular of all the cool-growing dendrobiums, this superb plant from India blooms during the spring. The flowers appear in ones and twos along the complete length of the previous year's bulbs, which are fairly tall and stoutish. The flowers, 5cm (2in) across, are rosy purple at the petal tips, shading to white towards the centre of the bloom. The lip carries a rich maroon blotch in the throat. *D. nobile* is semideciduous and requires a good rest during the winter; water should be withheld until the flower buds have started their development in the spring.
Photo X 1

Dendrobium pierardii
◑*Intermediate* ✤*Spring*

Left: This is a very handsome species from India which produces extremely long, cane-like pseudobulbs that assume a pendent habit unless trained upright in a pot. The plant becomes deciduous during the winter months, when it is important to allow full light to ensure successful flowering the following spring. The 5cm (2in) blooms are produced on the entire length of the previous year's canes and are extremely pretty. They are beautifully coloured a rosy pastel pink, while the rounded lip is creamy yellow, streaked with purple at the base. When in bloom the whole plant becomes transformed for a period of about three weeks.
Photo X ²/₃

Dendrobium secundum
◑*Intermediate* ✤*Spring/Summer*

Below: An extremely pretty and distinctive species with a wide distribution down the Malaysian peninsula and into the Philippine Islands. The unusual flowers are individually very small, clustered tightly together into compact sprays 8-10cm (3.5-4in) long. The rosy pink flowers, with an orange blotch on the lip, appear for an extended period through the spring and summer months. A free-flowering evergreen species, *D. secundum* should be grown in intermediate temperature conditions.
Photo X ¼

Dendrobium speciosum
◑●*Intermediate/Warm* ✤*Spring*

Left: A most attractive species from Australia, this plant enjoys warmth and humidity during its growing season, with a decided rest during the winter. It is not unusual for this rest period to last for many months. If ripened sufficiently the plant will bloom profusely in the spring producing a shower of flower spikes, each bearing numerous rather small, densely packed flowers, off white in colour with the lip lightly spotted in purple. The flowers have a delightful fragrance. This species grows exposed to the full sun in the wild, and produces leathery leaves from the top of stout, club-shaped pseudobulbs.
Photo X 1

Dendrobium superbum
● *Warm* ✿ *Summer*

Below: One of the finest dendrobiums from the Philippine Islands, this is a deciduous species that produces extremely long canes. The flowers appear during the early summer, along the entire length of the previous year's canes; they are 5-6cm (2-2.5in) across, and a rich magenta purple, the lip a deeper shade. Their powerful fragrance makes this a highly desirable species for the intermediate to warm section of the greenhouse. The very long canes make this species ideal for growing upside-down on a wooden raft.
Photo X 1

Dendrobium transparens
◐ *Intermediate* ✿ *Spring*

Above: This extremely pretty and free-flowering species from India grows well on bark in a pendent position. Its flowers, produced early in the year along the length of the previous season's canes, are 4cm (1.5in) across and pale rosy mauve, the colour heightening towards the tips of the petals; the lip carries two distinctive purple stains. It is a deciduous species which should be well rested before the next spring flowering season: it grows best in the intermediate section of the greenhouse.
Photo X 3

Dendrobium wardianum
○ *Cool* ✿ *Winter*

Above left: One of the most handsome of the cool-growing species, this too comes from India. The 5-6cm (2-2.5in) flowers, produced along the length of the previous year's canes, are white, with the petals, sepals and lip tipped with amethyst purple; the lip is also brightly stained with yellow and two maroon blotches at the base. The plant is deciduous and among the first to produce new growth and flowers in the early part of the year. The canes can become tall on a large plant and it grows well on wooden rafts.
Photo X 2

Dendrobium williamsonii
○ *Cool* ✿ *Spring/Summer*

Left: This is a stout species whose bulbs do not form very tall canes. The numerous flowers appear in early summer from the top of the newly completed bulbs and are ivory white, the lip handsomely marked with brick red. They are 4cm (1.5in) across, fragrant and long-lasting. This evergreen species requires a semi-rest during the winter and does well in the cool house.
Photo X 2

Dendrobium Hybrids

DENDROBIUM
Gatton Sunray (FCC/RHS)
◑Intermediate ❀Summer

Left: A magnificent hybrid, this is the largest of the cultivated dendrobiums, and requires plenty of growing space. It is a first generation hybrid from the yellow-flowered species, *D. dalhousieanum,* which is infrequently seen today, but was at one time regularly imported from Burma. The hybrid was registered in 1919 and has enjoyed immense popularity ever since. *D.* Gatton Sunray (FCC/RHS) is extremely robust, the canes growing to a height of 2m (5ft) or more. The extremely large and showy flowers, which appear in trusses during the early summer, are more than 10cm (4in) across and last in perfection for about 10 days. A large plant will produce numerous trusses, each carrying several flowers. This will extend the flowering period, as not all the trusses come into flower at once.

The plant succeeds best in an intermediate greenhouse where it can be given good light and a decided rest during the winter months.

Photo x ¼

DENDROBIUM
Louisae
●Warm ❀Autumn/Winter

Below: A very popular plant, this evergreen hybrid is widely grown and is readily available on both sides of the Atlantic. The plant was raised in Indonesia and resulted from the crossing of two showy species native to New Guinea, *D. phalaenopsis* var. *schroederanum* and *D. veratrifolium,* both of which bear long sprays of rose-mauve flowers. *D.* Louisae combines the characteristics of both parents and produces long arching sprays of flowers from the top of the bulbs. The 6cm (2.5in) flowers, which are a rich rose-purple, are extremely long lived and appear during the autumn and winter. The plant can be grown in a warm sun room or greenhouse where it enjoys an abundance of light. During the winter resting period it should be allowed to dry out almost completely.

Photo x ⅛

DENDROBIUM
Fiftieth State
●Warm ❀Summer

Right: This fine hybrid illustrates a completely different type of dendrobium, which has been bred from species of Australasian origin. *D. phalaenopsis*—the famous Cookstown orchid, discovered by Cook and depicted on Australian stamps—was crossed with *D.* New Guinea, a hybrid combining *D. macrophyllum* and *D. atrioviolaceum*—two unusual species not often seen in cultivation. The 6cm (2.5in) flowers of *D.* Fiftieth State are similar in shape to those of *D. phalaenopsis,* although the rich magenta colour of the species appears as overlying veins of soft red in the hybrid. Raised in Hawaii, the plant is warm growing and will succeed in high temperatures and almost full sunlight. It should be watered freely while growing but allowed a complete rest after flowering. The flowers, which open in summer are extremely long lasting and appear on lengthy sprays from the top of the completed bulb.

Photo x ¼

DENDROBIUM
Mousmee
○*Cool* ✿*Summer*

Right: Raised from the species
D. thyrsiflorum, this hybrid resembles the
species in appearance and flowering
habit. The 5cm (2in) blooms, which are
white with a rich yellow lip, are carried on
pendent trusses that appear in early
summer from the top of the robust
canes. An evergreen with stout dark
green leaves, the plant will lose an
occasional leaf from the oldest canes
each year. *D.* Mousmee will grow
successfully in the cool section of the
greenhouse, but requires abundant light
to flower well. It should also be well
rested during the winter when the
pseudobulbs will shrivel—a process
necessary to initiate the production of
flowers.
　Although not often seen in cultivation
today, this is a fine old hybrid well worth
looking out for.
Photo x ²/₃

DENDROBIUM
Sussex
○*Cool* ✿*Spring*

Above: This hybrid results from a combination of three Indian species *D. nobile,*
D. aureum and *D. findlayanum,*
with *D. nobile* exerting the most
influence. *D.* Sussex is cool growing and
easy to cultivate, blooming freely in the
spring. This hybrid is a good example of
what can be achieved by crossing the
hybrid *D.* Ainsworthii (*D. aureum* x
D. nobile) with further nobile hybrids to
improve the flower size and shape.
Although retaining the appearance and
flowering habit of *D. nobile, D.* Sussex
has larger flowers (7.5cm; 3in) of fuller
shape. The young plant pictured here
has only three flowers; when mature the
plant will bloom along the length of the
previous years' canes, which may remain
in leaf for several years.
Photo x ²/₃

DENDROBIUM
Tangerine 'Tillgates' (AM/RHS)
◐*Intermediate* ✿*Spring/Summer*

Left: Rather different from the 'traditional'
cultivated dendrobium, this outstanding
hybrid was raised from a little known but
beautiful species, *D. strebloceras,* which
comes from western New Guinea. Its
name means 'crumpled horn' and refers
to the long twisting petals. In the hybrid
these petals stand erect, closely
resembling the horns of an antelope. The
plant is more colourful than its parent
species, the 7.5cm (3in) flowers having
bright orange petals and mustard yellow
sepals and lip. Although the plant is little
grown outside the tropics, its unusual
and delightful flowers make it a desirable
addition to any collection. A subject for
the intermediate greenhouse, it would not
do well as a houseplant, as it requires full
light throughout the year.
Photo X ¹/₆

ODONTOGLOSSUMS

The genus *Odontoglossum* is well represented within the orchid family, containing approximately 300 species and including some of the most beautiful flowers. As a result, it is very popular with orchid growers. Odontoglossums are members of the subtribe Oncidiinae, which also includes such genera as *Brassia, Oncidium* and *Miltonia*.

They are native to the mountainous regions of Central and South America. Although they occur throughout an extensive range between latitudes 15°S and 20°N — which represents an area of the Andes from Peru to Mexico — their occurrence within this range is relatively limited. The main group of species is found at an elevation of between 1,525 and 2,745m (5,000-9,000ft) with some species to be found as high as 3,660m (12,000ft).

The natural environment for *Odontoglossum* species, which should be matched as far as possible in their culture, provides a temperature range from about 5° to 32°C (41-90°F) maximum, the mean annual temperature being about 13°C (55°F). The rainy season is almost continuous, because moisture brought on winds from the Atlantic condenses over the mountain ranges; as the temperature falls at night, mist envelops the region, leaving the plants moist with dew. The fact that these species grow at such heights must always be borne in mind, for continuous movement of air in a fresh, buoyant and moist atmosphere is essential.

A cultural calendar
Winter
In areas with a temperate climate, where the weather in the winter months is liable to be dull and cold and greenhouse conditions can easily deteriorate, careful use of the watering can, damping down and ventilation are essential. Supplementary heat should be in full operation to maintain a minimum night temperature of about 10°C (50°F); if during severe weather the temperature drops below this level, the plants should be kept drier at the root, with a lower atmospheric humidity, as damage is most likely to occur when they are cold and wet. On days when the outside temperature brings that in the greenhouse up to the required 16°C (60°F), you should take the opportunity to ventilate the house and refresh the atmosphere, provided the outside air is not too cold.

Shade should not be required, and any slight reddening of the leaves due to too much light will help to tone up the plants. As the hybrids will still be active during these months, they should not be allowed to become too dry at the roots for long periods; however, this is less dangerous than having the plants wet at the roots for days on end. The majority of species are either fully at rest or in a state of semi-rest in winter, so watering should be restricted

Right: Odontoglossums produce some of the most showy flowers of the orchid family. Today's hybrids combine large, richly coloured, long-lasting blooms with vigorous growth and relatively easy cultivation.

to once every three to four weeks, and then applied using a fine rose; experience and observation will determine how much they require. To prevent accidental watering of plants at rest it is a good idea to put a coloured label in the pot; alternatively, resting and semi-resting plants can be moved to a separate corner of the greenhouse.

Repotting and potting can be continued during this period for plants with new growths of about 4-5cm (1.5-2in).

Spring
As weather conditions improve during the spring months, plant growth will pick up in the greenhouse, just as it does outside. This is a period of very active growth for odontoglossums: many new shoots will appear, species will be coming out of their resting period, and correct conditions will be rewarded with strong plants and healthy flowers. The minimum night temperature should be about 10-13°C (50-55°F), and although it is sometimes tempting to turn heating off as warmer weather comes, supplementary heating will still be required. In areas where even late spring nights can be very cold a heater with a thermostat control really proves its worth.

The day temperature should rise to about 16°C (60°F), and up to 21°C (70°F) if the weather is sunny. Keep growth active by being prepared to use some supplementary heat on cold days. Ventilate as much as possible to give the plants plenty of fresh air, but be careful early on in this period not to use too much top ventilation and end up with cold air surrounding the plants; use some bottom ventilation instead. Frequent damping

down between pots and under benches will be necessary to ensure that the humidity remains fairly high; growth will be slowed down if the atmosphere becomes too dry.

As the new growths develop, new roots will be produced, and it is important to water correctly to encourage a healthy root system. Too much water at an early stage may rot the delicate new roots; on the other hand, for a plant that is growing well water is essential, so it is a question of achieving the right balance. The compost may be allowed to dry out between waterings, but should not remain dry for more than a day or two. Light feeding every two or three weeks is beneficial during this time, with a heavy watering between feeds to wash out excess salts.

The desirable average day temperature lies between 18° and 24 °C (65-75°F) and it is essential to keep the temperature within these limits if optimum growing conditions are to be maintained. The maximum temperature most odontoglossums can tolerate is about 27°C (80°F). Intergeneric hybrids have been bred to withstand higher day temperatures and are therefore more suitable for growing in the warm climates of such places as California and Australia. They are also able to withstand exceedingly hot summers in temperate climates.

Ventilation is necessary during the day throughout the summer to help maintain the fresh buoyant atmosphere and keep temperatures down. The atmosphere must not become too dry and more frequent damping down between pots and under benches will be necessary during hot periods. It is a good idea is to have troughs of moisture-retaining materials, such as Lytag (or perlite), capillary matting or sand, and an automatic damping system (see page 60).

Shading is essential during the summer. The amount of shade required depends on the ability to keep temperatures down. With good control the maximum temperature can be kept down to 24°C (75°F), when 60 percent shade will be adequate; otherwise 70 or 80 percent will be necessary. Extra shading, provided by shade cloth or lath blinds fixed to the outside of the greenhouse, helps to form an insulating barrier and keep the sun's heat out.

During these hottest months of the year, the plants should not be allowed to dry out too rapidly and they should certainly not remain dry for any length of time. Some orchid composts available today drain particularly well, which is beneficial for epiphytic orchids and during the cold damp winter months when it is all too easy to overwater, but extra care must be taken during hot weather to ensure that they do not bake dry. If plants do dry out they can be difficult to moisten again and you can easily be misled into believing that the plant has been well watered when, in fact, the water has merely trickled straight through the compost. Odontoglossums should be watered carefully during this period, little and often. If the compost is in good condition, and you are in any doubt about watering, the rule of thumb is to give them water.

It is not advisable to repot at this time of year, unless it becomes essential, as it is difficult to provide ideal conditions for settling the plants after potting.

Autumn
Autumn, like spring, is a time of good growing conditions and, for the most part, favourable weather. During early autumn there will probably be enough natural warmth to do without supplementary heating, but even so, preparations

Foliar feed in late spring will also help to tone up the foliage in anticipation of the better weather to come.

The spring can be a difficult time for shading, with days of bright sun when shade is necessary and dull days when every bit of light is needed. As odontoglossums scorch easily, it is prudent to provide permanent light shade at this time of year if you do not have automatic blinds or the time to put on or take off the shade as required. The colour of the foliage at this time should be a dark shiny green with a tinge of red denoting vigorous but not soft growth.

This is the best time of year to repot, ideally when the new growths are about 4 -5cm (1.5-2in) long. This coincides with the period of most root activity, when

new roots will be able to penetrate and ramify through the fresh compost.

Summer
This is probably the most difficult period of the year for odontoglossums. Normally, supplementary heat should not be required; in fact, high day temperatures can be damaging and proper use of shading, ventilation (including fans) and provision of correct humidity are essential to keep the plant in prime condition.

The minimum night temperature should be about 13°C (55°F), and usually the temperature will remain around this figure naturally. If very cold spells occur the use of thermostatically controlled heating is recommended to ensure that the rhythm of growth is maintained.

for heating during the cooler months to come should be made. The minimum night temperature should be about 10-13°C (50-55°F). Daytime temperatures should be allowed to rise to 21°C (70°F), and any excessive rise controlled by ventilation, damping down and shading.

Since it is not a good idea for the plants to enter the cool, dark winter months with soft lush growth, which is liable to be attacked by fungus, this is the time to harden off the foliage. Plenty of ventilation at all times during early autumn (certainly until supplementary heat is needed), reduction of the degree of shading and feeding with a high potassium plant food will help.

Many plants will be producing new shoots and this is therefore a good time for repotting. Select plants that have growths about 4-5cm (1.5-2in) long. Watering should be continued throughout this period for hybrids, but for species that are resting during the winter, reduce the amount of water as the pseudobulbs are completed.

Repotting odontoglossums

Odontoglossums are epiphytic and thrive in a compost that is open and free draining, but which retains moisture at all times, so that plants do not become dry during the growing season. They detest stale, lifeless and waterlogged compost. Bark-based composts, made up of graded pine bark, charcoal, perlite and sphagnum peat or good fresh sphagnum moss, are proving most satisfactory. For young seedlings and adult hybrids a fine moss is probably best as this will not dry out too quickly. Individual species may require different composts. Fertilizers that release their nutrient slowly over a period should not be used, as odontoglossums are not heavy feeders and root burn can easily result.

The best times to repot are spring and autumn, particularly when the new growths are about 4-5cm (1.5-2in) long, coinciding with the period of most active root growth. Potting can be done in summer and winter, but climatic conditions are not so favourable for the aftercare and settling down of the plants.

How often plants should be repotted depends to a large extent on the type of compost used. In bark-based compost the plants should be repotted every two years, and for young seedlings potting every year is advisable.

Potting procedure

Having selected the plant at the right stage of growth, knock it out of its pot and remove the old compost, dead back bulbs and any dead roots (the live roots will be white, green tipped and fleshy when felt gently between finger and thumb; dead roots will be brown, soft and the outer layer of cells will come away easily from the root core.). If the plant has a poor and rotten root system, dipping it in a solution of captan orthocide will prevent the spread of any further rot.

Pot size will be determined by the size of the plant and, in particular, the state of the root system. When potting a large adult plant with numerous bulbs, some of the surface back bulbs can be removed, leaving the plant a minimum of two to three bulbs and new growth.

There should be enough room in the pot for at least one new pseudobulb to form, but the pot should be on the small side rather than too large, as over-potting can lead to poor root action and subsequent deterioration.

First, place a layer of drainage material, such as clean, broken pot, polystyrene chunks or large gravel, in the bottom of the pot. Then, hold the plant so that the base of the bulb is just below the top of the pot with the new growth aimed in the direction of the most room and pour in the compost, working it gently among the roots and tapping the pot occasionally to help it to settle. Firm the compost gently with the fingers without using force: remember the roots are thin and fairly delicate and must be able to grow through the new compost with reasonable ease.

Aftercare of repotted plants

Using a modern compost the actual task of potting orchids is as easy as for any other pot plant, but aftercare is very important to enable them to settle down and continue their growth with a minimum of disturbance.

After potting, water the plant well (particularly if the compost has been stored and is very dry) to moisten the compost. However, it is important at this stage not to overwater and waterlog the compost and so deter new roots. Provide plenty of humidity by maintaining a buoyant atmosphere around the plant, so that it is able to take up all the water it needs through the new roots (which have just been disturbed), keeping water loss through the roots to a minimum. Keep in heavy shade with the maximum temperature below 21°C (70°F) if possible. Subsequent waterings should be light so that the roots are encouraged to search for water and thus build up into a strong system. A diluted foliar feed once a week will be beneficial at this time. Settling down after potting will depend on the state of the root system when repotted and how well you pot, but normally it will take four to five weeks, and after this time normal culture can be resumed.

Vegetative propagation

Odontoglossums are not noted for their ease of vegetative propagation (by division of back bulbs) because many varieties do not readily throw out more than one shoot at a time. Species that produce many new growths (such as *Odontoglossum pulchellum, cordatum, bictoniense, platycheilum* and *stellatum*) can be propagated by division, but do not be tempted to chop up a large specimen plant just to make many small plants, as large specimens should be your ultimate aim.

Each division should be made up of at least two to three bulbs and new growth; smaller divisions could take a year or more to come into flower. Back bulb propagation is another possibility and results can be outstanding. Take two bulbs at a time if possible, as there is then a better chance of getting an 'eye' to start. Pot in a fine bark mix or in sphagnum moss and place in a propagating case, where humidity can be kept high and excessive heat avoided; if a new shoot appears to be careful not to overwater and cause it to rot away. Once roots are visible resume normal cultural practice.

The most effective way of propagating odontoglossums, particularly the hybrids, is to divide the leading pseudobulb and new growth from the rest of the plant. Select a plant that has a growth of 4-5cm (1.5-2in) and, while it is still in the pot, cut through the hard rhizome connecting the newest bulb to the one behind it, then leave it undisturbed in normal conditions. After about eight weeks the bulb behind the severed front bulb and growth will produce a shoot and when this shoot has grown to 4-5cm (1.5-2in) remove both divisions and pot up separately.

Pests and diseases

Aphids are the main insect pests to attack odontoglossums, particularly during the summer months. New shoots and flower buds are especially susceptible. Regular spraying with an insecticide, such as malathion, will help to prevent attack.

Other pests which may attack the soft leaves, include red spider mites and mealy bugs, both of which can be controlled by spraying as above. Slugs and snails may also cause considerable damage to young shoots and flowers, and should be controlled with metaldehyde pellets or powder placed on the surface of the compost.

Provided the greenhouse is kept clean, and your original stock was healthy, odontoglossums should remain disease-free. However, plants may suffer from fungal rot if they remain wet in cold conditions. To prevent this, ensure that there is good air movement around the plants at all times, and reduce damping down during cool weather.

Species and hybrids

Although the species odontoglossums offered growers a superb range, in 1898, C. Vuylsteke in Belgium made the first hybrid, between *O. crispum* and *O. harry-*

Above: *Cochlioda noezliana* has had considerable influence on odontoglossum breeding over the years, contributing towards the brilliant colours of the modern *Odontioda* hybrids.

usually white or white with some purple markings. The latter have basically a white background with deep coloured markings. Names to note include: *O. Stropheon, Conncro, Philomel, Ardentissimum, Opheon.*

The species originally involved in the production of yellow hybrids were *O. luteo-purpureum, harryanum* and *triumphans.* Today's hybrids are deep golden yellows, often with attractive markings in red or chestnut-brown. Names to note include Moselle, Golden Guinea, Inca Gold, Stonehurst Yellow, Pacific Gold, Cornosa, Ascania.

In the red section the Odontioda hybrids are the most successful. Names to note are: Trixon, Chanticleer, Charlesworthii, Bradshawiae, Memoria Donald Campbell, Trixell, Salway.

Crosses between the large shapely odontoglossums and the brightly coloured odontiodas have resulted in some of the most beautiful colour combinations, ranging from white backgrounds with light markings through to deep rich imperial purples. Names to note include Florence Stirling, Memory, Brocade, Dalmar, Ingera, Memtor, Joe Marshall.

Many other genera have been crossed with odontoglossums and the results have been most interesting; many such crosses involve two or more genera and are therefore quite complicated. The full list of these to date is to be found in *Sander's List of Orchid Hybrids.* The most popular intergeneric hybrids are not only attractive for their flowers, but also are culturally more adaptable. Much breeding is being aimed at producing hybrids that will grow in climates such as Australia, South Africa or California that are normally too warm for odontoglossums and odontiodas. Some of the most popular types are odontocidiums, wilsonaras and vuylstekearas.

Odontocidiums are produced by crossing an *Odontoglossum* with an *Oncidium.* Species such as *Oncidium tigrinum, wentworthianum, leucochilum* and *incurvum* have been very successful, with noted progeny such as *Odontocidium* Tiger Butter, Tigerwood, Tigersun, Crowbrough, Solana, Tiger Hambuhren.

Wilsonaras result from crossing an *Odontioda* with an *Oncidium* or an *Odontioda* with an *Odontocidium.* The same species are generally used. Through the use of odontiodas, many of these crosses produce highly coloured flowers. Examples include: *Wilsonara* Widecombe Fair, Jean du Pont, Tigerman, Celle.

Vuylstekearas result from crossing an *Odontioda* with a *Miltonia* (the pansy orchids). Vuylstekearas are generally very tolerant of excessive heat and normally have the large flamboyant lip associated with the miltonias. Examples are: Vuylstekeara Cambria, Edna Stamperland, Heather Moore.

anum to make O. Crispo-harryanum, which opened up a whole new world. Hybridizing advanced quickly and crosses involving other genera were made as early as 1904, setting the scene for a deluge of interest that has lasted through the years to the present time, and their popularity is still increasing rapidly. The hybrids available to the grower today have over 70 years of breeding behind them and are necessarily complicated, but this should in no way deter the enthusiast from exploring the beauties and treasures to be found among them.

Odontiodas result from crossing an *Odontoglossum* with a *Cochlioda. C.*

noezliana, the most often used, was introduced because of its brilliant scarlet flowers. Many modern odontiodas are very similar to the odontoglossums because they have been bred back again and again to improve size and form.

There is a wide range of hybrids to choose from; new varieties are being raised all the time, and these quickly supersede the older ones. However, within the various colour groups there are certain breeding lines or parents that have been particularly successful and some of these are given below. The best way to make a selection is probably to visit a nursery, see the plants in flower, and take advice from the experts.

Odontoglossum crispum is the species most responsible for the whites; it produces large. well-shaped flowers—

Odontoglossum Species

Odontoglossum bictoniense
○*Cool* ✿*Summer*

Right: This must be one of the easiest and most popular species, and an ideal plant for beginners. Native to Guatemala, it is a very vigorous grower and will quickly grow into a specimen plant. Erect flower spikes appear at the end of the summer, growing quickly in the warm weather to reach heights up to 122cm (48in) and bearing 20 long-lasting flowers on each spike. The flowers open in succession so that there are usually eight or nine out at once over a period of several weeks. The flowers are about 3-4cm (1.25-1.5in) across, yellowy green with brown spots and a striking white or pink lip.

O. bictoniense, which can be grown successfully as a houseplant, requires cool conditions with medium shade and does not need resting in winter, though water should be reduced when flowering has finished, until new growth appears in the spring.

Photo X 1

Odontoglossum cervantesii
○*Cool* ✿*Winter/Spring*

Below: This delightful dwarf species comes from Mexico. The total height of pot, bulbs and leaves is only about 15cm (6in) and makes this an ideal subject for growers with limited space.

The flowers are produced on semi-pendent spikes, in winter and early spring, from the new growth as it starts to form a pseudobulb. In comparison to the size of the plant, the flowers are large — about 4 to 5cm (1.6 to 2in) across, beautifully white, almost round and marked with a distinctive band of chestnut rings towards the middle of the sepals and petals.

Being a species with fine roots it does not like to dry out during the growing season and thrives in a fine but free-draining compost. During the winter months water should be reduced and a small amount of shrivelling of the bulb is normal at this time. Give medium shade during the summer.

Photo X 1

Odontoglossum cariniferum
○*Cool* ✿*Winter*

Above: Perhaps this Central American species is not as widely grown now as it used to be, but this is probably due to difficulties of supply rather than any other factor. Given cool conditions it grows vigorously and produces long branching spikes which bear brightly coloured flowers. 4-5cm (1.5-2in) across, of dark greenish-brown with yellow tips to the sepals and petals, which open in the winter.

The new shoot appears in spring, developing through the summer growing season until the new bulb starts to form in late summer or early autumn, and it is at this time that the flower spike will first appear. A reduction in watering following the completion of the bulb is necessary and the gradual wrinkling of the bulb during winter is natural. Give medium shade during the growing season and use a medium grade compost.

Photo X ¾

Odontoglossum citrosmum
(syn. **Odontoglossum pendulum**)
○*Cool* ❀*Spring*

Above: The Mexican species has a distinct growth and flower cycle, which has to be respected if success is to be achieved; perhaps this explains why it has always been sought after but has never quite attained the popularity it deserves.

The plant needs a decided resting period during the winter, following the completion of the previous year's pseudobulb, when water should only be applied to prevent complete dehydration; full light at this time is necessary. Towards the end of the winter the new shoot will appear from the base of the pseudobulb, but the temptation to give water must be resisted as it is from an undeveloping new shoot that the flower spike appears; if water is given too early the new shoot will elongate and grow normally without flowering. It is therefore after flowering that normal watering should be carried out.

The flowers—about 4 to 5cm (1.6 to 2in)—are white flushed with pink and sweetly scented, and borne on pendular spikes, making this an ideal subject to suspend from the greenhouse roof. Give medium to light shade during the growing season and medium grade compost.
Photo X ½

Odontoglossum cordatum
○*Cool* ❀*Spring*

Right: This species is another native of Guatemala which has proved itself as one of the most popular odonto-glossums. It is a very vigorous grower and flowers freely in spring. As it readily produces new shoots it can soon be grown into a specimen plant and it is at this stage (with say six or seven flower spikes) that its beauty can be fully appreciated. The spikes are about 18 to 30cm (7-12in) long, bearing flowers of a bright golden yellow with attractive, eye-catching mahogany markings.

This is a thick-root species which can be grown in a medium to coarse compost and is ideal for growing in baskets suspended from the roof. Medium shade is required during the growing season.
Photo X 1

Odontoglossum crispum
○*Cool* ❀*All year*

Above: This is the most familiar species and has contributed more than any other to the development of manmade hybrids; it is a native of Colombia in South America.

Coming from high up in the Andes the plants need medium to heavy shade and cool, moist, humid conditions. The large waxy flowers, up to 10cm (4in) across, vary considerably in presence or absence of marking. Flower spikes develop from the side of the new bulb as it is forming and, as the seasons in its native environment are not clearly defined and growth can start at any time, the flowers may open at virtually any time of year, though spring and autumn are probably the most popular.

Over-collecting in the early days of the orchid craze, which swept England and Europe in the latter half of the nineteenth century, together with destruction of natural habitats during recent years, has made the direct supply almost dry up, but selective breeding of varieties has been continuing for many years and this has ensured that *Odontoglossum crispum* will still be available to enthusiasts without calling on the dwindling wild stocks; moreover, these cultivated plants are of higher quality. As an ancestor, *Odontoglossum crispum* has probably contributed more towards improving the flower size and shape of the *Odonto-glossum* and *Odontioda* hybrids than any other species. They should be grown in a fine to medium grade compost, with medium to heavy shade.
Photo X ¾

Odontoglossum grande
○Cool ✿Autumn

Right: Known widely as the 'clown orchid' due to the clown-like figure represented by the column in the centre of the flower, this is certainly one of the most widely grown in this genus, and popular as a houseplant. The flowers are very large up to 15cm (6in) across, yellow with bright chestnut-brown markings. Although it is now classified as a Rossii odontoglossum it is sure to be sold or known as *Odontoglossum grande* for many years to come.

It comes from Guatemala and is distinct from most odontoglossums, with the exception of *O. insleayi, schlieperianum* and *williamsianum,* for it has hard dark leaves and very tough pseudobulbs, and needs a decided rest during the winter months. During the growing season it needs plenty of moisture at the roots but excessive atmospheric moisture can result in unsightly black spotting on the foliage. As the new growth starts to make a pseudobulb towards the end of the summer the flower spike develops and the flowers usually open in autumn. Once flowering is finished and the pseudobulbs have fully matured, watering should be withheld until spring when the new growth appears and starts the whole cycle again. The plants need light shade and should be grown in a medium grade bark compost.

Photo X ¼

Odontoglossum harryanum
○Cool ✿Spring/Summer

Right: A native of Colombia, this is one of the most striking of the odontoglossums. It produces spikes of about 30cm (12in) or more in length with many large 7.5 to 10cm (3-4in) flowers of attractive coppery brown, dappled with yellow throughout, with a large and most distinctive white lip marked in bright lilac. Having been used a great deal during the early days of hybridizing, this species is very similar in its cultural requirements to the modern hybrids, and requires cool conditions, medium to heavy shade and a fine or medium grade bark mix.

Photo X ½

Odontoglossum insleayi
○Cool ✿Autumn/Winter

Above: A native of Mexico this species closely resembles *Odontoglossum grande* and has similar cultural requirements. The flowers are produced in autumn and winter from pseudobulbs that have just formed, they are about 7.5cm (3in) across, yellow with chestnut or reddish-brown markings. They should be grown in a medium grade compost and given light shade, with a rest in winter.

Photo X ⅙

Odontoglossum laeve
○*Cool* ✿*Spring*

Below: Opinions differ as to whether this species, a native of Mexico, should be classed as an *Odontoglossum,* an *Oncidium* or a *Miltonia,* but it is usually grown as *Odontoglossum laeve.* It produces long branching spikes and sweetly scented flowers, 5-7.5cm (2-3in) across, yellowish-green with markings of chocolate brown and a distinctive pink or purple lip. This is a vigorous species, producing large plump pseudobulbs at the end of the summer. The plants should be potted in fine or medium grade bark compost and given medium shade; they appear to enjoy a short hard rest after completion of the pseudobulb to initiate flower spikes, after which watering in winter should be kept to about once every three weeks. The spikes develop during the winter and come into bloom during the spring.
Photo X ⅓

Odontoglossum luteo-purpureum
○*Cool* ✿*Spring*

Below: This species is a native of Colombia and similar in cultural requirements of *Odontoglossum crispum* and the *Odontoglossum* hybrids, so it requires medium shade and medium or fine bark compost. In spring this attractive species produces long spikes of large flowers, 7.5cm (3in) across, basically yellow with heavy chestnut-brown markings.
Photo X ½

Odontoglossum maculatum
○*Cool* ✿*Spring*

Above: Very similar to *Odontoglossum cordatum* in both growth and flower habit, the culture should be the same. The flower spikes, about 30-44cm (12-18in) long, are produced in spring, bearing flowers of about 5-7.5cm (2-3in) across, which have a creamy yellow background with brown spots and blotches. Plants should be grown in cool conditions in a medium bark mix and given medium shade.
Photo X 1⅓

Odontoglossum nebulosum
(syn. **apterum)**
○*Cool* ✿*Spring*

Below: This popular Mexican species has flowers about 5-7.5cm (2-3in) across, white with orange-red or brown spots. The spike appears with the new growth and comes into bloom in the spring. The plants have thick fleshy roots so a medium grade bark-based compost is ideal; medium shade is required. The pseudobulbs are soft and fleshy so care should be taken not to overwater as this can result in rot.
Photo X ¾

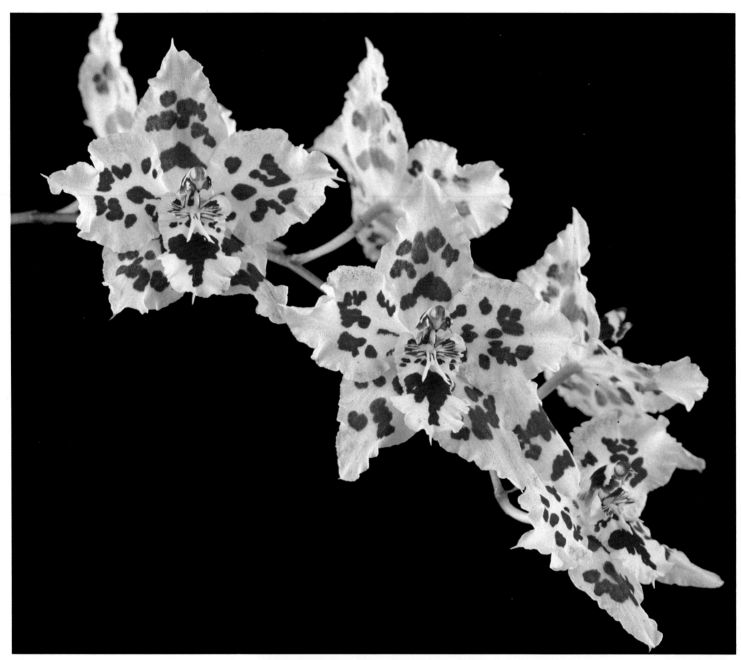

Odontoglossum pescatorei

○Cool ✿Spring and Autumn

Above: This is one of the loveliest of the Colombian odontoglossums with a branching spike and flowers which vary in size but are generally about 7.5cm (3in) across, white with spotting or flushing in lilac rose. Its growth habit and cultural requirements are similar to those of *Odontoglossum crispum;* cool conditions, fine to medium grade bark mix, and medium to heavy shade.
Photo X 1

Odontoglossum pulchellum

○Cool ✿Spring

Right: This is an extremely popular Guatemalan species as it is a vigorous grower. The waxy, white flowers, though small — 1-2cm (0.25-0.5in) across — bloom in masses and have a lovely scent, which explains why it is known as the 'lily of the valley orchid'. It flowers in spring and produces more than one shoot from each pseudobulb, making it ideal for growing into a specimen. The plants are thin-rooted and need cool conditions, a fine grade bark mix, and medium shade in the summer.
Photo X 1

Paphiopedilum rothschildianum

Intermediate ❀Summer

Above: This species from New Guinea, originally classified as *P. new-guineaense*, is one of the most striking paphiopedilums, and is much sought after by growers. The straight, leathery leaves are bright glossy green and can measure up to 60cm (24in) in length. The long flower stem carries two to five flowers, which can be as much as 29cm (11.5in) across. The flower markings are complicated, the overall colour being cinnamon yellow to greenish-brown, with dark brown stripes on the long petals and pointed dorsal sepal. The plant normally flowers in the summer.

Photo X ⅕

Paphiopedilum spicerianum

Intermediate ❀Autumn/Winter

Above: A native of Assam, this species has broad·leaves with wavy margins, dark green above and spotted with purple underneath. In autumn and winter one or two 7.5cm (3in) flowers are borne on a 30cm (12in) stem. They are distinctive in markings and shape and play an important role in the breeding of hybrids.

Photo X 1⅓

Paphiopedilum venustum

Intermediate ❀Spring

Left: The leaves of this species are heavily marbled with grey and green. One or occasionally two flowers, 7.5cm (3in) across, are borne on a 15-23cm (6-9in) stem. The petals and lip are basically yellow-green, tinged with rose-red, and the petals are slightly hairy. The dorsal sepal is white, strongly striped with green. The plant blooms in early spring.

Photo X ½

PAPHIOPEDILUM
Danella 'Chilton' (AM/RHS)
◑*Intermediate* ❄️*Winter*
Below: This plant illustrates one of the most
interesting new colours to be produced,
and is on the way to achieving the
sought-after perfect clear orange. In
addition, it is a lovely variety, being
vigorous and easy to grow. It flowers in
the winter, bearing beautifully shaped
flowers on long stems.
Photo X ½

PAPHIOPEDILUM
Honey Gorse 'Sunshine' (AM/RHS)
◑*Intermediate* ❄️*Winter*
Left: The first plant to combine the
characteristics of both the green and
yellow paphiopedilum groups, the
10cm (4in) flowers of this hybrid are dark
yellow-green. Deeper emerald green
hybrids are now being bred, but this plant
will take some beating for its heavy
texture—a feature usually lacking in the
green colour group.
Photo X 1½

PAPHIOPEDILUM
Miller's Daughter 'Snow Maiden'
◑*Intermediate* ❄️*Winter*
Above: This line represents the most
advanced breeding for white-flowered
hybrids in the world. There is nothing to
compare with the perfection of the
Miller's Daughter hybrids for flower sizes,
shape and vigour. The 13cm (5in)
flowers of this particular plant (*P.* Dusty
Miller 'Mary' AM/RHS & GMM ✕
P. Chantal 'Aloha') are white, lightly
speckled all over with pinkish-brown.
Photo X ⅓

PAPHIOPEDILUM
Royale 'Downland' (AM/RHS & GMM)
◐*Intermediate* ❄*Winter*
Right: This hybrid is a seedling from the illustrious *P.* Paeony 'Regency' (AM/RHS) line, and has very large flowers, 15cm (6in) across, borne on long flower spikes. The flowers, which are an interesting colour combination of soft rose-red shaded with green, open in the winter.
Photo X ¾

PAPHIOPEDILUM
Royalet 'Valentine'
◐*Intermediate* ❄*Winter*
Above: An example of how much a modern hybrid (*P.* Paeony 'Regency', AM/RHS) can improve the flower shape and texture of a species parent (*P. barbatum*), in just one generation. The flowers, which are not more than 10cm (4in) across, are rose-red with darker veining, and open in the winter.
Photo X ½

PAPHIOPEDILUM
Small World 'Adventure'
◐*Intermediate* ❄*Winter*
Right: Named in 1959, in honour of the crossing of the Atlantic by four people in a hot-air balloon, this hybrid has proved to be one of the most wonderful parents, giving only its best characteristics to its progeny. (Most of them have 'world' in their names.) The 13cm (5in) flower has warm rich amber-brown petals and lip, with mahogany overtones, and a green-flushed white dorsal sepal spotted with red. Like most paphiopedilum hybrids, the plant flowers in the winter.
Photo X ⅔

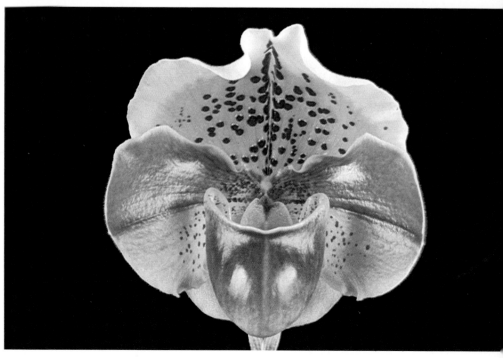

PAPHIOPEDILUM
Silvara 'Halo' (AM/AOS)
◑*Intermediate* ❄*Winter*
Left: An award winner in America, and a member of an extensive and vigorous group of hybrids, this plant has proved to be a useful and productive parent. The flowers, 9cm (3.5in) across, are white marked with yellow in the lip and on the petals, and open in the winter.
Photo X 1

PAPHIOPEDILUM
Vanda M. Pearman 'Downland' (AM/RHS)
◑*Intermediate* ❄*Winter*
Above: A recent cross between *P. delenatii* and *P. bellatulum,* this hybrid combines the rounded flower shape of the latter species with the longer flower stem and delicate colouring of the former. The beautiful 7.5cm (3in) flowers, which open in winter, are basically white, finely spotted with crimson, the spots becoming more dense on the pouch.
Photo X ²/₃

PAPHIOPEDILUM
Winston Churchill
◑*Intermediate* ❄*Winter*
Left: One of the most famous of modern paphiopedilums, this plant is generally thought of as an American hybrid because the stock was bought by American breeders in the 1940s. However, it is British-bred and is proving to be a very fine parent. The 13cm (5in) flowers are red, and the white dorsal sepal is spotted with red. The plant blooms in the winter.
Photo X ¾

PHALAENOPSIS

Phalaenopsis species have a characteristic elegance. Some bear many flowers: for example, on *P. schilleriana,* it is not unusual to find as many as 70 flowers on a single spike. The more flamboyant species have beautifully marked foliage, greys and silver overlying the rich green of a tongue-shaped leaf, and pink or white flowers 7.5cm (3in) or more across. In recent years various hybrids of *Phalaenopsis* have been grown extensively for the cut flower trade, the white flowers being popular for wedding bouquets.

Phalaenopsis in the wild

All species are native to the Far East, but are found specifically in an area stretching from Assam and Burma to the Moluccas and, especially, the Philippines. The name *Phalaenopsis* is derived from *phalaina,* a moth, and *opsis,* the appearance, and was suggested by the Dutch botanist Blume, who, when the first specimen was found in 1852 and named *Phalaenopsis amabilis,* likened them to tropical moths in flight.

Phalaenopsis are epiphytic or lithophytic plants, which grow attached to the branches and trunks of trees, rocks and mossy banks overhanging water, and are almost always found in deep shade. A few species grow so close to the seashore that they receive salt spray at times. (A gardener in charge of an early orchid collection in England, who was particularly successful with this genus, is said to have dressed the gravel of the staging and paths periodically with salt; this could do no harm but it is doubtful whether it had any bearing on his success!)

Three species, *P. lowii, P. parishii* and *P. esmeralda,* are deciduous in their native habitat, where they grow on small bushes and limestone rocks. But in cultivation, where they are not subject to such drastic changes in the seasons, they usually keep their leaves. The leathery leaves can be quite large, up to 46cm (18in) long and 7cm (2.8in) wide, and are succulent to the extent that they can store water. The majority of species flourish in the wild where the temperature is naturally uniform, ranging from 24 °C (75°F) at night to 35°C (95°F) during the day, with a rainfull around 2,030mm (80in) a year, so that the atmosphere is nearly always saturated. For this reason *Phalaenopsis* plants do not have pseudobulbs.

The roots are remarkably freely produced and adhere firmly to whatever supports them, be it tree or rock. In cultivation, when the plants are repotted, it is virtually impossible to release the roots from the sides of the pot without leaving half the root covering—and inevitably the growing tip—behind. In *P. schilleriana* and *P. stuartiana* the roots are silver-coloured, wide and flattened, and grow to some length, not so much in

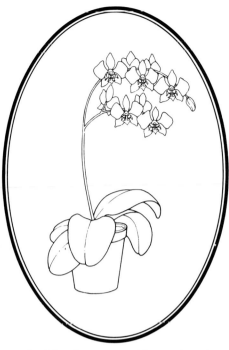

search of food as to provide good anchorage. Food is mainly supplied by the humid atmosphere, well laden with contributions from the rotting vegetation below, and absorbed through roots and leaves.

In the natural habitat the flower spikes hang in cascades, as do the long, heavy leaves. The plants are almost continually in flower, and often flower more than once from the original spike. When the first crop of flowers has dropped, branches on the spike will often produce another crop of buds. If you want to use the flowers for decoration, fully cut the spike to just above the uppermost node. The plant will then produce a secondary spike within a short time. Flower spikes are usually staked upright under cultivation.

When conditions are favourable, plants are capable of producing keikis, or 'eyes', which grow into young plants that make their own roots. In the wild it is not uncommon to see large clumps of plants whose flower spikes have produced keikis that have established themselves further along the branch, producing flower spikes of their own.

In some species, including *P. violacea, P. amboinensis* and *P. mariea,* after the flowers have been fertilized and the seedpod is being formed, the petals and sepals become thickened and green like the leaves and presumbly function in the same way.

Phalaenopsis in cultivation

The natural environment of *Phalaenopsis* species provides high average temperatures, high humidity and good shade. Therefore, the plants succeed best when an entire greenhouse is devoted to them. The ideal structure is a low-span house, preferably with the first 61cm (2ft) of the building below ground level. Nevertheless, rewarding results are now being achieved

in less exacting conditions. When a mixed collection of orchids is being grown it is usually possible to provide a small area which receives more heat, humidity and shade than the rest of the house.

Many hybrids are now being grown successfully in centrally heated homes, but these are generally fully matured plants, comparatively tolerant if humidity is lower than ideal. At least warmth and shade can be provided in home culture, and a tray or saucer of wet gravel will give some immediate humidity. An increasing number of home growers are installing fully automatic growing cases which provide controlled conditions.

Temperatures for growth

Phalaenopsis usually start growing in early spring, when the night temperature should not be allowed to fall below 18°C (64.5°F), with a daytime rise to 24 °-27°C (75°-80.5°F). These temperatures should be maintained until late autumn when a reduction in temperature to a minimum of 15°C (59°F) at night, rising to 18°-21°C (64.5°-70°F), will be required. Some variation may occur as the weather outside dictates, and an occasional drop to 10°C (50°F) on winter nights will do no harm provided the plants have not been heavily watered and humidity is low. Some commercial growers use the lowering of the temperature to 10°C to initiate flower spikes if the timing of flower production is important for marketing.

Ventilation

Conventional roof ventilation must be operated with great care: as a rule the ventilators should only be opened on the hottest summer days, when the temperature may rise above 27°C (80.5°F). How much they are opened will depend partly on the direction and force of the wind: draught should be excluded at all costs and the aperture should never be so great that there is a heavy loss in humidity. On the other hand, whatever the season, the overall conditions must be kept buoyant to avoid pockets of stagnant air, and good air movement is especially important during the flowering season. In recent years electrically operated fans have given excellent results.

Shading

During the winter months, when the plants will be in a state of least activity, no shading is required unless there is exceptionally bright weather. But from early spring shading will be necessary. As the important factor is not only to provide shade but to keep the glass cool, the ideal form of shading is one suspended

Right: If shaded from strong sun by blinds during the growing season and given humid conditions, phalaenopsis orchids will provide a colourful display from spring to late autumn.

above the glass, allowing sunlight to filter through. Lath blinds suspended 15-23cm (6-9in) above the glass on a metal or wooden frame have proved satisfactory, as the blinds can be rolled up or down according to weather conditions. A colour wash applied to the glass is less satisfactory as it is liable to wash off and thus require several applications, with the possible risk of scorch occurring between. Where seedlings are grown, heavier shading is required.

Composts and potting

When selecting a compost it is again advisable to remember the native environment and to think in terms of root anchorage rather than of compost as such. As already mentioned, fir or pine bark has the properties required, and can be broken down to a size suitable for the plant to be potted. In general, plants of flowering size are potted in bark crushed to pieces of about 5-12mm (0.2-0.5in); for small seedlings just produced from culture flasks, a much finer grade should be used. In both cases the addition of a little charcoal helps to keep the compost sweet.

Repotting should normally be done during the growing season, but if the condition of the rooting medium has deteriorated badly, the plant should be repotted immediately, whatever the season. Mature plants need fresh material in their second year. Seedlings should be repotted at least twice in the growing season until they have reached full maturity in the third or fourth year.

The potting procedure is simple. After shaking off all the old compost, trim away dead roots and shorten any that are excessively long before settling the plant in its new container and topping up with the selected compost. Polypropylene pots or pans are preferable to the conventional clay. Some growers prefer to use hanging baskets but these dry out more rapidly and will therefore require more frequent watering.

Propagation and division

Generally, vegetative propagation is associated with the *Phalaenopsis* species rather than hybrids and is limited to keikis, or new plantlets produced from the nodes on the flower stalk. In the natural growing conditions of high humidity and heat keikis are formed readily. Under cultivation, they can be cut from the parent plant when a number of roots have appeared and then potted up in the normal way.

Hybrids do not produce keikis as readily as the species, but where more stock is required of a specific clone, this can be achieved by subjecting the nodes to laboratory treatment. This is a highly scientific process and generally practised only by commercial growers (see page 95). New hybrids can be grown from

Above: Phalaenopsis often produce plantlets, or keikis, at the nodes on the flower spikes. When they have formed several roots, these keikis can be cut from the parent plant and potted up.

Below and Right: Be careful not to get water in the crown of phalaenopsis as this will cause rot, which can be devastating. Although the plant appears to be dead, a new shoot (right) may grow if given correct conditions.

seed, but special facilities are required. Details are given on page 94.

Watering and feeding
Because the atmosphere of their native habitat is virtually saturated, it is necessary to maintain very high humidity during the growing season. From early spring to late autumn sprinkling all surfaces with water two or three times a day will help, particularly in the late evening during the height of summer. The overall moisture and general conditions of the greenhouse will determine how often the plants should be watered. As a guide, large plants may require watering once a week, while smaller ones need more frequent attention. The density of the rooting medium is also important, as the denser it is, the more water will be held. The epiphytic nature of phalaenopsis necessitates a compost that retains some moisture, is well aerated, and does not decompose too quickly; for all-round good results, pulverized fir bark is best as it is nearest to natural conditions.

Phalaenopsis are fast-growing plants with no pseudobulbs in which to store food and they therefore require feeding. A fertilizer with a high nitrogen content should be applied at fortnightly intervals, when the plants are watered.

Pests and diseases
The main pests are slugs and snails and you should keep a lookout for these at all times. Occasionally water will lodge in the centre growth of a plant and rot will ensue. If this happens little can be done other than to dry out the area as quickly as possible and treat it with captan. The original plant will be permanently disfigured, but occasionally secondary growths appear from its base.

Species and hybrids
In the following pages, some of the most popular varieties are illustrated. Phalaenopsis are very free-flowering and it is possible with only a small collection to have several plants in flower throughout the year. They are easy to grow provided the few basic requirements are met.

The first species to be discovered, *Phalaenopsis amabilis,* has pure white flowers with a red-spotted lip and yellow throat. This species was used extensively in the early days of breeding, and has provided the backbone of all the present-day high quality white phalaenopsis hybrids.

Although many of the species have pink or white flowers, with hybridization and selective breeding new colours and contrasts are continually being produced, notably the 'peppermint striped' varieties, such as *P.* Hennessy.

Phalaenopsis Species

Phalaenopsis amboinensis
●*Warm* ✿*Spring-Autumn*

Above: There are essentially two forms
of *P. amboinensis*. The best known and
perhaps more extensively used in
breeding has flowers with rich dark
brown bars on a pale green base. In the
second form the base colour is almost
cream with bars of pale mustard yellow.
The plants are of compact growth, with
pale yellow-green foliage, and tend to
produce several flower spikes at the
same time, normally 15 30.5cm (6-12in)
long. The flowers, 2.5-5cm (1-2in)
across, are borne singly over a long
period through spring to autumn.

Given appropriate conditions, this
species responds well in cultivation.
The first hybrid was made with *P. amabilis*,
and was registered as *P. Deventeriana*
in 1927.
Photo X 1½

Phalaenopsis aphrodite
●*Warm* ✿*Autumn*

Right: This species was first discovered in
1837 in the Philippines, and at that time
was thought to be the same as
P. amabilis. However, as more
phalaenopsis were introduced into cultivation and knowledge of the genus
increased, *P. aphrodite* eventually came
to be recognized as a distinct species.
The leaves are deep green with a high
gloss. Arching flower spikes, carrying
many exceptionally long-lasting blooms
of a pure glistening white, 5cm (2in)
across, are produced in late autumn. The
plants grow well in cultivation.
Photo X 1½

Phalaenopsis lueddemanniana

●*Warm* ✸*Spring/Summer*

Above: This is a free-flowering species, which is easy to grow and one of the most variable of the *Phalaenopsis* genus. The leaves are usually light green, broad and long. The flower spikes, several of which may be produced at the same time, each carry up to 20, 2.5cm (1in) flowers that open in succession through-out spring and summer. The sepals and petals are almost white or yellow, marked with bars or spots ranging from pink to deep purple, and the small lip is usually purple. If the plant is given cooler and more shady conditions when the first buds appear, richer colours will be produced. The flower spikes readily produce keikis at their nodes.

The species has been widely used in breeding with great success, two of the best known hybrids from *P. lueddeman-niana* being *P.* Golden Sands and *P.* Cabrillo Star. As the name suggests, *P.* Golden Sands is a fine yellow hybrid, and *P.* Cabrillo Star is a large white bloom heavily spotted with red.

Photo X 2

Phalaenopsis equestris

●*Warm* ✸*Autumn/Winter*

Above: This species (for many years synonymous with *P. rosea*) is said to be the commonest phalaenopsis of the Philippines. It was introduced into England in 1848 by James Veitch. The plant is comparatively compact in growth and has leathery, dull green leaves some 15cm (6in) long and 7.5cm (3in) wide. The very graceful arching flower spikes bear pale rose flowers, 2.5cm (1in) across, with a darker oval lip. The flowers open in autumn and winter.

P. equestris was used as a parent to produce the first manmade hybrid phalaenopsis, *P.* Artemis, in 1892. It still plays a part in modern hybridizing where compact, small-flowered plants are in demand.

Photo X ¾

Phalaenopsis mannii

●*Warm* ✸*Spring/Summer*

Left: This species grows wild at high altitudes in Assam, where *Vanda coerulea* is also found. It is the least flamboyant of the *Phalaenopsis* genus, and not a large grower. The flowers, deep yellow in colour, heavily barred with chestnut-brown and borne on short branched spikes during spring and summer, are about 5cm (2in) across. Although a subject for the warm house, the plant is able to withstand temperatures as low as 7°C (45°F) without being harmed. *P. mannii* has had great influence by contributing yellow flower colour to its hybrids.

Photo X 1¼

Phalaenopsis mariea
○*Cool* ✿*Spring/Summer*

Below: Little is known about this species. Closely related to *P. lueddemanniana,* it was found in 1878 growing in the Philippines at high altitudes in deep shade. In cultivation the plant should be grown in the coolest section of the greenhouse.

The flowers, which open in spring and summer, are pale yellow, banded with chestnut and are 2.5-4cm (1-1.5in) across. Although the plant has been little used in hybridization in the past, it is possible that some interesting progeny may result from its use as a parent.
Photo X ½

Phalaenopsis sanderiana
●*Warm* ✿*Spring*

Below: It has been suggested that *Phalaenopsis sanderiana* is a natural hybrid between *P. aphrodite* and *P. schilleriana.* But both parents are not found in the same locality, and it is now generally accepted as a species in its own right. The foliage resembles that of *P. aphrodite,* being bright glossy green, and the plant is a strong grower. The flush pink flowers, produced in the spring, are 7.5cm (3in) in diameter, and particularly beautiful.

By 1946 some 17 hybrids of this species had been registered, and it is still being used in breeding today.
Photo X ⅔

Phalaenopsis schilleriana
●*Warm* ✿*Spring*

Above: This is the best known of all phalaenopsis, and is held in great esteem. It was discovered in Manilla in 1858 growing on trees, often very high up. The plants fix themselves to the branches and trunks by numerous flattened roots. In cultivation these roots grow to considerable lengths along any firm surface within their reach, and are almost impossible to release without breaking. As they mature they develop a beautiful silver sheen.

As a decorative plant, *P. schilleriana* is hard to beat; the handsome leaves, up to 46cm (18in) or more in length, are deep green, marbled and blotched with grey and silver. The flowers 5-7.5cm (2-3in) across, of a delicate rose purple, are often borne in great numbers during early spring on a branched arching spike, which may grow to 91cm (3ft) in length.
Photo X 1

Phalaenopsis stuartiana

●*Warm* ❀*Spring*

Above: This species is very similar to
P. schilleriana, and when not in flower it is
virtually impossible to tell them apart: the
foliage is the same deep green, marbled in
grey and silver, and the roots have the
same flattened appearance. In the wild it
is said to be found always closely
associated with water, sometimes close
to the shoreline, where the plants are
subjected to salt-water spray. The spike
habit and quantity of flowers are also like
those of *P. schilleriana,* but in
P. stuartiana the upper sepal and two
side petals are white. Of the two lower
sepals one half is white and the other
heavily spotted with reddish-purple; the
orange-yellow lip is also spotted. The
overall appearance when in flower is thus
distinct and striking. The flowers open in
spring.

Many hybrids have been registered
from this species, all showing the
characteristic spotting, and it is valuable
for introducing orange shades to the lip,
when crossed with white hybrids.
Photo X ¾

Phalaenopsis violacea

●*Warm* ❀*Summer*

Left: This species, first discovered in
1859, has two distinct types, one from
Borneo, the other from Malaya. Although
it may not be the easiest species to
maintain in good flowering condition, it is
nevertheless very attractive, as it
combines beauty with fragrance. The
7.5cm (3in) flowers of this plant from
Borneo, which have the fragrance of
violets, are borne in summer on a short
pendulous spike, often in succession.
The Malaysian form is smaller and of a
fuller shape, about 6.5cm (2.5in) across.
The plant requires deep shade and high
humidity.

The first hybrid, *P. violacea* × *P.
amabilis,* was registered by James Veitch
in 1887 as *P.* Harrietiae. In recent years,
P. violacea has been used extensively in
breeding, with great success.
Photo X 2½

Phalaenopsis Hybrids

PHALAENOPSIS
Barbara Moler
●*Warm* ✽*Spring-Autumn*

Right: The parents of this important hybrid are *P*. Donnic Brandt and *P*. Spica (syn. Yardstick). *P*. Spica is the result of a two species cross between *P. fasciata* and *P. lueddemanniana*. *P*. Barbara Moler is a comparatively compact grower, with leaves some 30cm (12in) long and 10cm (4in) wide. The flower spikes, which are long—up to 46cm (18in)—and branched, bear flowers for many months from spring to autumn. Individually, the flowers are 7cm (2.75in) across, and of very heavy texture. There are two colour forms. The best known is white with heavy pink spotting, giving an overall appearance of rich pink. The second form can best be described as yellow; the base colour is greenish-yellow overlaid with yellow-chestnut blotches.

 P. Barbara Moler is already proving to be a very important parent in breeding for heavy texture and new colour breaks. *P*. Space Queen is an example of the type of hybrid produced from *P*. Barbara Moler breeding.
Photo X 1

PHALAENOPSIS
Hennessy
●*Warm* ✽*All year*

Below: This hybrid is an example of a peppermint-striped phalaenopsis. The plant is very free-flowering, blooming throughout the year, and the branched spikes may bear up to 30 flowers at a time. The individual flowers are 9-12cm (3.5-4.75in) across, white to light pink in basic colour, with red or pink stripes or, in some forms, spots. The lip varies in colour from deep rosy pink to orange.
Photo X ½

PHALAENOPSIS
Party Dress
●*Warm* ✽*Season varies*

Below: This hybrid produces many small, round pink flowers on branched spikes. Large specimen plants are particularly beautiful.
Photo X ⅔

PHALAENOPSIS
Purbeck Sands
● *Warm* ✾ *Season varies*
Above: With this hybrid a new colour was introduced into the genus. The result of crossing *P.* Golden Louis (a small yellow) with *P.* Zada (a rich round pink) has been to produce flowers, 5cm (2in) across, in very pleasing shades from light primrose to mustard pinks. The foliage also carries shades of brick red. Plants are small, compact and free-flowering at any season.
Photo X ½

PHALAENOPSIS
Space Queen
● *Warm* ✾ *Season varies*
Left: This hybrid is the result of crossing *P.* Barbara Moler with *P.* Temple Cloud, thus producing beautiful flowers of heavy substance, 9-10cm (3.5-4in) across, soft pink or white, heavily spotted with red.
Photo X 1

PHALAENOPSIS
Temple Cloud
● *Warm* ✾ *Season varies*
Below: Resulting from the crossing of two outstanding hybrids, *P.* Opaline and *P.* Keith Shaffer, this hybrid took on the finer points of both parents, producing pure white 11.5cm (4.5in) round blooms of heavy texture, and in turn proved to be a very successful parent. It can be in flower at any season.
Photo X ¾

VANDAS

Few orchids can surpass the beauty and drama of the vandas in foliage or flower. There are about 80 species of evergreen plants, native to China, the Himalayas, New Guinea and northern Australia.

The genus is remarkable for the great differences in the colour and sizes of the flowers. Most vandas have erect leafy stems, evergreen leaves and fleshy roots, and flowers are borne on lateral spikes, produced from the axils of the leaves. Vandas are monopodial orchids, and most are epiphytic. For horticultural purposes the leaves of vandas fall into two categories: terete, or cylindrical, as in *Vanda teres*, and strap-leaved as in *v. coerulea*. (A third group, semiterete, whose leaves are a cross between the two, is sometimes included.)

Vandas have thrived on the Hawaiian islands for many decades because of the islands' climate and ocean breezes, but the plants are not indigenous to Hawaii. Today many hybrids of vandas are available, and the plants are often prized as cut flowers. *Vanda sanderana* and Vanda coerulea are perhaps the two most important species of the genus. The flowers of *V. sanderana* are a beautiful lilac or pink colour; those of *V. coerulea* are noted for their striking blue, and thus this species is frequently cultivated.

The sepals and petals of vanda flowers are similar in size, rounded and rather flat. The lip is affixed to the base of the column; the lateral lobes may be either large or reduced in size, and the middle lobe, a part of which is usually fleshy and ridged, is also variable in form.

Vandas in cultivation

Vandas are highly epiphytic, preferring an arboreal existence on tree trunks and branches. The plants can attain heights of 2.2m (7ft), although the average height indoors is 1.2m (4ft). Their long aerial roots, measuring up to 1.2m, store food and water if necessary during periods of drought. All vandas enjoy the light, and with sufficient sunlight they may bloom two or three times a year, with as many as 50 or more flowers. Most vandas bloom in the winter, although some species come into flower in the late summer or early autumn. A healthy plant can produce as many as three or four flower spikes, each bearing up to 12 flowers that last perhaps three to four weeks on the plant.

Requirements for growth

Because vandas are tall plants, they must have sufficient vertical growing space. Most plants should be grown in the warm or intermediate greenhouse as they thrive on sunlight and heat during the day, doing best at a temperature of 26.5°C (80°F). They can survive lower daytime temperatures if absolutely necessary but not for any length of time. At night, plants should be kept in cooler tempera-

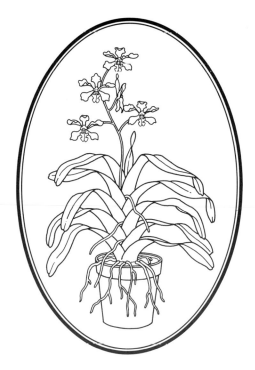

Right: A flamboyant display of vanda orchids at the World Orchid Conference in Bangkok, where they thrive in the warm, sunny climate. Although cultivated commercially, large numbers also adorn many parks and gardens.

tures: 15.5°C (60°F), if they are to be brought to perfection. Some species, such as *V. coerulea* and *V. kimballiana*, need cool daytime temperatures of about 21°C (70°F).

Because vandas thrive in sun and bright light it is a good idea to hang plants high up in the greenhouse so that they receive all light possible. And, because the position of the sun in the sky changes with the season, you may need to move vandas around to obtain optimum light at all times.

The higher the temperature, the higher the humidity should be. Vandas require high humidity so daily spraying for most of the year (except in winter) is essential. Minimum humidity for plants should be about 50 percent; in lower humidity plants will not grow well (although they will not die). Higher humidity increases the risk of fungal infection, especially if days are cloudy and conditions wet. Regular damping down of the greenhouse surroundings will create excellent humidity and is especially recommended during summer months. If you are growing vandas at a window in your home, spray-mist plants with water.

A free circulation of air is necessary to keep vandas at the peak of health, as they are naturally arboreal plants and like a buoyant atmosphere. Even in winter, open vents or windows whenever possible (even if for only 30 minutes) without causing a drastic drop in temperature inside the growing area. If you cannot keep vents or windows open, run an electric fan at low speed near, but not directly at, the plants to keep the air moving. Also, try to avoid water becoming

lodged in the axils of the leaves as this can cause rot.

Composts and potting

Large-grade fir bark is the accepted growing medium for vandas in containers, but they can also be grown in gravel or charcoal chunks. A good potting mix is fir bark and broken charcoal (half and half). Some growers cultivate plants successfully in cracked bricks, pumice stones or even gritty sand. The selection of the proper growing medium for your plants depends on where you live—in warmer climates you may opt for fir bark, while in cooler climes a mixture of bark and charcoal may be best.

Vandas resent being disturbed, so repot them only when absolutely necessary—about every three years. To remove the plant from a clay pot you will need to break the pot with a hammer because the roots adhere so tightly to the container. Repotting is best done in spring when most vandas are starting new growth (when the root tips are green).

Plants should be potted rather high in the container with only the basal parts of the stem and roots in compost. Plants do best in wooden baskets or clay pots, with additional holes around the base—the more air circulation at the bottom of the pot, the better for the health of the plant. But no matter what potting material is

used or what kind of container, drainage must be perfect.

Although plastic pots may be suitable for other orchids it is best not to use them for vandas. Such pots have a tendency to hold water too long and, furthermore, they are top heavy. They are, therefore, unsuitable for growing such tall plants.

Some growers cultivate vandas on large slabs of wood, and in this situation the plants require daily watering. Osmunda compost is anchored to the slab with wire and the plant roots are tied to the osmunda. It is a tricky method but after several months roots grow into the osmunda and the plants are then securely anchored.

Vegetative propagation

Vandas produce offshoots, or keikis, at various times during the year, usually in the late autumn. When these offshoots are 5-7.5cm (2-3in) high they can be cut from the 'mother' plant, using a sharp, sterile knife, and started in small pots of fir bark. The cut marks should be dusted with charcoal. To ensure maximum humidity, drape polyethylene over four sticks pushed into the container. When the offshoots are 15-18cm (6-7in) tall, move them into larger containers. Now you no longer need the polyethylene cover, but the humidity must be maintained.

If you keep your vandas for several years, and the plants become large (over 1m [39in] in height), new plants can be propagated by cutting off the top of the parent plant. You will need to remove about 30.5-46cm (12-18in) from the top. Make a clean cut on the central stem, and dust both the cut surfaces with charcoal. Place the cuttings in pots of fir bark.

Watering and feeding

During the spring and summer months vandas need plenty of moisture, so flood the pots daily in mid-summer. (Also, hose down any wood slabs if you are using them.) Make sure that containers have sufficient drainage holes because vandas do not like stagnant water.

Their aerial roots should be allowed to hang loose since they are highly specialized moisture-absorbing structures. Vandas require as much water in winter as at other times of the year, but it is best at all times to allow plants to dry out before watering them again.

After flowering, the plants need a resting period of about two weeks. During this time the growing medium should be kept just damp but never bone dry, and spray-misting continued. Increase the amount of watering again in early spring.

Although most orchids do not need much feeding, vandas thrive on plant food, which should be applied at least twice a month in spring and summer. A balanced nitrogen-phosphorus-potassium fertilizer (10-10-5) is best.

Pests and diseases

Vandas are remarkably free of pests and diseases; the leaves are too tough to be chewed by insects. Apart from snails or slugs, which sometimes attack leaves, other common plant pests are rarely found.

Occasionally, vandas develop dark, almost black, streaks, on their leaves. This is generally the result of water remaining on leaves too long or, in some rare cases, it may be due to a virus disease. When due to disease, the black streaks, which are 5cm (2in) in diameter, do not usually affect the plant but they are unsightly.

Species and hybrids

In the last few decades vandas have been used for the production of an incredible number of hybrid orchids and they can be successfully crossed with a large number of orchid groups in their subtribe Sarcanthinae. Crossing *Vanda* with *Ascocentrum,* for example, produces *Ascocenda*; and with *Renanthera, Renantanda.*

The following list is merely a sampling of the many lovely *Vanda* species and hybrids. You can buy your plants from orchid suppliers or, in some cases, at plant shops.

Vanda Species

Vanda sanderana
●*Warm* ✿*Summer*
Above: This magnificent summer-flowering orchid grows to about 61cm (2ft) or more in height, and comes from the Phillippines. The leaves are 30-38cm (12-15in) long, and the flower spikes semi erect with 7 to 20 flowers clustered together. The flowers, 13cm (5in) across, are almost flat, with the upper sepal soft rose to white in colour suffused with whitish-pink, and the lower sepals round, slightly larger, and tawny yellow crossed with red markings. The petals are smaller than the sepals and are white to rose coloured with red blotches near the base; the lip is tawny yellow, streaked with red. Although this species adjusts to varying conditions and will, if necessary tolerate some coolness, it generally grows best in the warmth and sun.

Photo X ½

Vanda coerulea
◑*Intermediate* ✿*Autumn/Winter*
Above: This is perhaps the showiest and most popular vanda for collectors. Blooming in autumn and winter with lovely pale blue flowers, *V. coerulea* is found wild in the Himalayas, Burma and Thailand, growing at about 1,220-1,830m (approx. 4,000-6,000ft). The leaves are leathery and rigid, about 25.5cm (10in) long and 2.5cm (1in) wide, and the flower stems are erect or arching to about 61cm (2ft) with from 5 to 20 flowers per spike. The flowers can be variable in colour, shape and size, but are generally 10cm (4in) across with pale blue sepals and petals and a network of darker markings. The lip is purple-blue marked with white. While most vandas revel in warmth, *V. coerulea* is a subject for the intermediate greenhouse, requiring temperatures between 13° and 18°C (15.5°-64.5°F).

Photo X ½

Vanda cristata
◐*Intermediate* ✿*Spring-Summer*
Right: This small orchid, which grows only to about 25cm (10in), is a good subject for indoor growing. It is native to high altitude areas of Nepal and Bhutan. The leaves are 15cm (6in) long and the flowers waxy and fragrant, about 5cm (2in) across. The sepals and petals are mostly yellow-green, and the entire flower is marked with blood-red longitudinal stripes and spots. Blooming from early spring until mid-summer, this is a fine orchid for those with limited space, and will tolerate evening temperatures of 13°C (55°F).

Photo X 1

Vanda sanderana var. *alba*
●*Warm* ❋*Summer*

Left: Unusual and pretty, this lighter coloured form of *V. sanderana* is highly prized by collectors and produces rounded flowers, 12.5cm (5in) across, of heavy texture. The upper sepals and petals are white, and the lower sepals are pale mustard yellow. The flowers open in the summer.

Photo X ½

Vanda suavis var. *tricolor*
●*Warm* ❋*Autumn/Winter*

Below: Coming from Java and Bali, this free-flowering strap-leaved epiphyte bears colourful flowers in autumn and early winter. The stems are densely leafy with curving leaves about 25cm (10in) long and 2.5cm (1in) wide. Flower spikes are horizontal, shorter than the leaves and carry 5 to 10 flowers that vary in shape and colour. Typically they have whitish-yellow sepals and petals barred or spotted with red-brown, usually flushed with pale magenta near the base. The fragrant waxy flowers are about 7.5cm (3in) across. This is an easy vanda to coax into bloom in warm sunny conditions, with temperatures of 25°C (75°C).

Photo X 1

Vanda Hybrids

VANDA
Jennie Hashimoto 'Starles'
●*Warm* ✿*Summer*
Above: This recent cross between *V. sanderana* and *V.* Onomea shows good flower form and is becoming popular with collectors. In the summer, mature specimens may bear as many as 200 flowers, with pink sepals and orange-red petals. This orchid requires growing conditions in the warm house.
Photo X ⅓

VANDA
Nelly Morley
◐●*Intermediate/Warm* ✿*Spring and Autumn*
Right: A semiterete orchid bearing many flowers, this is a cross between *V.* Emma Van Deventer and *V. sanderana*. It has become a very popular hybrid for the collector because it generally blooms twice a year, in spring and early autumn. It requires intermediate to warm conditions.
Photo X ¼

Above: *Stanhopea wardii*   Photo x ½

Above: *Trichopilia tortillis*   Photo x ½

Above: *Sobralia macrantha*   Photo x ⅓

Trichopilia suavis
◑*Intermediate*   ✿*Winter/Spring*

This species produces a short, semi-arching spike, which bears two to five flowers of about 10cm (4in) in diameter and cattleya-like in appearance; the basic colour is white or cream, with rose-pink spotting on the sepals and petals, and heavier blotching of the same colour on the broad lip.

Trichopilia tortillis
◑*Intermediate*   ✿*Winter/Spring*

This plant carries a single flower, up to 13cm (5in) across, on a pendent spike. The sepals and petals, which are narrow and twisted throughout their length, are brown, bordered by a narrow yellow-green band; the trumpet-shaped lip is white with some rose-red spotting.

Trichopiliu fragrans
◑*Intermediate*   ✿*Winter/Spring*

One of the larger species, *Trichopilia fragrans* produces arching sprays of two to five 10cm (4in) flowers. The sepals and petals are white with a greenish tinge, and the lip is white with yellow markings in the throat.

Zygopetalum

This genus comprises 20 species, most of which come from Brazil. They are mainly terrestrial, producing rounded pseudobulbs with long but fairly narrow leaves. One of their great attractions is the contrast between the colour of the sepals and petals and that of the lip.

These are plants for the intermediate house and require good light, with plenty of moisture at the root when in full growth. Air movement around the plant in conditions of high humidity is very important, otherwise the leaves soon become badly spotted; and, for this reason, they should never be sprayed. Both of these species flower during the winter, producing heavily scented flowers that last for four or five weeks.

Zygopetalum intermedium
◑*Intermediate*   ✿*Winter*

Often known as *Z. mackayi,* this plant produces an upright flower spike 45-60cm (18-24in) in height, from inside the first leaves of a new growth. The spike bears four to eight flowers each 7.5cm (3in) across. The sepals and petals are of equal size, and bright green blotched with brown. The lip, in contrast, is broad, flat and basically white, heavily lined with purple.

Zygopetalum crinitum
◑*Intermediate*   ✿*Winter*

This is similar to *Z. intermedium,* although in some forms the blotching on the sepals and petals is very much darker and the markings on the lip are almost blue.

Above: *Zygopetalum intermedium*   Photo x ½

GLOSSARY

Words in *italics* refer to separate entries within the glossary

Adj. = Adjective
Cf. = Compare
Pl. = Plural

Adventitious Usually applied to roots, or any growth produced from a site other than the usual or normal.

Aeriel Living without contact with compost or the ground.

Anther The part of the *stamen* containing *pollen*.

Anther cap The cap covering the *pollen* masses.

Articulate Jointed; possessing a *node* or joint.

Asexual Without sex.

Asymmetrical Not symmetrical; without regular shape.

Axil The upper angle between a stem or branch and a leaf.

Back bulb Old *pseudobulb,* usually without leaves.

Bifoliate Having two leaves.

Bigeneric Involving two *genera* in the parentage of a plant.

Bisexual Two sexed, the flowers possessing both *stamens* and *pistils.* (cf. *unisexual*).

Bract A reduced leaf-like organ protecting a flower stalk.

Bulbous Having the character of a bulb.

Calceolate Slipper-shaped.

Callus The protective tissue covering a cut or bruised surface.

Cellular Composed of cells.

Chlorophyll The green pigment in plants, essential for the manufacture of food.

Chlorotic Excessive yellowing due to a breaking down of the *chlorophyll.*

Chromosome A structure within the cell nucleus, which carries the *genes.*

Clone An individual plant raised from a single seed, and all its subsequent *vegetative propagations.*

Column The central body of the orchid flower formed by the union of the *stamens* and *pistil.*

Crest A raised, fringed or toothed ridge found on the *lip.*

Cross-pollinate The *pollination* of one flower with the *pollen* from another flower. (cf. *self-pollination*).

Cultivar An individual plant in cultivation, including its *vegetative propagations.*

Deciduous Losing leaves at the end of the growing season.

Diploid Having the normal complement of a double set of *chromosomes* in the cell nuclei.

Division The means by which a single *cultivar* is divided into two or more plants.

Dorsal Pertaining to the back or outer surface. (cf. *ventral*).

Ecology The study of organisms in relation to their environment.

Endemic Occurring only in a given area, and not elsewhere.

Epidermis Outer layer of cells.

Epiphyte A plant that grows on another plant but is not a *parasite,* as it obtains nourishment from the air.

Eye The bud of a growth.

Family A group of related *genera.*

Filiform Long, slender or thread like.

Fimbriate Fringed.

Flaccid Soft and limp.

Fragrans Sweet scented.

Gene The unit of inheritance, located at a specific site on a *chromosome.*

Genetics The study of heredity and variation.

Genus A subdivision of a *family,* consisting of one or more *species* which show similar characteristics and appear to have a common ancestry. Adj. generic. Pl. genera.

Grex A group, applied collectively to the progeny of a given cross between two plants.

Habitat The locality in which a plant normally grows.

Hirsute *Pubescent,* the hairs being coarse and stiff.

Hybrid The offspring resulting from the cross between two different *species* or hybrids.

Hydroponics A method of growing plants using nutrient solutions alone.

Inbreeding *Self-pollinating.*

Indigenous Native; not introduced.

Inflorescence The flowering part of a plant.

Intergeneric Between or among two or more *genera.*

Internode The part of a stem between two *nodes.*

Keel A projecting ridge.

Keiki A plantlet produced as an offset or offshoot from another plant. (A Hawaiian term used by orchidists.)

Labellum The *lip,* or modified *petal* of an orchid flower.

Lateral Of or pertaining to the side of an organ. (cf. *terminal*).

Lead A new *vegetative* growth.

Linear Long and narrow, with parallel margins.

Lip The *labellum,* usually quite distinct from the other two *petals.*

Lithophyte A plant which grows on rocks. Adj. lithophytic.

Mericlone A plant produced by *meristem* culture.

Meristem *Vegetative propagation* of plants by cultivating new shoot tissue under special laboratory conditions.

Monofoliate Having only one leaf.

Monopodial Growing only from the apex of the plant.

Mutation A departure from the parent type; a *sport*.

Natural hybrid A *hybrid* produced by chance in the wild.

Nectary A gland or secreting organ that produces nectar.

Node A joint on a stem.

Nomenclature A system of names or naming.

Ovary The central female part of a flower.

Parasite A plant that lives on and derives part or all of its nourishment from another plant. Adj. parasitic. (cf. *epiphyte*).

Pedicel The stalk of an individual flower.

Pendulous Hanging downwards, or inclined.

Petal One of the three inner segments of an orchid flower, which is not modified to form the *lip*.

Pistil The seed-bearing organ of a flower consisting of the *ovary, stigma* and *style*.

Plicate Pleated, or folded like a fan.

Pollen The fertilizing grains borne by the *anther*.

Pollination The transfer of *pollen* from the *anther* to the *stigma*.

Pollinia The masses of pollen grains found in the *anther*.

Polyploid Containing one or more additional sets of *chromosomes* beyond the normal *diploid* number.

Proliferation Offshoots; the growth of buds that normally remain dormant.

Protocorm A tuber-like structure formed in the early stages of a plant's development.

Pseudobulb The thickened portion of a stem, but not a true bulb.

Pubescent Covered with fine hairs or down.

Quadrigeneric Pertaining to four *genera*.

Raceme A simple *inflorescence* of stalked flowers.

Recurved Curved downwards or backwards.

Rhizome A root-bearing horizontal stem, which, in orchids, usually lies on or just beneath the ground surface.

Rib The primary vein of a leaf.

Rosette A cluster of leaves arranged around a short stem.

Saccate Pouched, or bag-like.

Saprophyte A plant which lives on dead organic matter. Adj. saprophytic.

Scape A flower stalk without leaves, arising directly from the ground.

Self-pollination The *pollination* of a flower by its own *pollen*. (cf. *cross-pollination*).

Semiterete Semicircular in cross-section; semicylindrical. (cf. *terete*).

Sepal One of the three outer segments of an orchid flower.

Sheath A tubular envelope protecting the developing *inflorescence*.

Species A group of plants sharing one or more common characteristics which make it distinct from any other group. Adj. specific.

Spike A flower stem.

Sport A deviation from the usual form; a *mutation.*

Spur A hollow tubular extension of the *lip*.

Stamen The male organ of a flower, bearing the *pollen*.

Stigma The part of the *pistil* which is receptive to the *pollen*.

Style The part of the *pistil* bearing the *stigma*.

Symbiosis The close association of dissimilar organisms, with benefit to both. Adj. symbiotic.

Sympodial A form of growth in which each new shoot, arising from the *rhizome* of the previous growth, is a complete plant in itself.

Synonym A surplus name, arising when a *species* has been given two or more names.

Systemic A pesticide that is absorbed by the plant and poisons the cells against pests.

Terete Circular in cross-section; cylindrical. (cf. *semiterete*).

Terminal At the end of the axis (cf. *lateral*).

Terrestrial Growing in or on the ground.

Transpiration The loss of water from the plant tissue by evaporation.

Tribe A group of related *genera*.

Trigeneric Pertaining to three *genera*.

Tuber A thickened, normally underground stem.

Unifoliate With one leaf.

Unilateral Arranged only on one side.

Unisexual Having flowers of one sex only. (cf. *bisexual*).

Variety A subdivision of a *species;* a group of plants that differ slightly from the main *species* type.

Vegetative propagation The increasing of a particular plant by *division,* or by *meristem* culture.

Velamen The thick layer of cells covering the roots of *epiphytic* orchids.

Ventral The front (cf. *dorsal*).

Verrucose Covered with wart-like projections.

Virus An infectious agent which increases in living cells causing disease.

Whorl An arrangement of leaves or other organs in a circle around an axis.

FURTHER READING

Arditti, J., *Orchid Biology: Reviews and Perspectives, 1,* Cornell University Press, New York and London, 1977.

Birk, L.A., *Growing Cymbidium Orchids at Home,* L.A. Birk, California, 1977.

Blowers, J.W., *Pictorial Orchid Growing,* J.W. Blowers, Maidstone, 1966.

Bowen, L., *The Art and Craft of Growing Orchids,* Batsford, London, 1976.

Cohen, B. and Roberts, E., *Growing Orchids in the Home,* Hodder and Stoughton, London, 1975.

Curtis, C.H., *Orchids – Their description and Cultivation,* Putnam, London, 1950.

Darwin, C.,*The various contrivances by which orchids are fertilized by insects,* John Murray, London, 1862.

Dodson, C.H. and Gillespie, R.J., *The Biology of the Orchids,* Mid-America Orchid Congress, Tennessee, 1967.

Freed, H., *Orchids and Serendipity,* Prentice-Hall, New York and London, 1970.

Hawkes, A.D., *Encyclopedia of Cultivated Orchids,* Faber & Faber, London, 1965.

Kramer, J., *Growing Orchids at your Windows,* D. van Nostrand, New York, 1963.

Kramer, J., *Orchids: Flowers of Romance and Mystery,* Harry N. Abrams, New York, 1975.

Nicholls, W.H., *Orchids of Australia,* Thomas Nelson, Sydney, Australia, 1969.

Noble, M., *You Can Grow Orchids,* M. Noble, Florida, 1964.

Northen, R.T., *Orchids as House Plants,* Dover Publications, New York, 1955.

Northen, R.T., *Home Orchid Growing,* Van Nostrand Reinhold, New York, 1970.

The Orchid Stud Book, Hurst & Rolfe, London, 1909.

Paul, M., *Orchids – Care and Growth,* Merlin Press, London, 1964.

Reinekka, M.A., *A History of the Orchid,* University of Miami Press, Florida, 1972.

Richter, W., *Orchid Care: A Guide to Cultivation and Breeding,* Macmillan, London, 1969.

Rittershausen, P.R.C., *Successful Orchid Culture,* Collingridge, London, 1953.

Rittershausen, B. and Rittershausen, W., *Popular Orchids,* Stockwell, Devon, 1970.

Rittershausen, B. and Rittershausen, W., *Orchids – in Colour,* Blandford, Dorset, 1979.

Sander, D.F., *Orchids and their Cultivation,* Blandford, London, 1962.

Sanders' Complete List of Orchid Hybrids, Royal Horticultural Society, London, 1966, available from the American Orchid Society, Cambridge, Massachusetts.

Sessler, G.J., *Orchids – and how to grow them,* Prentice-Hall, New York and London, 1978.

Skelsey, A., *The Time-Life Encyclopedia of Gardening: Orchids,* Time-Life Books, Virginia, 1978.

Sunset Books, *How to Grow Orchids,* Lane, California, 1977.

Swinson, A., *Frederick Sander: The Orchid King,* Hodder and Stoughton, London, 1970.

Thompson, P.A., *Orchids from Seed,* Royal Botanic Gardens, Kew, 1977.

Waters, V.H. and Waters, C.C., *A Survey of the Slipper Orchids,* Carolina Press, N. Carolina, 1973.

Williams, B.S., *Orchid Growers' Manual,* Wheldon and Wesley, Herts, 1894; reprint Hafner, Connecticut, 1961.

Withner, C.L., *The Orchids: A Scientific Survey,* The Ronald Press, New York, 1959.

Withner, C.L., *The Orchids: Scientific Studies,* Wiley, New York and London, 1974.

Veitch, J. and Sons, *Manual of Orchidaceous Plants,* H.M. Pollett, London, 1887.

Journals

American Orchid Society Bulletin, American Orchid Society, Cambridge, Massachusetts, USA.

Australian Orchid Review, The Australian Orchid Council, Sydney, Australia.

Die Orchidee, Deutsche Orchideen-Gesellschaft, Frankfurt, West Germany.

Orchids In New Zealand, the New Zealand Orchid Society, Wellington, New Zealand.

The Orchid Digest, The Orchid Digest Corporation, Orinda, California, USA.

The Orchid Review, The Orchid Review, Ltd., Kingsteignton, Newton Abbot, Devon, England.

The South African Orchid Journal, the South African Orchid Council, University of Natal, South Africa.

Above: *Coelogyne cristata*　Photo x ¾

SOURCES OF PLANTS

Adelaide Orchids Pty, Adelaide, South Australia

Keith Andrew Orchids, Plush, Dorchester, Dorset, England

The Beall Company, Vashon Island, Washington, USA

Burnham Nurseries Ltd, Kingsteignton, Newton Abbot, Devon, England

Duckitt Nurseries, Darling, Cape Town, South Africa

Artur Elle & Co., Hambühren, Celle, W. Germany

Floricultura, Haarlem, The Netherlands

Hanes Orchids, San Gabriel, California USA

Wilhelm Hennis Orchideen, Hildesheim, W. Germany

J. & L. Orchids, Easton, Connecticut, USA

Jones & Scully Inc., Miami, Florida, USA

Kultana Orchids, Bangkok 4, Thailand

Lemförder Orchideen, Lemförde, W. Germany

Mansell & Hatcher Ltd, Rawdon, Leeds, Yorkshire, England

McBean's Orchids Ltd, Cooksbridge, Lewes, Sussex, England

Orchideen Hans Koch, Unna, Dortmund, W. Germany

Orchids by Hausermann Inc., Elmhurst, Illinois, USA

Ratcliffe Orchids Ltd, Chilton, Didcot, Oxfordshire, England

Santa Barbara Orchid Estate, Santa Barbara, California, USA

'T' Orchids, Bangkok 4, Thailand

Vacherot & Lecoufle, Boissy-Saint-Léger, France

Valley Orchids Pty, Reynella, South Australia

H. Wichmann Orchideen, Celle, West Germany

Wildroot Orchids, Constantia, Cape Town, South Africa

Wondabah Orchids Pty, Carlingford, New South Wales, Australia

Wyld Court Orchids, Hampstead Norreys, Newbury, Berkshire, England

Zuma Canyon Orchids Inc., Malibu, California, USA

Above: *Cymbidium* Elmwood   *Photo x ½*

GENERAL INDEX

Figures in *italics* indicate illustrations in place of, or in addition to, a reference in the text. Figures in **bold** type indicate major treatment of a subject.

INDEX TO PLANTS

Above: Oncidium cheirophorum   Photo x

CREDITS

Picture credits

The publishers wish to thank the following photographers and organizations who have supplied photographs for this book. Photographs have been credited by page number and position on the page: (B) Bottom, (T) Top, (C) Centre, (BL) Bottom left, etc.

Photographs

A-Z Collection: 109(B)

Alec Bristow: 128(TC), 131(TR)

Gloria Cotton: 170-1

Eric Crichton: Endpapers, Half-title, Title page, Copyright page, Contents page, Foreword, 12(CL), 13(CR), 15(TR,CL), 16(T), 24-5, 31, 33-4, 36, 39(TC), 45, 49(C), 50, 53(T, CR), 54-5, 63(B), 64-5(C), 66-7, 68(TC, C), 70-1, 75(B), 82-5, 87-9, 92(B), 93(B), 94(T), 95, 98-9, 103-5(CL, BL, TR), 106-109(T), 110-111, 116-25, 128(L,CR), 129(TC,L), 130 (T,B), 131(TL,CL,B), 132 (T,BR), 133(B), 134-5, 137-141(T,BL,BC), 142-59, 161, 164-9, 172(TL,B), 173(B), 176-80(R), 181(B), 182-3(T), 184(TR,CR,BC), 185(T), 186(B), 187(TR), 188(T), 189(T), 190-1(T,CR), 192(T), 193-4(T,B), 195(T), 196-7(CL,CR,B), 200-1, 202, 207
© Salamander Books Ltd: 14(C), 15(CR), 26-7(L, RHS Lindley Library), 28-9(R, RHS Lindley Library), 30, 32, 41(T), 46, 49(T), 51(TL), 53(CL), 56-7, 59, 60-1, 62(L), 63(T), 65(T), 68(R),

69, 72, 74-5(T), 76-81, 90-92(C,TR), 94(B), 96-7, 104, 162-3

Derek Fell: 114-5

Alan Greatwood: 129(B), 141(BR), 180(TR), 181(T), 183(B), 184(B), 185(B), 186(T), 187(TL), 188(C,B), 189(B), 191(LC,B), 192(B,C), 194(C), 195(B), 197(T,CR)

Jack Kramer: 40-1

Mansell Collection: 27(CR), 29(TL)

Charles Marden Fitch: 174(T)

John Mason: 12(BR), 13(TL), 20(B), 38-9(T)

National Monuments Record: 34(B)

J.R. Oddy: 172(TR)

Orchid Society of Great Britain: 132(BC), 133(C,R)

Alwyn Y. Pepper: 21(TR)

Herman Pigors: 173(T), 174(B),175(T,B)

Ratcliffe Orchids: 44

Gerald Rodway: 105(BR), 128(BR), 130(CR)

Edward Ross: 12(T), 14(CR), 18-19, 22-23, 39(C)

B.J. Wallace: 21(TL)

Peter Ward: 13(TR), 20(T)

Tom Wheeler: 58

Joyce Wilson: 42-3, 47(R)

Artists

Copyright of the drawings on the pages following the artists' names is the property of Salamander Books Ltd.

Lydia Malim: 11, 14-16, 19, 43, 72-4, 76, 81, 83-4, 86, 93-4, 101-2, 112, 126-7, 134, 146, 160, 170, 179

Diana MaClean (Linden Artists) 17,162

Brian Watson (Linden Artists) 35, 38, 48, 52

Acknowledgements

The publishers would like to thank the following individuals and orchid nurseries for their help in supplying material for a major portion of the photographs in the book.

Eddie Anderson, Derek Cotton, Gloria Cotton, Ben Darby, Alan Day, Alan Greatwood, Josephine Kelleher, David Leigh, Molly Pottinger, Sir Robert and Lady Sainsbury: The Bucklebury Collection, Eric Young, Brian Williams, Burnham Nurseries Ltd, Keith Andrew Orchids Ltd, Mansell and Hatcher Ltd, McBeans Orchids Ltd, Neville Orchids Ltd, Phalaenopsis Ltd, Ratcliffe Orchids Ltd, Twyford Laboratories Ltd, Vacherot & Lecoufle, Wyld Court Orchids.

PRINTED IN BELGIUM BY

INTERNATIONAL BOOK PRODUCTION

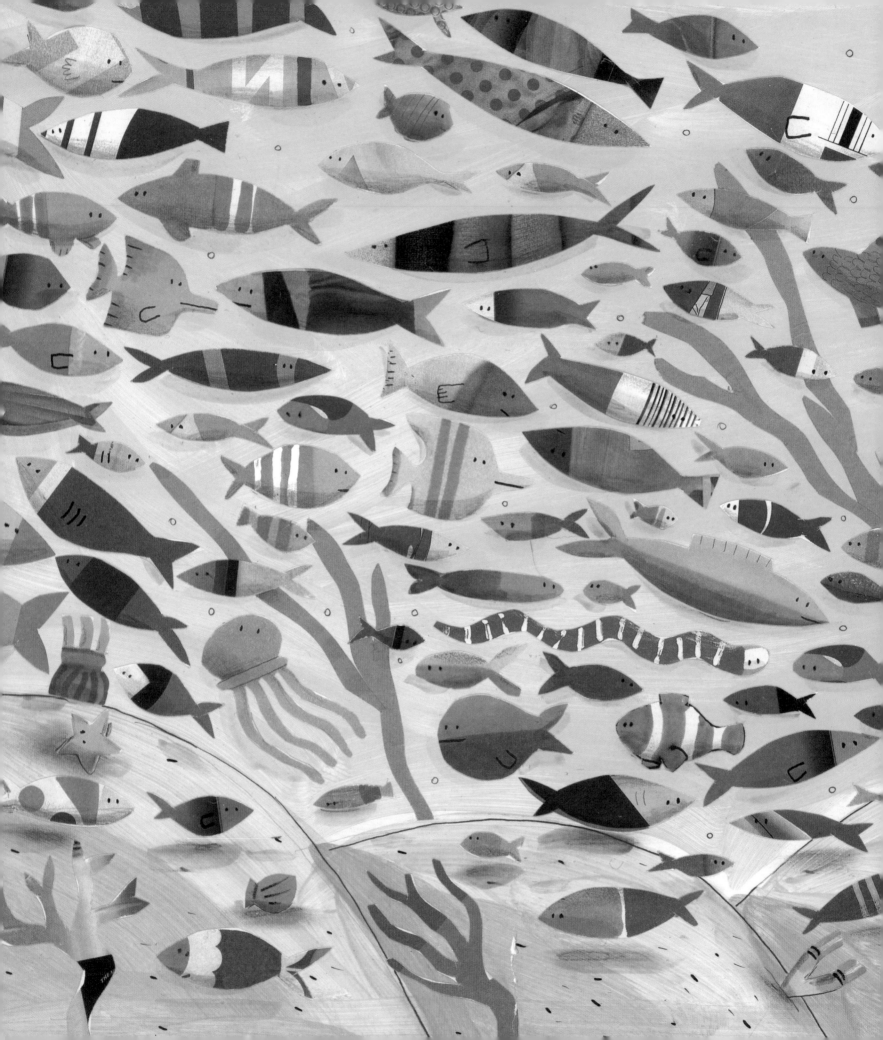

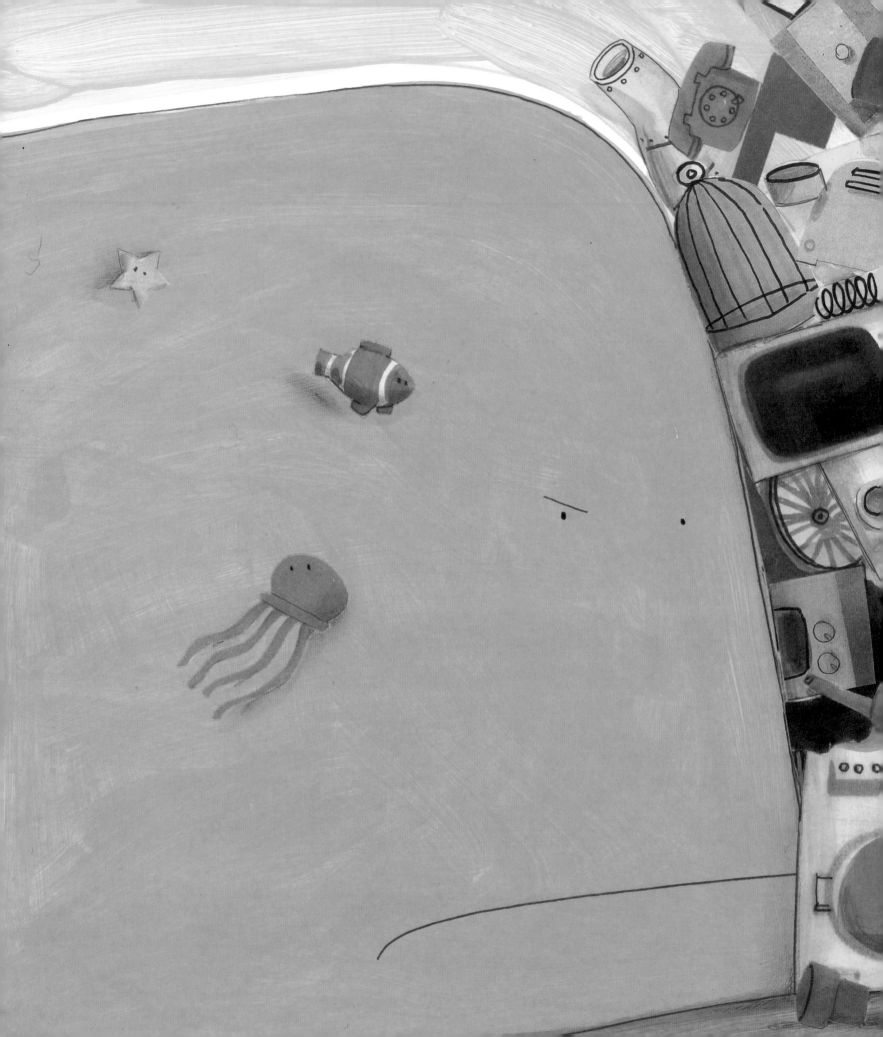

"Next, throw your wings back. Now open your beak as wide as you can. And *cock-a-doodle-doo!*

"Good!" said Rupert. "But louder—way, way louder. Remember, Sherman, your voice is going to have to wake up everybody on this whole big farm."

"Don't worry," Sherman called back.

When nighttime came, Rupert put his fuzzy slippers over his ears and held them in place with his sleeping cap. Nothing was going to wake *him* up early!

He fell sound asleep.

Out in the pasture,
Sherman slept too.
But it wasn't very long
before Sherman had a dream.

He dreamed it was already morning. The sun was
high in a bright blue sky and he had slept right
through the six ringing alarm clocks!

"OH NO!!!" He gasped.

"I'm too late!"

He looked down on the farm with pride as lights came on and voices filled the air. Everything was back to the way it always was.

Well, almost. There was one thing that was new. After they all crowed in the middle of the night, Sherman and his friends and relatives loved how they sounded together and decided to form a chorus.

They were rehearsing a song when Rupert walked by the pasture.
Sherman stopped conducting for a moment and called over, "Come
to our show tonight, Rupert! Everyone's invited."

INTRODUCTION

Almost everything about orchids is touched with the quality of fantasy, and nothing in all the plant world quite equals their power to fascinate both eye and mind. They are the newest and most advanced plants on the evolutionary ladder, and analysis of their structure and state of development places their origin between 60 and 130 million years ago. No fossils of orchids have ever been found, and perhaps none ever will be; and so there is a huge gap in the record of their development where theory must substitute for fact. Although fossil-forming conditions have existed continuously during the last 500 million years, not once in all that time do they seem to have preserved an orchid. Just why that is so is still an unanswerable question, and must rest with other orchid-related queries until future developments provide answers.

Another mystery is the question of exactly how many kinds of orchids exist at the present time. Conservative estimates run to about 450 genera with some 12,000 species, while others claim there are 750 genera and 35,000 species. The reason for the discrepancy is that an exhaustive analysis of the described species has yet to be completed. The inevitable duplications and errors, when brought to light, will probably reduce the final figure to somewhere around 15,000 species. In the meantime, new species are still being discovered and new hybrids developed, so a somewhat chaot-

ic condition is very likely to continue.

Despite the vagueness of some data, there *are* certain positive statements that can be made about orchids. For one thing, they have an enormous range of habitats, from above the Arctic Circle, 72° north (the uppermost limit of the coral root orchid) to 52° south, in Tierra del Fuego, where *Chiloglottis cornuta* may be found. Ninety percent of all orchids originate in the tropics or subtropics, but the rest are well distributed over the temperate and cold regions of every continent except Antarctica. And even though orchids show a preference for tropical areas, many of them avoid the steamy lowlands thought to be typical of those regions, choosing instead cool mountain heights at almost alpine altitudes. This fact was once widely misunderstood, with the result that orchids died by the countless thousands in conservatories, where they were being grown in heat and humidity suited only to a minority of them. Yet even under the most abysmal conditions a few did live on, which was less a miracle than a tribute to the orchid's powers of survival.

Once established, most orchids hold a tenacious grasp on life, even outliving the trees that are their hosts. The versatile plant can be found growing happily in every type of ecological situation, from semiarid beaches to the steaming rain forests to windswept mountains, where the drifting, low-lying clouds supply the plants with moisture. They can make themselves at home in sand, loam, or earth, or upon rocks and trees; some few are aquatic, and there are even species, such as the Australian *Rhizanthella gardneri*, that are completely subterranean throughout their entire life cycle. No environmental adaptation seems impossible for the orchid family to attempt, and the very process of their evolutionary experiments can be seen on almost every hand.

One particularly notable instance has to do with the seed that orchids produce. It is little more than a dry envelope surrounding a mass of undifferentiated cells, each of which carries all the molecular information needed to make an entire plant. To assure maximum dispersal by the wind, each seed is kept small—about one hundredth of an inch in diameter—and it sacrifices its food supply to keep itself as light as possible. Despite their apparent fragility, such seeds have a tremendous capacity for survival, especially if they are desiccated and frozen—conditions that they readily encounter when borne aloft into the upper atmosphere, where they can remain viable for at least ten years in the dry and frigid stratosphere.

Germination of the seeds, however, is much chancier, for the developing plant is totally reliant on exterior sources to supply it with food. It must land in a suitable spot where available light, moisture, and temperature meet its special needs. In addition, its nourishment must be provided by certain fungi, whose threadlike mycorrhizal structure penetrates the coating of the seed and then furnishes it with a flow of sugar and other nutrients. Remarkably few orchid seeds encounter the proper conditions, and mortality among them is extremely high. The orchid, of course, counters that danger by producing enormous quantities of seed. One species, the green swan orchid, has been known to create 3,770,000 seeds in one pod; if all of them matured it would take only a few orchid generations for them to cover the earth.

The orchid's complete dependence on outside agencies is somewhat disadvantageous and wasteful, forcing them to rely heavily on a combination of very high productivity and luck. One genus, however, *Catasetum*, seems to be developing a more efficient system, and may very well be turning a new page in the evolutionary process. Professional orchid growers have long since learned how to bypass the need for mycorrhiza in germinating seeds by substituting nutrient cultures held in flasks. This results in a higher rate of successful germination than occurs in nature, and is one of the reasons that orchids are no longer the exclusive province of the wealthy. But now some catasetums have unexpectedly managed to germinate outside of their laboratory flasks, eliminating the services of mycorrhiza altogether; and the same thing may very well be happening out in nature. Perhaps they have found a way of providing a store of food for the developing embryo, as most other plants have always done, but how they are doing that remains a mystery. Only one thing can be said with certainty about orchids: they seem endlessly capable of exceeding their limitations.

There are three major classes of orchids: epiphytes, terrestrials, and saprophytes. Epiphytes grow on trees but are not parasitic, since their aerial root systems provide their food. This is the largest section of the orchid family. The terrestrials, as their name implies, are rooted in earth, while the saprophytes, the smallest group, live in, on, and under decaying vegetable matter which is fed to them through the digestive action of mycorrhizal fungi. They live out their lives in the same dependent state as do germinating orchid seeds, since they have no chlorophyll of their own with which to make food.

Cultivated orchids come from the terrestrial and epiphytic groups, and much of the mystery and mythology that once surrounded their cultivation has since been exploded. Recent advances in horticultural methods and increased knowledge about orchid structure and environmental needs have made orchid raising much easier than it once was; some are now no harder to raise than common house plants. Some species will even tolerate a certain amount of neglect, as long as their specific temperature requirements are met within reason. Artificial light, small ventilating fans, water pans and humidifiers, aquarium heaters, and the use of gravel or chopped fir bark as a growing medium have taken much of the risk out of raising orchids, and make possible year-round supplies of bloom. We may not have fully realized the concept of "orchids for the millions'' that Benjamin Williams formed in 1851, but we aren't very far from it.

The prospect of living with an orchid collection, even a small one, is one of the most rewarding things that the plant world can offer. To introduce you to orchid growing, horticultural directions have been added to the descriptions accompanying every species pictured in this book. However, all instructions that follow are to be considered as guidelines rather than dogmas, for horticulture is full of variables and is as much an art as it is a science.

First, all temperatures mentioned, both minimum and maximum, may be exceeded for brief periods of time. Orchids are tough organisms capable of standing some abuse, though they prefer kindly treatment when possible. Second, all the directions, except for lady-slipper, refer to raising orchids indoors. They may be grown in your window or in any suitable place in the house; but if it is possible to place them in terrariums, Wardian cases, or the like, you will have almost complete control of their cultivation, particularly if you add supplemental light.

If your orchid's leaves turn yellow, it is getting too much water. If they become bluish green and the pseudobulbs (the plant's storage organs for food and water) grow hard, it is getting too much light. Always err on the conservative side; more orchids have been killed by too much heat or water than too little. Always give the plant adequate drainage. Avoid drafts, but provide gentle, indirect circulation of air. Maintain humidity around orchids by placing their pots on stages (planks, boards, boxes, trays, etc.), set over pans filled with pebbles and water. In very warm or dry weather, sprinkle the stages and surrounding areas frequently with additional water.

Fir bark takes up water slowly at first, so it should be thoroughly soaked before being used for planting. It is also difficult to re-wet once allowed to dry out completely. When it feels resilient between your fingers it is just right. In inactive seasons let it dry to the point where only the slightest moisture, a damp-dry state, is present. Always test it below the top surface.

The mysterious formulas repeated in so many commentaries, such as 30–10–10 or 10–20–10, refer to liquid fertilizers available at your garden shop. The numbers indicate the nitrogen, phosphorus, and potash content, respectively. Dilute in the proportion of one teaspoon per gallon of water and follow manufacturer's instructions for application.

A final word of caution: orchids are insidious and habit-forming. One innocent victim of their spell ended up with ten greenhouses filled with thousands of specimens. He also gained lifelong contentment and longevity and said goodbye to boredom forever. May orchids bring you the same good fortune.

AN ILLUSTRATED TREASURY OF

Orchids

Dendrobium superbum variety *giganteum*

There are some 1600 species in the genus *Dendrobium,* many of which were originally misidentified. There is no way of succinctly describing their distinguishing characteristics, as they are extremely varied even at the species level. The result is a botanist's nightmare, a floral Augean stable that nobody has dared to clean up since the last incomplete effort in 1910. More and more species have been added to the genus, with more and more names revised and shifted about, but the end result is still a confused mass of data that obscures its subject rather than illuminating it.

Horticulturists, however, don't care very much what a plant is called, just so long as they can grow it. So whether it is one inch or ten feet tall; evergreen or deciduous; bears twenty blossoms or nine thousand—and dendrobiums do all three of those things, and more—the horticulturist revels in the variety before him and even adds to it by crossbreeding.

Many of the varieties of *Dendrobium superbum* are fragrant; they give off the scent of either rhubarb or raspberries, depending on the variety and on whose nose is making the decision. As to the confusion mentioned above, one botanical "bible" lists this species as a synonym for *D. anosmum* (meaning *scentless* dendrobium), and adds the comment that it is very fragrant—or not!

Growth: 60°–75° F., feed dilute 30–10–10 once or twice a week, water freely. *Flowering:* In spring. Feed dilute 10–20–10 once or twice a week, drop temperature to 55°–60° F.; very little water. *Maturity:* 60°–75° F., dilute 30–10–10, gradually reduce water. *Rest:* 55°–60° F., no food, keep compost barely moist. New growth will become evident in from one to four weeks. *Light:* As bright as possible; shade only to prevent foliage from drying or burning. *Compost:* 3 parts fir bark, 1 part sphagnum moss, in pots filled to within 2 to 3 inches of the top with mixed perlite and charcoal. Bind plants firmly to compost with nylon thread.

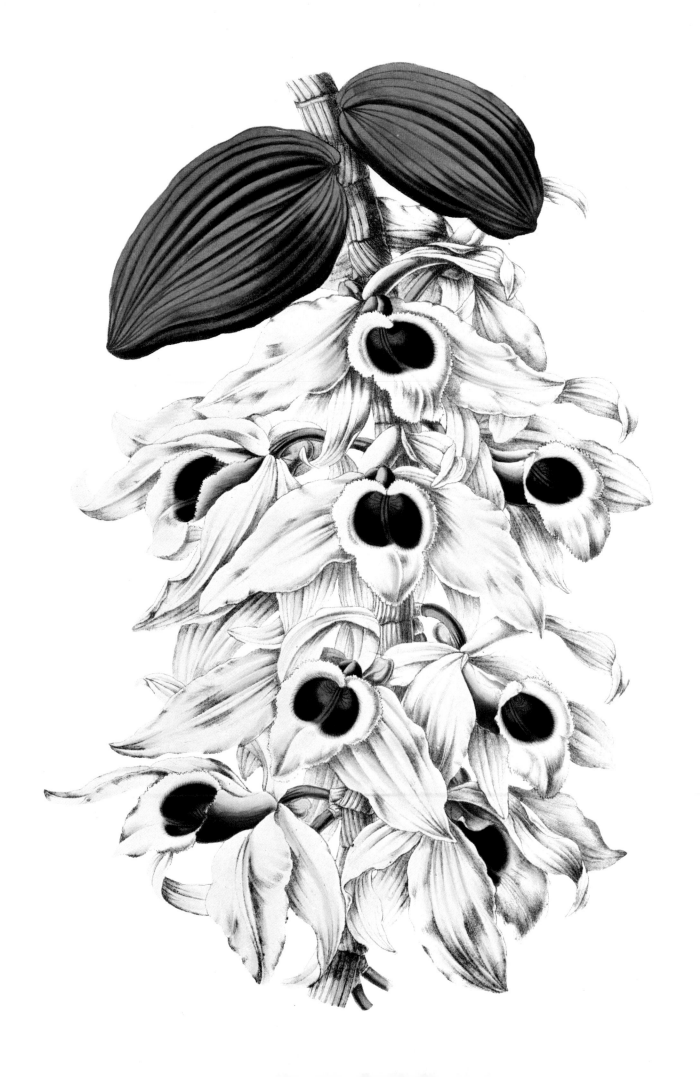

Chysis laevis

Melting and smooth is the English translation of this orchid's botanical name, and those terms do convey a good idea of its appearance. The smooth waxy petals look like molten gold that still bears a sign of fire, as evidenced by its orange tones flecked with red. But truth to tell, the botanist who named *C. laevis* didn't have that kind of melting in mind. He was referring instead to the fused condition of the pollinia, those pollen-bearing organs that firmly attach themselves to certain insects and are then carried off to fertilize the stigma of another blossom.

The genus *Chysis* is a rather small one, consisting of only six species or so. Plant hunters have been searching for more species in the wild ever since the orchid first came into cultivation in 1840. Not much has resulted from various expeditions, so the genus is unlikely to be greatly enlarged in the future. However, one of its members, *C. aurea,* has the ability—rare among orchids—to fertilize itself and thus ensure propagation. Since this process also prevents hybridization, it is just as well that *C. laevis* lacks such a capacity, or its lovely hue could not be crossbred into other species.

Growth: 65°–75° F., feed dilute 30–10–10 twice weekly; water plentifully, both directly at roots and by mist-spraying, but gently dry off young foliage. *Flowering:* Generally in June. Feed dilute 10–20–10 from appearance of buds until flowering ends. Decrease water by at least one-third, and increase ventilation. *Maturity:* Keep same temperature and water supply, but resume 30–10–10 formula. *Rest:* In winter. 55°–60° F., keep compost barely moist, no food. *Light:* Bright, indirect, but give some direct sunlight in autumn. *Compost:* Fir bark in wire or slat baskets half filled with lump charcoal.

Cattleya velutina

Because of its unusual coloring, this orchid was originally thought to be a natural hybrid. It was first described in 1870 after flowering in the collection of Mr. Joseph Broom of Didsbury; then began a fruitless twenty-year search for its supposed parents. It seemed to be a cross between *Cattleya bicolor* and one of the *C. guttata* varieties with which it was often imported from Brazil. It was not until the early 1890s that large numbers of this velvety cattleya were discovered—far too many to be produced by a hybrid. Only at that point did botanists first suspect it to be a species in its own right, which it eventually proved to be. Discerning and interpreting the truth about orchids has always been as much an art as a science; the study of orchids constantly raises new and baffling questions, as these flowers seem to change even in the process of being studied.

Besides its great visual appeal, *C. velutina* offers another pleasure for the senses; it is delightfully fragrant, giving off the aroma of violets.

Growth: 70°–75° F., feed dilute 30–10–10 once or twice a week. Water thoroughly, letting compost nearly dry out between waterings. *Flowering:* Flowering of the cattleyas and related groups occurs in every month of the year, depending on the species. When buds first swell give dilute 10–20–10; continue through flowering. Maintain temperate climate with 10°–15° F. drop at night. Water as above. *Maturity:* 70°–75° F.; can go up to 90° F. for a few days. Water less as pseudobulbs ripen. *Rest:* 50° F. is ideal. No food, no water, for one to three weeks. *Light:* Bright as possible, indirect. *Compost:* Fir bark in pots one-third filled with mixed perlite and charcoal. Place pseudobulbs level with top of pot.

Epidendrum phoeniceum

The obvious common name for this species is the purple epidendrum, which also explains to some degree the term *phoeniceum*. It was ancient Phoenicia that provided purple for the Caesars—the imperial purple of Roman times. But that is the only connection this native of Cuba has with the Old World, since it was unknown elsewhere until described by Dr. Lindley in 1838. In fact, Lindley anticipated its first flowering in England by three years, for it was not until the nursery firm of Loddiges brought it into bloom in 1841 that it entered European cultivation.

During the nineteenth century, orchid stock had to be brought from native habitats, since propagation was too slow to keep pace with the demand for plants, and expeditions were sent to areas known to be rich in orchids. As it so happened, Cuba had relatively few species, and few orchid growers journeyed there with any regularity. Aside from those specimens propagated by private collectors, almost no examples of *E. phoeniceum* were available in Europe, and the plant became a very rare item among orchid collections. Today, by means of germinating orchid seeds in nutrient-filled flasks and through cloning, all orchids can be supplied in abundance, and orchid raising is no longer the exclusive pursuit of the wealthy. Of course, money is never a disadvantage in setting up special greenhouses with temperature and humidity control; but ingenuity can—and often does—substitute for expensive equipment.

Growth: 70°–75° F., feed dilute 30–10–10 once or twice a week, water abundantly. *Flowering:* 70°–75° F.; as flower buds form, feed dilute 10–20–10. Maintain ample water supply throughout flowering season. *Maturity:* 70°–75° F., feed dilute 30–10–10 after flowering. Reduce water gradually when pseudobulbs end growth. *Rest:* 45°–50° F., no food, no water until new growth appears. *Light:* As bright as possible, with occasional slight shading to prevent leaf burn. *Compost:* Pack fir bark firmly into pots or hanging baskets; set orchid on top, using nylon thread to hold it in place.

Rhynchostylis retusa

Once again, the layman has proved more sensitive in the naming of plants than the scientists. Simply compare the common names fox-tail or cat's-tail orchid with *Rhynchostylis retusa,* which translates as "beaked pillar with a curved end." Despite the undoubted accuracy of the botanical terms and the scientific necessity of using them, the plant deserves something with a sweeter sound. The process of naming is, after all, somewhat arbitrary, so a little effort should be made to invent more euphonious names. This orchid was similarly ill-treated when it was first known as *Saccolabium blumei,* which means Blume's bag-lipped orchid. Ugh!

Discovered in Java in 1823 or 1824 by Karl Ludwig Blume, a German-born physician, explorer, and botanist, this orchid was found to have an extensive range that ran from Indonesia up to the Philippines and over into Burma and India. On the Subcontinent, it grew in the jungles alongside sluggish rivers where the air was filled with insects carrying malaria and other diseases, while venomous reptiles made the ground equally danger-ous to tread upon. An odd feature of this fragrant orchid in its native area is that it is always found by itself, and with long distances between individ-ual specimens—still one more orchid puzzle for the botanists and plant hunters to solve at some future date.

Growth: Usually March–August. 70°–85° F., feed dilute 30–10–10 twice weekly, water amply. *Flowering:* Maintain temperature, reduce moisture to less than half. Feed dilute 10–20–10 as buds begin to appear. *Maturity:* Plant ceases growth after flowering. No pseudobulbs. *Rest:* 50°–60° F. from November to end of February, when new growth appears. Keep compost and plant moist by daily misting. No food. *Light:* Bright but indirect. *Compost:* Sphagnum moss in wire or slat baskets suspended over water pans. Fill bottom of basket two-thirds full with charcoal lumps.

Miltonia spectabilis variety *moreliana*

Miltonia spectabilis (showy *Miltonia*) barely escaped the cruel fate of being called by the most unmusical name of *Macrochilus fryanus*. The orchid was originally sent from Brazil in 1835 to a Mr. Fry of Birmingham, whom the specific name *fryanus* was intended to honor. Another specimen, however, reached Loddiges's Nursery in London at about the same time and flowered a couple of weeks before the one in Birmingham did. As a result, Dr. John Lindley of the Horticultural Society was able to describe and classify it first by a very narrow margin. By publishing his findings before Fry, Lindley was able to establish priority for *Miltonia* as the name of the genus and for *spectabilis* as the species name.

A few years later, in 1846, a French orchid grower, M. Morel, received this variety of *M. spectabilis* from Brazil, one that exactly reversed the typical color pattern of the species. It flowered in his orchid house at St. Mandé, near Paris, and the variety was accordingly named *moreliana* for its discoverer. Independence and initiative seem to be characteristic of orchids, and an insight into their genetic engineering might well teach us some things about the evolutionary process that we haven't yet guessed at.

Growth: 65°–75° F., feed dilute 30–10–10 twice weekly, keep compost evenly moist. *Flowering:* Maintain temperature and moisture, but give dilute 10–20–10 at end of summer until flowering ends. *Maturity:* Maintain temperature and moisture; give dilute 30–10–10 after flowering ends. *Rest:* None. *Light:* Bright, but indirect and shaded from intense, direct sun. *Compost:* Fir bark in pots over layer of perlite. Keep constantly moist, though never dripping wet; give more water in very warm weather, but reduce feeding and water in winter.

Dendrobium fimbriatum variety *oculatum*

The botanical name of this orchid, once translated, provides a pretty good description of the plant: "the fringed dendrobium (life on a tree) that has eyes." This variety differs somewhat from the parent type, having maroon eyes instead of orange ones. It is also a very prolific plant in terms of flowers; one specimen is known to have yielded 1216 separate blossoms by actual count.

Dr. Nathaniel Wallich, a nineteenth-century director of the Calcutta Botanical Garden, was the first to find the parent type, *D. fimbriatum*, in Nepal in 1820. He promptly sent specimens back to England, where it bloomed in the Liverpool Botanic Garden some two years later. The variety *oculatum* was discovered in Burma in 1836 and in Assam the following year. In its native habitat it encounters summer temperatures of 90° F. or more and a rainfall of six hundred inches per year. Its long, reedlike stems bend under the weight of a heavy floral load, and the blossoms sparkle in the light even when there is no dew or rain on them, for the flowers have a crystalline texture. Of the thousand or more species of dendrobiums, *D. fimbriatum* variety *oculatum* is one of the most rewarding to raise; its visual appeal has caused it to displace the parent type almost entirely in cultivation.

For cultivation see *Dendrobium superbum* variety *giganteum* (page 12).

Cypripedium calceolus

The yellow lady-slipper of Europe, a plant familiar for generations past, seems to be losing its battle for survival in the wild. The reason lies in the structure of the plant, which, like the Oriental genus more *Paphiopedilum,* traps and kills its pollinators more often than not; only the largest and strongest insects can force their way back out of its pollen-bearing pouch.

Until the mid-nineteenth century it was thought impossible to cultivate these lovely wildlings, for nobody had realized that it was essential to duplicate the soil conditions that prevailed where they grew. Today these plants are available from nurseries, where they have been adapted to garden conditions. It is best to procure them from such places, for most wild species are on the endangered list and it is illegal to lift them from their native places.

Because man has long known this beautiful and conspicuous terrestrial orchid, it has acquired a long list of names in addition to lady-slipper; Virgin Mary's shoe, parson's shoe, Venus's slipper, Lord's shoe, wooden shoe, maiden's shoe, cuckoo's shoe, yellow shoe, and Our Lady's little shoe among them. Its range extends from Britain to Siberia and southward into the temperate zones of Europe, Asia, and even North America. Three varieties of it may be found from Newfoundland to Missouri and Georgia, always growing in mountain woods or in bogs and swamps.

Cypripedium calceolus is a hardy terrestrial orchid, the only one in this volume that can be easily grown outdoors. Plant in spring, placing rhizome 1 inch deep in a neutrally acid bed of loam, rich humus, and sand over 3 to 4 inches of broken crockery. Choose a site with a northern or northwestern exposure so as to delay growth until all frost is over. Water frequently once growth begins, and give occasional dressings of humus. Set plants where they will be in light shade. They flower in the summer. Protect from snow with piled brushwood or a layer of mulch.

Catasetum macrocarpum

This widespread catasetum may be found anywhere from Trinidad to as far south as Venezuela and Brazil. Its scientific name simply means the catasetum with large fruit; but don't expect much sustenance from this plant, because orchids are notoriously poor providers of nutrition—even to their own progeny. Certain species, however, produce a substance in the pseudobulbs which is utilized by rural Brazilians as a kind of glue. Beauty, of course, rather than nourishment is the chief stock in trade of the catasetums, and it is not confined solely to their form and color but extends to their fragrance as well.

A jasminelike scent is fairly common among catasetums, but some, such as *C. discolor,* remind us of the aroma of caraway seeds in freshly baked rye bread, while *C. roseum* fills the air with the smell of cinnamon. Such perfume is borne in special oil-producing cells scattered throughout the tissue of the labellum; it strongly attracts male bees, who extract it while pollinating the flower. Although male bees gather the perfume avidly, they get no food value from it, and may use it solely to attract females (who ignore the flowers) during the swarming process when new colonies are established. Such is the theory, but swarming doesn't happen frequently and one might wonder why females pass up the perfume in the flowers while finding it desirable on the male bee. Only further research may supply the answer.

Growth: 70°–80° F., feed dilute 30–10–10 twice weekly, water regularly and fully. *Flowering:* Maintain 70°–80° F., feed dilute 30–10–10, regular watering until flowering ends. *Maturity:* Indicated by leaf-fall and flowering. Maintain all procedures until flowering ends. *Rest:* 60° F. after leaves and flowers die back. Mist-spray pseudobulbs when they show signs of shriveling. Keep compost very slightly moist, nearly dry. *Light:* Bright, with an increase during maturity, usually in autumn. *Compost:* 3 parts fir bark, 1 part sphagnum moss over a layer of charcoal in shallow slat boxes suspended over water pans.

Brassavola glauca

This genus was named for a sixteenth-century doctor, Antonio Musa Brasavola of Venice, who taught logic, natural philosophy, and the theory of medicine at Ferrara until he became physician to Pope Paul III. Both gourmet and gourmand, he probably shortened his life by his intemperate eating habits, for he died in his prime at fifty-five. He became eminent in the fields of botany and pharmacy, which were almost synonymous practices in an age when most medicines were derived from plants. It is fitting that botanical science should have memorialized his name, even in misspelled form, through this group of attractive tropical orchids. These exotic plants were unknown in his day (1500–1555), so short is the documented history of orchids, and one cannot but wonder at what Brasavola would have thought of their many marvelous characteristics and oddities.

This species is termed *glaucus* from the fact that its pseudobulbs are often covered with a white powder, giving them the grayed appearance that the Latin word designates. The plant has a neat look about it, with smooth, thick leaves and flowers that combine deep lemony hues with creamy yellow ones. It was first cultivated early in 1837 and blossomed at Chiswick in the spring of the following year, proving thereupon to be a fragrant orchid as well as a lovely one.

For cultivation see *Cattleya velutina* (page 16).

Schomburgkia undulata

This genus of orchids is dedicated to the British naturalist Sir Richard Schomburgk, director of the Botanic Garden in Adelaide, South Australia. He served as botanist on the expedition that attempted to establish the boundary between Venezuela and British Guiana (now Guyana) between 1840 and 1844; he also discovered the giant water lily *Victoria amazonica*.

Schomburgk, however, was not the man who discovered this species. That honor belongs to Jean Linden, who found it in 1841 growing on rocks near Truxillo, Venezuela. Subsequent discoveries extended its range to Icononzo, Colombia and to the neighborhood of Caracas.

This orchid grows at an altitude of about 2000 feet. It spends half the year in heavy rain and the other half in drought while exposed to the full intensity of the tropical sun. Luckily, that exact environment does not have to be reproduced in order to grow the plant, but it obviously requires plenty of dry heat, and lots of water while growing. Other members of the genus cover a territory from Haiti and Cuba to Colombia, Venezuela, and Guyana. Its closest botanical relative is the genus *Laelia,* in which it was once included. The specific term *undulata* refers to the undulating, roller coaster line formed by the edges of its flowers.

For cultivation see *Cattleya velutina* (page 16).

Laelia harpophylla

The name of this species of laelia has nothing whatever to do with music, despite the resemblance of its Greek root, *harpé* (sword), to the English word harp. The term certainly does not identify the species with much precision, since most laelias have swordlike leaves (which is all that *harpophylla* really means). Its truly distinctive flame-red color would have been far more suitable as a term of identification: it is a rather rare color among orchids, and *Laelia flammeus* would have had a pleasing sound.

When first discovered *Laelia harpophylla* was a very rare species; only two specimens were known to the early orchid collectors and enthusiasts. It was not until the final decades of the nineteenth century that a lucky find in southern Brazil suddenly brought about a dramatic increase in the number of specimens under cultivation. The result was that considerable numbers of *L. harpophylla* entered into hybridizing experiments being carried out in ever-increasing numbers. Like all laelias, it was well suited to crossbreeding, being compatible with at least six genera (*Brassavola, Broughtonia, Cattleya, Epidendrum, Sophronitis,* and *Schomburgkia*). This quality, and its generous endowment of forty chromosomes, ensure enough genetic versatility to satisfy even the most demanding hybridizer.

For cultivation see *Cattleya velutina* (page 16).

Euanthe sanderiana

If ever an orchid made a dramatic entrance into the world of horticulture, *Euanthe sanderiana* certainly did. It was the object of a perilous search on the Philippine island of Mindanao, where its discoverer, Roeblen, suffered near drowning and the hazards of intertribal warfare before coming upon his prize. Nor were things eased for him even at the last. Put up in a treehouse overnight, he was awakened by an earthquake, which carried away the ladder by which he had climbed up and also tore away large sections of the roof and walls. What was more, the earthquake drove all the natives away in terror. Trapped in the darkness, Roeblen didn't dare make a move until dawn, but then, looking up through the hole in the roof, he saw his long-sought precious orchid hanging right above him. However, the port from which he had hoped to ship it had also been wiped out by the earthquake, and Roeblen was forced to return empty-handed and wait two more years before collecting another specimen in 1882. No wonder orchids were once so expensive!

This orchid was until recently called *Vanda sanderiana,* but even from the first it was recognized as somewhere between the genera *Vanda* and *Arachnis,* hence a new genus has now been created for it. It grows on trees overhanging the beaches of Mindanao, where its lengthy, trailing roots seem unaffected by the salty spray.

Growth: Almost continuous, but the aerial roots occasionally become dormant briefly. 75°–85° F. in summer, 65°–75° F. in winter; will withstand 55°–100° F. for short periods. Feed dilute 20–20–20 weekly, water abundantly, and be sure to spray the aerial roots. *Flowering:* Vandas may flower at intervals through the year; however, the peak blooming season is late spring and summer, when dilute 10–20–10 should be fed. *Rest:* None. *Light:* The brightest possible. Supplemental light needed outside of tropical and subtropical regions, where vandas are regularly grown outdoors. *Compost:* Fir bark chips and charcoal in firm but open mixture, placed in baskets.

Laeliocattleya amanda

While orchid growers were still struggling to keep their plants alive, much less germinate and crossbreed them, nature had long since been hybridizing them out in the forests. *Laeliocattleya amanda* is one of those natural crosses, resulting from the normal proximity of both parents and from the fact that both genera were closely related. Once technical proficiency in orchid culture had been attained, growers followed the lead given to them by nature; thus, the first experimental generic cross, made by John Dominy of Exeter, was between a laelia and a cattleya.

Laelias have entered into countless such crosses since then, for they have very desirable color characteristics and the genes they possess for those traits are dominant ones. Cattleyas, on the other hand, usually offer dominant genes in the matter of size. Special qualities, such as texture, fragrance, long-lasting flowers, disease resistance, and other properties have also been bred into orchids, often by a complex series of crosses that takes several years. Today not only two genera are crossed, but three or four may be brought into the process.

L. amanda, which translates as the charming laelia, was brought from Brazil in 1882 by Mr. William Bull. Its presumed parents—for the jungle kept no record—are *Cattleya intermedia* and either *Laelia crispa* or *L. lobata.* For a time it was given the name *Cattleya rothschildiana,* until it was recognized to be a hybrid.

For cultivation see *Cattleya velutina* (page 16).

Galeandra baueri

In the early days of orchid raising *Galeandra baueri* was a very rare species, so scarce that it was even lost to science for several years. First found in French Guiana, it was finally rediscovered some one thousand miles away from its original site, this time near Oaxaca, Mexico. Later collectors came upon it in Guatemala and Brazil, in widely separated locations, good evidence of the efficient airborne dispersal of its nearly weightless seed.

The name comes from the Latin word *galea*, meaning helmet, while *baueri* honors Francis Bauer, who was official artist at Kew Gardens and probably the finest one ever to hold that title. Happy in the simultaneous pursuits of science and botanical art, he became internationally famous for the delicacy, precision, and minute detail of his drawings, though he never made any money from them beyond his small official salary. Nonetheless he loved Kew and worked there from 1790 to 1840, when he died at the age of eighty-two. He is buried in the churchyard on Kew Green, beside the famous portrait artist Thomas Gainsborough.

Growth: 80°–90° F.; water sparingly at first, gradually increasing amount and frequency as growth develops. Feed dilute 30–10–10. *Flowering:* Maintain heavy watering as flower buds develop and feed dilute 10–20–10 until flowering ends. During flowering and afterwards drop temperature to 65°–75° F. *Maturity:* When flowering ends resume 30–10–10 formula, gradually decrease water. *Rest:* Change of foliage color signals resting period. 55° F., no food, water at intervals to keep compost moist. *Light:* Slight shading until flowering is over, then bright but indirect light. *Compost:* 3 parts fir bark, 1 part sphagnum moss, 1 part fibrous loam in pots half filled with charcoal lumps and broken crockery.

Odontoglossum nevadense

A rare species when first brought to Europe in 1868, *Odontoglossum nevadense* is still an uncommon item in orchid collections. But its cinnamon-red sepals and petals edged with pale yellow, and its snowy lip, with chestnut-brown and yellow markings, make it a prime candidate for renewed interest.

It was first discovered by Gustav Wallis, a plant hunter for the Ghent nursery of Jean Linden. Although he only sent four specimens back to Europe, Wallis wasn't being remiss or stingy; he simply didn't know that this species was included among the plants he had collected. They must have been in a dormant state when he found them, for they were mixed in with a batch of *Odontoglossum wallisii* from the Sierra Nevada in Venezuela. That location, incidentally, is the inspiration for the name *Od. nevadense,* or snowy odontoglossum.

Despite the fact that the plant was only offered for sale on the Continent, it was an Englishman from Manchester, Mr. S. Mendel, who purchased a specimen and had the honor of being the first to bring it into flower, around 1870. It must have been a delightful surprise for its owner, who had purchased it as the rare *Od. wallisii* but found himself in possession of beauty and rarity greater still.

Growth: 45°–70° F., feed dilute 20–20–20 twice weekly. Water freely, but for other odontoglossums in this book let compost nearly dry out between waterings. *Flowering:* Same procedures as above for all types of odontoglossums. *Maturity:* Continue same procedures. *Rest:* 45°–50° F., no food, no water until new growth becomes visible. Resting period is brief. *Light:* Bright with partial shade for *Od. nevadense,* all others very bright. *Compost:* Fir bark in pots; leach out accumulated salts once a month. Use slightly undersized pots to increase flowering.

Angraecum sesquipedale

No one would believe a story called "The Moth and the Orchid: A Romance by Charles Darwin"; but that title would come very close to the truth about this unusual orchid. While examining the flower, which holds a few drops of nectar at the very bottom of a twelve-inch nectary, Darwin predicted that only a moth with a flexible sucking organ just that long could fertilize this species. Such an insect was still unknown in 1862, but fifty years later it was found, and named—with a nod towards Darwin's prophecy—*Xanthopan morganii praedicta*.

The species name *sesquipedale* means "a foot and a half," a slightly exaggerated reference to the long spur of the flower's nectary. The generic term *Angraecum* comes from the Malay word *angrek,* meaning air plant, although no angraecums grow in Malaysia. Instead they come from Africa, Madagascar, and neighboring islands. One sole exception is a hardy miniature found in Japan, almost half a world away from the rest of its tropical family; the question of how *that* ever happened is as yet unanswered.

Even though *A. sesquipedale* was first discovered about 1798 by the French botanist Thouars, nothing was published about it until 1822. And then it took until 1855 to get some live specimens into England, where they flowered in 1857. It was very rarely seen outside of Madagascar until after the Suez Canal opened in 1869, making shipment quicker and easier. But the raising of angraecums hasn't become any less troublesome, for they have stems forty inches high and roots twelve to eighteen feet long. Like many other things from Africa, they are a marvel and a wonder.

Growth: Continuously active. 65°–80° F., give dilute 30–10–10 twice weekly until plant is ready to flower; water amply. Provide high humidity, about 70%, at all times. *Flowering:* Generally in December. Water a little less and keep temperature at 65° F. in winter. Feed dilute 10–20–10 during flowering. *Maturity:* None. Plant grows continuously. *Rest:* None. *Light:* Shade before, during, and for some time after flowering. Give partial shade in summer only. *Compost:* 2 parts fir bark, 2 parts sphagnum moss, well mixed with charcoal grains. Place in large pot two-thirds filled with broken crockery. *Note:* Long, tenacious root will eventually develop, and this plant likes room.

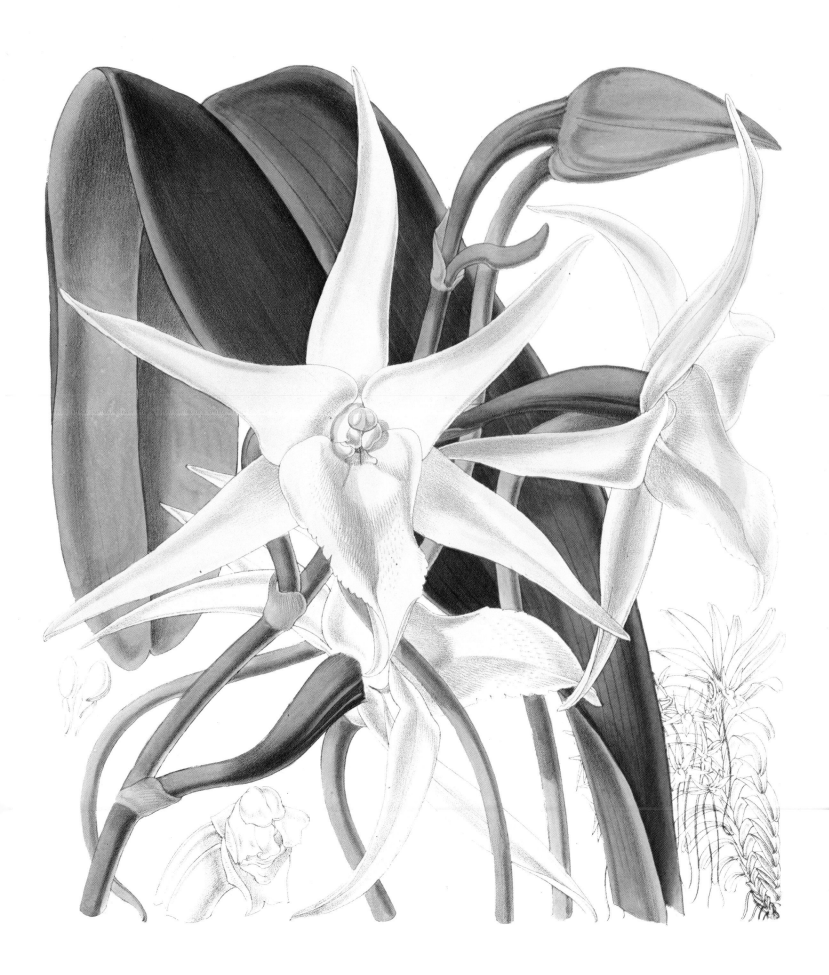

Orchis morio

Not all orchids come from the tropics; this one, *Orchis morio,* may be found the length and breadth of Europe, from England south to Cyprus and north to Archangel on the White Sea. It has been known since ancient times and was recommended as an aphrodisiac in a herbal dating from the first century A.D. Proof that it is no such thing lies in all the fields of Europe; if it had been effective not a single plant would have been left alone to survive until now.

The generic name *Orchis* commemorates a young satyr who was killed by angry bacchantes. A medieval synonym for *Orchis* was satyrion, the popular belief being that this was the food which drove satyrs to sexual excesses. The specific term *morio* means fool and may indicate that this species was useless as a venereal aid, for it was fed, in Elizabethan times and later, to invalids and ailing infants, who certainly had no need for its supposed ability to incite lust.

The food derived from the tuberous roots of *O. morio* was called salep, a highly nutritious, bland, starchlike substance with a somewhat sweet taste. It used to be sold in Turkish and Persian bazaars, whence came the Arabic name of sahlep, and was also dished up in shops on London's Fleet Street. According to Charles Lamb, it was sold for a halfpenny and made a good breakfast for a chimney sweep. Salep was also a popular hot winter beverage in Istanbul up to the time of the First World War. Although small in size, it has long been of considerable stature in cooking and medicine.

Orchis morio is not suitable for cultivation, as it requires the presence of special organisms in the soil.

Paphiopedilum lawrenceanum

This orchid was discovered in North Borneo in 1878 by Mr. F. W. Burbidge, a plant hunter for the Royal Exotic Nursery of Chelsea. It was promptly named for Sir Trevor Lawrence, Baronet, President of the Royal Horticultural Society. His interest in orchids, and in all other aspects of gardening, came about because his mother, Mrs. Lawrence of Ealing, was one of the nineteenth century's greatest patrons of horticulture and had several species of orchids and other tropical plants named after her. Her collection of orchids was one of the most notable in England and led Sir William Hooker to dedicate the sixty-eighth volume of Curtis's *Botanical Magazine*, the foremost botanical and horticultural journal of the time, to her in 1842. Her son, Sir Trevor, not only carried on the tradition she had established but intensified and extended every means of increasing interest in horticulture throughout England.

When found, *Paphiopedilum lawrenceanum* was seen to occur along riverbanks, shaded by trees, and it grew in a layer of humus overlying a layer of yellow clay. One notable ecological feature was its accompaniment by a dwarf palm, *Pinanga veitchii*. A variety of *P. lawrenceanum* exists in which the purple streaks, so conspicuous in the upper sepal, are completely absent, being replaced by veins of bright grass-green. The petals also differ in color, being yellowish green with deep green veins, while the pouch, or lip, is of brightest green with dark green veins and netting. It is considered one of the handsomest examples of its genus.

Growth: More or less continuous since they lack pseudobulbs. These orchids receive the same cultural treatment as all other phragmipediums and all paphiopedilums and cypripediums, save for temperature. Species with plain leaves are grown at 65°–75° F., those with mottled leaves at 70°–80° F. Feed dilute 30–10–10 twice weekly. Keep compost consistently moist, never soggily wet. *Flowering:* In spring drop temperatures for both types 10° F. below normal levels and feed dilute 20–20–20. Reduce water slightly until flower buds open. After flowering begins, resume 30–10–10 and normal watering. *Rest:* None. *Light:* Semishade at all times. *Compost:* Layer of sphagnum moss over mixture of 2 parts fine fir bark, 1 part humus, in pots.

Cattleya violacea

Whenever the word orchid is mentioned, the image that probably springs to mind is that of the cattleya, everyone's idea of what an orchid should look like. It is *the* orchid that almost every florist offers for sale as a corsage and is probably the world's most widely raised orchid. Its genus is comprised of some sixty-five species, an untold number of varieties, and literally thousands of hybrids, a good percentage of which occur in nature.

In the early days of orchidology such works as John Lindley's *Sertum Orchidaceum (A Garland of Orchids)*, from which this illustration is taken, supplied a lavish and luxurious answer to a genuine need. A large folio volume, it was filled with precise and detailed botanical descriptions of orchids and magnificent full-color lithographs of each species discussed. Lindley received much deserved praise for his efforts, but his artist unfortunately did not. Nothing much is known of her besides her surname, Miss Drake, and the hypothesis that she may have been one of Lindley's relatives and a member of his household. Many Victorian ladies were skilled at painting flowers but few could equal Miss Drake, and Lindley paid her the tacit compliment of letting her share the task of illustrating his *Ladies Botany* with Francis Bauer, one of the greatest botanical artists of all time. As to the *Sertum Orchidaceum*, although Lindley's text is authoritative enough, it is Miss Drake's illustrations that cause collectors to bid wildly for its possession.

For cultivation see *Cattleya velutina* (page 16), but give *C. violacea* a little extra water. It blooms through the summer.

Lycaste virginalis
varieties *delicatissima, picturata, purpurata*

Three varieties of the diversely colored species *Lycaste virginalis* are seen here: *delicatissima* (daintiest), *picturata* (stained or colored), and *purpurata* (empurpled). They are particularly delightful examples of one of the most popular of all nineteenth-century orchids, for they combine great beauty with ease of cultivation and reward their owners with longlasting blossoms from fall right into winter.

Because George Skinner published a full botanical description of the plant in the same year it was discovered, he is officially credited with having been the first to find *L. virginalis* and introduce it into cultivation. But some nineteen years later that claim was disputed by one Jean Linden, who had traversed the same region as Skinner in 1838; Linden asserted that he, not Skinner, had been the first to send the flower back to Europe. Whatever the merits of his case, they were set aside and disallowed once botanists adopted the rule of prior publication to govern such disputes. Linden had never published a word about his find until 1861, and thereby forfeited all the credit for such a fine discovery.

Having learned the hard way, Linden never again committed such an oversight. He published two journals on plants, *Lindenia* and *Illustration Horticole*, and became one of the most formidable rivals to the great English horticultural establishments. In fact, his nursery, Horticulture Internationale, became a model for the entire profession. So perhaps this one error of omission became the impetus for the commission of many beneficial horticultural deeds.

Growth: 60°–70° F., feed dilute 30–10–10 fertilizer every third day. Water freely every day. *Flowering:* November–March; 70° F., feed dilute 10–20–10 twice weekly until flowering ends. Steady, ample water supply. *Maturity:* 70°–75° F., feed 30–10–10 every third day, water freely. *Rest:* 4–6 weeks, midsummer; no fertilizer, keep compost moist but not wet. *Light:* As much as possible, but keep slightly shaded from summer sun. *Compost:* 3 parts fir bark, 1 part sphagnum moss in a pot three-quarters full of mixed perlite and charcoal. Set pseudobulbs level with top of pot.

Schomburgkia superbiens

Besides its present name of *Schomburgkia superbiens*, this orchid has been known as *Laelia superbiens* and also by the common name of St. Joseph's staff *(baculo de San José)*. George Skinner discovered it in the small town of Sumpango, where the villagers planted it before their doorways. At that time the name differed slightly from the more recent one, using "wand" in place of "staff"—thus making it *la vara del Señor San José* in Spanish. Even the common names for orchids seem to be afflicted with the same restless need for change as the scientific ones.

Skinner was evidently able to get a specimen, probably a dried one, back to Dr. Lindley at the Horticultural Society, and he described it in 1840, the same year Skinner found it in Guatemala. However, it was not introduced into cultivation for another two years, nor did it flower in England until 1844.

Skinner, not satisfied with his location of the orchid, since it was being used where he found it as a cultivated plant, decided to seek it out in its native habitat. He succeeded, after a brief excursion, in coming upon wild specimens growing outside the town of Comalapa (since lost to the mapmakers), about sixty miles north of Guatemala City. On the day he found it, the ground was covered with frost, and those orchids which were not screened on the north side were quite stunted in comparison with those that had shelter. Tropical latitudes, one may infer, do not always imply tropical temperatures.

For cultivation see *Cattleya velutina* (page 16).

Vanda insignis

The generic name *Vanda* comes from ancient Sanskrit and is used not only for parasitic growths such as mistletoe, but for all kinds of orchids as well. This reflects a widely held notion that all orchids are parasites, which they are not. Even among people supposedly familiar with these plants as part of their everyday life, such as the Indians of Latin America, there is a persistent tendency to consider orchids parasitical, a notion that is furthered by their epiphytic habit of growth. An uninformed observer would have to be a genius to realize that these orchids obtain their nourishment from moisture, light, and air, not from the trees they happen to have perched upon.

Vanda insignis has been an innocent cause of confusion among orchid growers, simply because a species of *V. tricolor* is often sold in its place. *V. insignis* has a leaf that is notched on one side of its tip, whereas *V. tricolor* has a notch in the center of the tip, with a broader leaf throughout. This vanda comes originally from Timor, the island that provided a haven for Captain Bligh (of H.M.S. *Bounty* fame) at the end of his four-thousand-mile ordeal in an open boat. The island, however, was not so kind to one orchid collector, who lost all the specimens of *V. insignis* that he had gathered when the two horses carrying them were swept away while crossing a torrential stream. Not often grown today, *V. insignis* is readily replaced by one or more of the similarly marked species, *V. tricolor*.

For cultivation see *Euanthe sanderiana* (page 36).

Diothonea imbricata and *Maxillaria eburnea*

Diothonea is a small genus of about twelve species that is found in the high Andes of Colombia. As it is rarely mentioned even in modern times, it is all the more remarkable that Dr. John Lindley gave it notice in his *Sertum Orchidaceum (A Garland of Orchids)*, published serially between 1838 and 1841. The one species he described and had illustrated (by the industrious Miss Drake) was *D. imbricata*, a small red flower that might easily be overlooked despite its vivid scarlet coloration. It is cultivated at Kew Gardens and almost nowhere else, an indication that it is not only rare but also difficult to keep alive and well.

Maxillaria eburnea, the ivory-like maxillaria, is another species that receives little or no attention in current orchid literature. The virginal white of the plant gives it the appearance of having been carved out of ivory. Like *Diothonea imbricata*, it is found high in the Colombian Andes, and if we are to judge from Lindley's juxtaposition of the two plants, they would seem to associate with each other—a not uncommon habit among orchids—and thus would have the same requirements for cultivation.

For cultivation see *Maxillaria luteoalba* (page 58).

Huntleya wallisii variety *major*

Only one species of this genus appears to be in present-day cultivation: *Huntleya meleagris*. Such a condition verges on the disastrous, for there are probably no more than three other members of this genus extant, and none are common in the wild, nor are any of them easy to keep in cultivation. This orchid, *Huntleya wallisii* variety *major*, was found in Colombia sometime after 1867, while that country was still called New Granada. However, the plant was rare even then, and no plant hunter who reported its presence made mention of its location; its scarcity made it far too valuable to divulge its whereabouts to rivals in the orchid trade.

Back in the early days of orchid hunting, when it seemed that there was an inexhaustible supply, whole regions were plundered and stripped. In one instance, over four thousand trees were cut down so as to get at their entire accumulation of orchids, some ten thousand or more plants. That territory was quite effectively rendered useless for future orchid production, and its ravager then moved on to repeat the act elsewhere. One plant hunter even stated that his shipment represented the last that could be sent of a particular species, for "they are now extinguished in this spot." In other places the inroads of civilization and agriculture have leveled areas for miles, and no one knows how many orchids (some of which were never classified) have disappeared.

Venezuela alone seems to have taken some ecological responsibility, and now prohibits the exportation of orchids. Let us hope that *Huntleya wallisii* variety *major* is alive and well somewhere, even though the practices of the past 150 years make that happy ending doubtful.

Growth: 65°–75° F., feed dilute 30–10–10 twice weekly, water abundantly. *Flowering:* Give dilute 10–20–10 in midsummer to initiate flowering; maintain temperature and watering. *Maturity:* Maintain temperature and watering, but resume feeding dilute 30–10–10 after flowering is under way. *Rest:* 55°–60° F.; reduce water during winter rest and give only occasional feeding. *Light:* Semishade at all times, never any direct sun. Diffuse light is best. *Compost:* Set plants atop slightly mounded compost of fir bark and sphagnum moss mixed together. Add a light covering of the moss on top. Fill pots two-thirds full with broken charcoal before putting in compost.

Vanda tricolor variety *warneri*

For a considerable time this variety of *Vanda tricolor* was regularly confused with *V. insignis*, although the latter is much less common and a separate species besides. Such errors have a way of perpetuating themselves, but you may avoid the confusion by looking for a broad notch in the center of the ends of the leaves, the mark of the true *V. tricolor*. But if you just want to enjoy the beauty of orchids, forget the leaf ends and be happy with whichever species you have.

This beautiful orchid originally came from Java in 1846, but was seldom raised in Europe because of the great amount of light it needed. As the north temperate zone is not noted for the abundance or intensity of its sunlight in the winter season, vandas appeared likely to remain desirable but only rarely grown. But Oriental immigrants brought them to Hawaii and began commercial cultivation there on a large scale, so that today millions of vanda flowers are exported annually. The same growers began experimenting with new cultivation techniques, drastically shortening the usual fifteen-year lag between seed and flowering. They also hybridized the vandas in every possible way, widening the color range of the genus and bringing its excessive demand for light down to manageable levels for indoor growers. Thanks to the Hawaiian breeders, these orchids have fully adapted now to outdoor environments in Florida and Puerto Rico as well as Hawaii, and to indoor conditions almost everywhere.

For cultivation see *Euanthe sanderiana* (page 36).

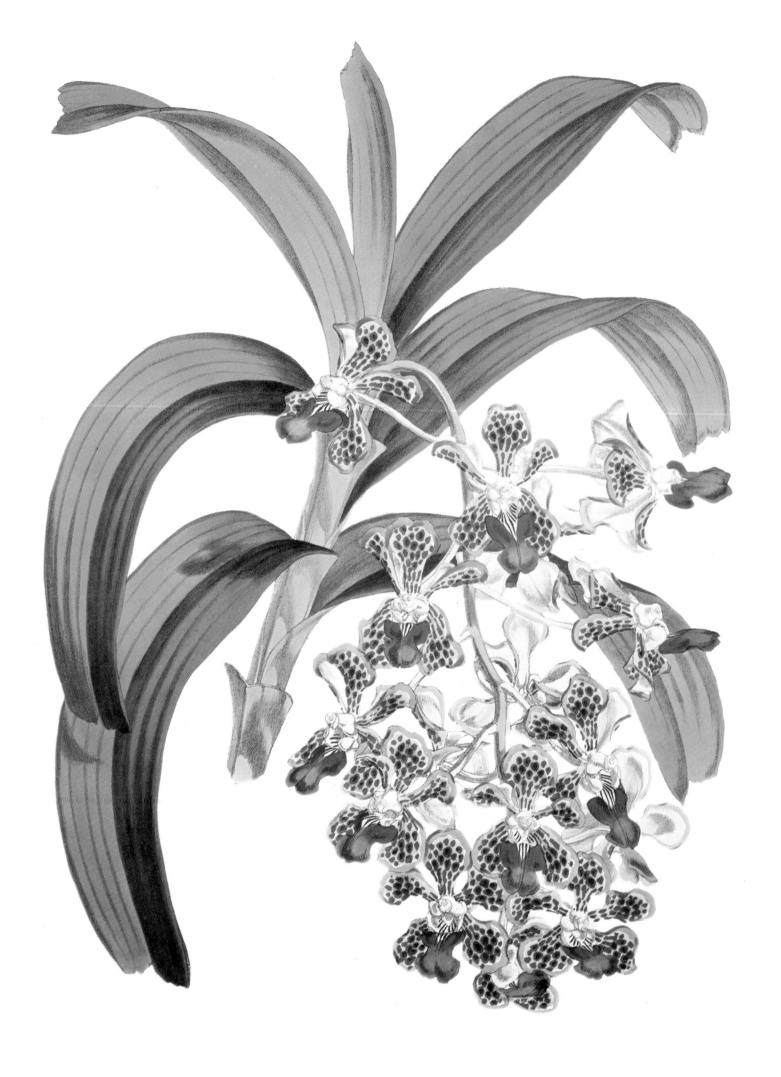

Oncidium lanceanum

Introduced from Surinam in 1834 by Mr. John Lance, for whom the species is named, *Oncidium lanceanum* is a splendid orchid which comes in two different color combinations. Both have sepals and petals of yellow or yellow-green spotted with chocolate brown; but the prominent labellum, or lip, can be either a combination of dark purple and rose-violet, or rose-purple and white—a particularly lovely form.

Although it is an epiphyte, drawing its nourishment from the atmosphere rather than the soil, this orchid lacks the pseudobulbs in which many other members of its clan store food and water for future use. Nonetheless, the plant never experiences a lack of water in its habitat. Projecting from its rhizome are a number of green-tipped, whitish roots, looking rather like thick lengths of spaghetti. These aerial roots have a covering of very light, loose tissue called *velamen*, after the Latin word for veil. This tissue is filled with cells that contain nothing but air when the roots are dry, but which absorb water with the ease of a sponge whenever moisture is present. In areas of high humidity the velamen is always smooth and plump, but in times of drought it becomes stringy and tough, preventing the stored fluids from evaporating.

At the time of its discovery, *On. lanceanum* was almost always found growing on tamarind, sapodilla, or calabash trees, and it still prefers those trees to all others. It is an extremely fragrant plant, and retains its aroma even when dried, although then the odor is a bit fainter and spicier.

Growth: 60°–75° F., feed dilute 30–10–10 fertilizer twice weekly, water abundantly. *Flowering:* Maintain temperature condition and feed dilute 10–20–10 twice weekly, from budding to end of flowering. Reduce water but keep compost moist. *Maturity:* Maintain temperate condition, feed dilute 30–10–10 twice weekly, do not overwater but keep compost constantly moist. *Rest:* Drop temperature to 45°–55° F., stop feeding, and keep compost barely moist, until new growth begins. *Light:* As much as possible, but shade from very strong sun. *Compost:* Fir bark packed tightly in pots filled half full with mixed perlite and charcoal. Leach out accumulated salts once a month.

Catasetum chrystianum

For the moment it is still uncertain whether or not this orchid is a true species or only a variety of *Catasetum saccatum*. Agreement on orchids' names is still, to say the least, in a state of flux, so the name that Warner and Williams gave this one in 1883 will do as well as any other. In any event, the name assigned to a particular orchid depends to a large extent on the opinion of whichever botanical authority you may be consulting, and the differences between them may not be resolved for another century. In the meantime life goes on, and the plants must be called something if they are to be discussed.

Catasetum chrystianum looks somewhat like a hobgoblin riding on a blackbird, and like many catasetums, has more than a hint of the sinister about it. In fact the genus seems to have been designed by the Witch of Endor, and the properties of some species certainly further that idea. For instance, what plant but a catasetum would develop two kinds of roots, one set twining down while the other rises up like tiny spears? Still other catasetums may grow and thrive as terrestrials, yet if allowed to grow on trees they become luxuriant epiphytes. And while oak trees produce a substance that is toxic to almost all orchids, *C. integerrimum* will live and thrive upon them. Catasetums are a force to be reckoned with, and as with women, their power should never be underestimated.

For cultivation see *Catasetum macrocarpum* (page 28).

Oncidium sarcodes

This entire genus was once lumped together with *Epidendrum* by Linnaeus, the father of classification, but the two genera were soon separated by one of his better pupils, Olof Swartz. Even expert botanists commit errors and have to accept the corrections science makes—though they may grind their teeth while doing so.

The botanical term for this species does it somewhat of an injustice, for it means "tumorous with fleshlike (i.e. meatlike) color." Less scientific, but much more attractive and accurate, are the common names of butterfly orchid and dancing doll, both suggestive of the plant's motion in a gentle breeze. The gold and brown coloration catches the sunlight and gives the whole plant a joyful aspect, conveying an infectious gaiety—decidedly not an orchid for gloomy people.

Oncidium sarcodes was found in 1849 near Nova Friburgo, Brazil, north and east of Rio de Janeiro, but almost nothing more is known of its history other than the name of its discoverer, Mr. P.N. Don. This skimpy record seems to indicate that its location was concealed for commercial reasons, because in the early days of orchid growing such knowledge was a gold mine. Although long known and admired, oncidiums have only recently begun to come into their own, and they are now being incorporated more and more into the processes of cultivation and hybridization.

For cultivation see *Oncidium lanceanum* (page 78).

Laelia purpurata

This magnificent orchid, with flowers six to eight inches wide, is a native of the southern Brazilian province of Santa Catherina, which is a rather vague but very roomy address for an orchid. It was found there in 1847 by a plant hunter from Verschaffelt's of Ghent, a Belgian horticultural establishment. Although it was distributed promptly throughout England and the Continent, it was not until 1852 or 1853 that the orchid was first recorded botanically—by Dr. John Lindley, as usual.

There would seem to have been no problem about this species, but orchids being as unpredictable as they are, a controversy arose. Another Belgian plant hunter, orchidologist, and publisher, Jean Linden, claimed that the plant had been brought to Belgium before 1847 by a Monsieur Brys of Antwerp under the name of *Cattleya brysiana*. The argument was raised around 1860, a bit late for claims of priority, but the dispute apparently had a good measure of durability built into it, for it was still going strong some twenty-five years later.

Laelia, the generic name, honors a vestal virgin of ancient Rome. She was a lady of the patrician family Laelius, one of whose members, Sapiens Laelius, was immortalized in Cicero's essay *On Friendship*. Another link between the flower and classic Rome is in the deep amethyst-purple of the labellum, so like the Tyrian purple reserved for the Caesars. This royal orchid certainly has every bit as much right to wear the color.

For cultivation see *Cattleya velutina* (page 16).

Phaius tuberculosus

Although *Phaius tuberculosus* was known at the beginning of the nineteenth century, when it was described from dried specimens by at least four botanists, no live plants were available in Europe until 1880. Up until 1856 the plant even bore a different name, *Bletia tuberculosa*, and had been called *Limodorum tuberculosum* before that, at the time it was first described in 1822 by the French orchidologist Aubert du Petit-Thouars. The current name serves well enough botanically, but does the plant gross injustice otherwise, for it means swarthy and tubercular. Perhaps the botanists were taking revenge on the flower, whose structure they found very difficult to describe.

P. tuberculosus is a plant of remarkable beauty, having spotlessly white sepals and petals plus a labellum that strikingly combines orange-yellow with reddish-purple spatters and then adds white with rose splotches. It has often been judged the loveliest plant of its genus. It is a native of Madagascar, from whence the Humblot brothers, plant hunters for the firm of Messrs. Sander and Company, sent it to England in 1880, thus introducing it to horticulture. For almost fifteen years thereafter the only specimens grown came from that first shipment, for the plants resisted cultivation until a means was found of giving them a suitable substitute for their normally boglike habitat.

Growth: 65°–75° F., feed dilute 30–10–10 twice weekly; water abundantly, but *never* wet the leaves. *Flowering:* Usually flowers around April, but *Phaius tankervilliae* may do so earlier. Maintain temperature and moisture as above. Give dilute 10–20–10 when buds form. *Maturity:* Maintain same temperature and moisture, but give dilute 30–10–10 after flowers have opened. *Rest:* Only partial, since plant simply slows down its normal processes in the winter (December–February). Reduce water, keeping compost moist but not wet; feed dilute 30–10–10 once a month. *Light:* Medium shade. *Compost:* Fill pot half full with lump charcoal, covered with a mixture of 3 parts fir bark to 1 part sphagnum moss.

Phragmipedium caudatum

This unusual orchid is a South American relation of the European and North American cypripediums and of the Asiatic paphiopedilums. Like them, it is of rare occurrence in the wild, and is found in remote areas that experience little if any disturbance by man. There has been some uncertainty about their proper classification: they were first placed with the cypripediums, then moved to the selenipediums, and finally (?) to their present genus.

One of the most remarkable characteristics of *Phragmipedium caudatum* is the great length attained by two of its ribbonlike petals, which sometimes grow thirty inches long. The petals are about three inches long when they first appear, but lengthen at the rate of two inches per day for the next seven days, slowing growth as they near maximum length. It has been thought that the petals act as ladders for insects to fertilize the flowers, but this has not yet been proven. The orchid's name, which means the screened foot with a tail, comes from the fact that the stems rise from partially concealed rhizomes and the petals look like long tails dangling from the flower.

Discovered by Ruiz and Pavon about 1787 in the Peruvian Andes, *P. caudatum* remained in obscurity until 1847, when a specimen reached England; it flowered two years later. There is some reason to believe that all the "slipper" orchids may not really be orchids at all, but are instead remnants of an intermediate form lying between the true orchids and the unknown flower family from which they originally evolved.

For cultivation see *Paphiopedilum lawrenceanum* (page 62).

Paphiopedilum superbiens

Until the beginning of this century, and in all probability right up to the era of air transport, all specimens of this orchid sold in commerce had been derived from only two plants. With just a set of two to account for, it might be imagined that all data concerning the pair would be complete, correct, and in perfect order. Not so, however; one specimen, which was described in 1855, was said to have come from either Assam or Java—a trifling difference of some seventeen hundred miles!

From London, where it was sold to the German consul Schiller, it went to Hamburg, and from there it was dispersed among a number of European collections by plants divided from it. Since orchids have considerable longevity, some of the progeny from Schiller's plant may still be around.

The second specimen of *Paphiopedilum superbiens* to reach the orchid market arrived in 1857 from Mount Ophir in southern Malaysia. Both this specimen and its offspring bore all the same characteristics as the one that had been so vaguely placed geographically. Actually, Mount Ophir is midway between Assam and Java and has long been thought to be the actual point of origin of the genus.

Paphiopedilums, because of their long-lasting qualities, are very important in the cut flower trade. The waxy surface of the flowers, which protects them in their rainy habitat, probably serves also to retain vital substances, and thus prevents rapid deterioration of the blossoms.

For cultivation see *Paphiopedilum lawrenceanum* (page 62).

Catasetum longifolium

Here is an orchid that once clearly demonstrated that botanists hadn't really absorbed their lessons about the birds and the bees. Like the other catasetums, it possesses both male and female forms plus an androgynous one, but the nineteenth-century botanists were slow to recognize that fact. They even reached the point of classifying the three sexes as separate genera, but later decided that two of them were sterile aberrations of catasetum. Sometimes scientific pronouncements should be labeled "Shake well before using."

Catasetums have a decisive way of pollinating themselves. They have a hair-trigger mechanism that hurls compact masses of pollen onto the backs of visiting bees, sometimes nearly staggering them with the load, yet always with an accuracy that places the pollen in an optimum position for transfer to the stigmas of the female plant. The bee has no option of shedding its burden, for the pollen is stuck fast to him until the female surfaces remove it.

For cultivation see *Catasetum macrocarpum* (page 28).

Odontoglossum grande

As with many other orchids in a number of different genera, tiger stripes form a common pattern on these blossoms. The six- to seven-inch-wide flowers of *Odontoglossum grande* not only attract attention, they command it, coming as close to a tiger roar as ever a plant can. The slightly varnished appearance of its flowers is a token of their durability, and their yellow and mahogany coloring is appropriate for their autumnal season of bloom, which begins in October. These orchids come from the lowermost levels of the Central American highlands and can survive temperatures that vary from as low as 45° F. to more than 80° F.

In spite of the difficulty of pronouncing *Odontoglossum*, which means tooth-tongue, it is little trouble to raise these plants. In fact, they are a very good start for any prospective orchid fancier, for their forgiving nature allows a lot of latitude in their cultivation. Some growers go as far as to suspect them of enjoying a certain amount of neglect, though even a masochistic species does require some attention from time to time.

For cultivation see *Odontoglossum nevadense* (page 42).

Cattleya dowiana

Although this species is one of the loveliest yellow orchids known, it had a very difficult time coming to public notice. Its discovery resulted from a wildly impractical and almost totally unfinanced venture by a Lithuanian gardener, Josef Warszewicz. Accompanied only by one Indian, probably as imprudent as himself, he set out on foot to journey through Central America, eating and living in Indian huts most of the way.

In Costa Rica he found the magnificent *Cattleya dowiana*, and eventually succeeded in shipping specimens to London, with instructions to name it for a benefactress, Mrs. Lawrence of Ealing. But the shipment arrived in such a bad state that none of it survived in cultivation. The next bit of bad luck was that the orchid could not be found again in its native habitat; worse yet, all the dried specimens were destroyed in transit to Germany, where they had been sent to be classified.

Not until 1865 was the plant rediscovered and sent to George Skinner in London. Not knowing of Warszewicz's request to honor Mrs. Lawrence, he asked that the plant be named for Captain Dow of the American Packet Service, a gentleman who had done great services for orchid hunters and had carried numerous shipments of flowers across the Atlantic. With its adventures out of the way, *C. dowiana* became a hybridizer's dream, and was crossbred innumerable times thereafter.

For cultivation see *Cattleya velutina* (page 16).

Epidendrum lindleyanum

Once known as *Barkeria spectabilis*, or showy *Barkeria*, this orchid was shifted to the genus *Epidendrum* by the taxonomists, those botanical scientists responsible for the proper classification of plants. The early literature of orchids mentions wide variability among the *Barkeria* species, a good indication that some revision would take place if the botanists began to sift their data more thoroughly. This procedure of renaming plants does cause considerable confusion and contention between horticulturists and botanists, but there is sound reason behind it. As one taxonomist said in defending his actions: "We stop changing the classification when we finally arrive at the truth." And coming to the truth about anything in this bewildering world is never easily done.

For cultivation see *Epidendrum phoeniceum* (page 18).

Epidendrum lindleyanum

Once known as *Barkeria spectabilis*, or showy *Barkeria*, this orchid was shifted to the genus *Epidendrum* by the taxonomists, those botanical scientists responsible for the proper classification of plants. The early literature of orchids mentions wide variability among the *Barkeria* species, a good indication that some revision would take place if the botanists began to sift their data more thoroughly. This procedure of renaming plants does cause considerable confusion and contention between horticulturists and botanists, but there is sound reason behind it. As one taxonomist said in defending his actions: "We stop changing the classification when we finally arrive at the truth." And coming to the truth about anything in this bewildering world is never easily done.

For cultivation see *Epidendrum phoeniceum* (page 18).

Odontoglossum williamsianum

Up until 1881, any specimens of this orchid in cultivation would have been considered varieties of *Odontoglossum grande*, but in that year it was granted the status of a full species by the orchidologist Reichenbach, writing in the *Gardener's Chronicle*. Three years later Warner and Williams' *Orchid Album* concurred, but that does not mean that the entire orchid world agreed with them. In fact, many modern works on orchids make no mention of *Od. williamsianum*; and the name of its discoverer, its place of origin (other than Costa Rica), and the date of its introduction into horticulture all remain elusive.

Confusion is especially prevalent among the odontoglossums because they vary greatly in appearance, frequently hybridize naturally, and may be found growing in various habitats—on rocks, trees, or sometimes as terrestrials. As a consequence their classification is badly in need of revision, but then that is the case with quite a few other plant families.

This species, if indeed it remains a species, is one of the *grande* group, and is considered to be among the easiest of all orchids to grow, especially in the northeastern and northwestern United States. Its blossoms are a little smaller than the five- to six-inch ones of *Od. grande*, but the general distribution and patterning of its colors is more graceful and subtle.

For cultivation see *Odontoglossum nevadense* (page 42).

Paphiopedilum venustum

It was not until about 1886 that botanists became certain that this was an entirely new genus of orchids, although they had been suspecting it for some time. Originally it had simply been considered an Asiatic branch of the *Cypripedium* or lady-slipper family, but it proved to be otherwise. Two other genera, both from South America, also had to be granted separate status, and thus one genus split into four. Florists and horticulturists fought the change tooth and nail (and many still do), for they had sold countless specimens under the name of cypripediums, which they had even shortened to the more popular term "cyps."

Paphiopedilum venustum, which means "the beautiful lady-slipper," was first found in 1816 by Dr. Nathaniel Wallich near the town of Sylhet, India, in the foothills of the eastern Himalayas. Through Wallich's efforts, this orchid became the first of its genus to reach Europe, where it flowered in 1819. In its native habitat, it grows in soil or on mossy rocks at the three- to five-thousand-foot level, where its heavy three-inch-wide flowers bloom from January to March. As cut flowers they can last as long as a month.

All four genera of lady-slippers seem to be in trouble currently out in nature, although they thrive mightily in cultivation. In the wild they seem to be retreating on every hand, seeking out locations that are ever more remote and localized. In their individual stands they may be abundant, but the stands always tend to shrink in size. For once, it is not man but rather the orchid that is to blame. Although these orchids are totally dependent on insects for pollination, their structure more often than not traps their insect visitors, who die where they have been lured without ever completing pollination.

For cultivation see *Paphiopedilum lawrenceanum* (page 62).

Paphiopedilum stonei

Another native of the Sarawak region of Borneo, this orchid grows on low-lying limestone hills at about one thousand to fifteen hundred feet. It is usually found on rocks where only a thin covering of humus has accumulated, and always in places where the surrounding forest gives it shade.

Paphiopedilum stonei was discovered by Hugh Low of Messrs. Low and Company's Clapton Nursery in 1860, and was sent to England by him the same year. Low, who had been sent to collect plants in southeast Asia and Borneo about 1840, became fascinated by the region and stayed on to study the languages and customs of the people. In 1848 he was made a colonial treasurer in Borneo, and finally, in 1876, Hugh Low became Chief Resident in the colonial government there. During the intervening years he enriched horticulture with numerous new species of orchids and other tropical plants, introduced reforms in government policy, and improved the island's agriculture by bringing in fine strains of cattle from England and India. Low was knighted in 1883 by Queen Victoria for his notable achievements in many fields, not the least of which were in orchidology. In fact, the natives of Borneo named two species of orchids after him, calling both *Daun lo*, or "Low's leaf."

P. stonei first flowered in cultivation for the first time in 1861, and its species name *stonei* honors the gardener who brought it into bloom.

For cultivation see *Paphiopedilum lawrenceanum* (page 62).

Oncidium tigrinum

This orchid has long been associated with the dead by the people of its native Mexico, as evidenced by their own name for the flower, *flor de muertos*, which it has borne since the sixteenth century, and probably well before that. In Mexico it blooms in the winter months and probably has an intimate connection with some forgotten Toltec or Mayan funeral ceremony. Certainly its bright blossoms, sunny yellow streaked with stripes of dark, reddish brown, are not suggestive of death to us, but to the minds and eyes of the Meso-American Indians they might have signified human blood revivifying the sun in a time of danger.

First seen in 1825 near Valladolid, about ninety miles east of Merida, Yucatan, this species could no longer be found there one generation later, a common occurrence in botanical collection throughout Latin America. For a time, *On. tigrinum* was called *Oncidium barkeri*, because a Mr. Barker of Birmingham, England was the first to cultivate it outside of Mexico; but the earlier, more appropriate term prevailed. Whatever the cause of its disappearance from the Yucatan, it turned up twice elsewhere, some twenty and sixty years later, journeying across Mexico from Valladolid to Michoacan and finally to Colima, near the Pacific Coast—six hundred miles from its point of origin. Plants may not have the power of movement, but they somehow manage to get around.

───────────

For cultivation see *Oncidium lanceanum* (page 78).

Cymbidium hookerianum

This genus derives its name from the Greek word for boat, *cymbid*, and is native to the Orient in an area stretching from India to Japan and southward to Australia. It is an evergreen plant, whose blossoms can last in perfect condition from a minimum of six weeks to as long as three months. That kind of durability is rare even among orchids, many of which are noted for their long-lasting qualities. Cymbidiums are such a natural item for the cut-flower market, and for amateur growers who have heard of their reputation, that almost everybody wants to grow one or another of them.

Cymbidium hookerianum was named for Sir Joseph Dalton Hooker, Director of the Royal Botanic Garden at Kew from 1865 to 1885, and active in a number of scientific endeavors and societies up to his death in 1911 at the age of ninety-four. The orchid comes from Nepal, Sikkim, and Bhutan, regions explored by Hooker between 1847 and 1851, and has a striking color combination of clear green, pale yellow, and spots of reddish purple. It formerly had one major defect, which breeders have now eliminated: a habit of shedding its buds before they ever opened. The orchid is still occasionally called *C. grandiflorum*, a name it formerly bore but which has since been invalidated. This is a story repeated time after time in orchidology, but one that is excused as a necessary consequence of its relative newness as a science.

Growth: Continuous. 70°–90° F. in daytime; at night temperature may drop to 45° F. Water amply, keeping compost consistently moist. Feed dilute 30–10–10 twice weekly. *Flowering:* January and February. Feed dilute 10–20–10 from mid-December until flowering ends. Reduce water by half or a bit more. Most important, let night temperatures drop to 45°–50° F., daytime to 50°–60° F.; this is essential to the flowering process. *Maturity:* None. *Rest:* Little or none. *Light:* Bright, indirect. *Compost:* 2 parts coarse fir bark, 1½ parts perlite, 1 part humus. Mist-spray plants and compost to maintain 30–40% humidity.

Paphiopedilum hirsutissimum

Even among a family of plants noted for its splendor and strangeness, this orchid stands out. It first arrived in British gardens in 1857, sent there by a plant hunter named Simons, who neglected to include any information as to where he had obtained it. It took twelve full years to discover its point of origin, and it is a wonder that it didn't take much longer, since it came from one of the wildest and most remote regions of Asia, the Khasia Hills. These are located north and west of Burma, just south of Bhutan and the Himalayas—most certainly not a neighborhood as highly frequented as Hollywood and Vine or Piccadilly Circus.

The horrendous syllables of this orchid's name boil down to meaning "the very hairy Venus's slipper," and one can only hope that Venus didn't have extrasensitive soles. During its period of bloom from March to May, it is one of the most spectacular of exotic orchids, fully deserving all the additional qualities that the term "exotic" implies. Its combination of bright violet-pink and yellowish-green colors, together with its oddly shaped petals and sepals, spotted with deep purple and studded with clusters of dark, knobby bumps, give it a fantastic and faintly sinister look. Paphiopedilums, with their waxed and almost artificial appearance, are either warmly loved or thoroughly disliked; but all growers agree that they are very undemanding plants. In fact, these orchids could once be found growing with unrestrained vigor as house plants par excellence in almost every kitchen and parlor throughout Europe; and they seem once more to be regaining all the favor they formerly knew.

For cultivation see *Paphiopedilum lawrenceanum* (page 62).

Stanhopea wardii

Stanhopea wardii is a spectacular orchid that is a favorite with bees, who come crowding to taste its nectar almost as soon as the flower releases its fragrance. But after watching the treatment that the bees receive, one quickly decides that they are either morons or masochists, or both. Lured into the recesses of the flower, they deposit whatever pollen they are carrying onto the stigmatic surfaces, and are then dumped down a chute that slaps a new load of sticky pollen on them for the next orchid they visit. All without so much as a sip of nectar or a "thank you" from the plant. Only certain types of bees are tricked into this act, so perhaps they may learn to go out on strike one day when they find that their services are never paid for.

This genus is named for the Earl of Stanhope, President of the Medico-Botanical Society of London during the mid-nineteenth century. Its native territory ranges from Mexico to Venezuela, and it blooms from July to September, each blossom lasting about three days.

Growth: 65°–75° F., feed dilute 30–10–10 twice weekly, give ample water. *Flowering:* Maintain temperature, water amply; give dilute 10–20–10 in late July and early August. *Maturity:* Maintain watering and temperature but resume feeding dilute 30–10–10 until growth ceases. *Rest:* During winter months. Reduce temperature to 55°–60° F., and let compost become moderately moist. *Light:* Bright to very bright, indirect. *Compost:* Best placed in shallow wire or slat boxes suspended over water pans. 1 part fir bark, 2 parts sphagnum moss over layer of lump charcoal.

Laelia autumnalis

Laelia autumnalis is one of those rare orchids that bears a pleasing name. Dr. John Lindley of the Horticultural Society must have been in a poetic mood on the day he christened the genus, for Laelia was the name of one of Rome's most gracious vestal virgins. The specific, *autumnalis*, which refers to this plant's blooming in the fall, adds a musical touch of its own, making the orchid as delightful to talk about as to look at. Its durable blossoms come into flower from October through January, providing a welcome note of beauty, delicate color, and fragrance in the dark winter season. With foresight, the orchid grower can arrange a year-round succession of bloom, bringing different species into flower throughout the seasons. *Laelia autumnalis* is often crossed with its related genera of *Cattleya, Brassavola, Epidendrum, Schomburgkia*, and others, for it is one of the hybridizer's favorites.

For cultivation see *Cattleya velutina* (page 16).

Dendrobium phalaenopsis

This orchid is said, on authority of those contemporary with its introduction, to have been brought into cultivation by a certain Captain Broomfield of Balmain. Its discoverer remains unknown, but it was procured from North Australia, and has also been found in New Guinea and Timor. It reached England about 1880, when it was first described in *Gardener's Chronicle*. That popular journal, incidentally, was issued weekly beginning in 1841, and was responsible for bringing much orchid information before the botanical and horticultural worlds. In fact it kept abreast of all important developments in orchidology almost from the beginning, due to the keen interest of its first editor, Dr. John Lindley. Nor did the tradition die out once established, but was continued instead by regular weekly contributions from the great German orchidologist, H. G. Reichenbach. Without the aid of the early issues of the *Gardener's Chronicle,* it would be almost impossible to write a history of orchid culture.

Dendrobium phalaenopsis was so named from a fancied resemblance of its flowers to those of another genus, the moth orchids, known as *Phalaenopsis*. For a time it was thought to be simply a variety of *D. biggibum,* which has nothing to do with large tramps, but does translate as "two-humped." On closer examination, the orchid proved to be a truly new species, which is just as well, for *D. biggibum* variety *phalaenopsis* would probably have broken the jaws of a few botanists in the mere mention of its name.

For cultivation see *Dendrobium superbum* variety *giganteum* (page 12).

Stanhopea tigrina

This very fragrant orchid, with flowers that can measure up to seven inches when fully extended, is often considered the finest of the genus *Stanhopea*. First discovered in 1835 near Jalapa, Mexico, it was found flourishing at an altitude of about 7500 feet, where temperatures remain moderate despite the tropical location. Many other tropical species grow in similarly cool habitats, a fact that was long misunderstood during the era when all cultivated orchids were routinely subjected to the high heat and humidity believed to be typical throughout the tropics.

A collector from the Clapton Nursery was the first to gather *Stanhopea tigrina* while on a plant hunting expedition commissioned by his London firm. In the early nineteenth century, when orchids were first becoming popular, such expensive and often hazardous journeys had to be made in order to obtain the plants at all, and orchid fanciers of that day had to face heavy expenses in order to pursue their hobby. Not until recent years has it been possible to raise orchids on a large scale and so reduce the cost of building a collection.

For cultivation see *Stanhopea wardii* (page 112).

Cattleya skinneri

This species honors two of the men who were largely responsible for developing an interest in the art of raising orchids. One is William Cattley of Barnet, whose introduction of *Cattleya labiata* in 1818 first made orchid growing fashionable among British horticulturists. The other, George Skinner, was an English merchant living in Guatemala who became a major collector for the orchid trade; he introduced almost one hundred new orchids into England.

Cattley, who was constantly enlarging his collection of tropical plants, received his first orchid more or less by accident when it was included in a shipment of plants from Rio de Janeiro. Out of curiosity, he cultivated it and brought it into flower a few months later. The orchid expert John Lindley recognized it as a new kind of orchid, and thereupon named the genus for Cattley. Skinner was accorded the same honor by James Bateman, who received from him the first example of this species ever to reach England. Skinner soon became such an avid plant hunter that when his ship, the *Spartan,* was wrecked on the Pacific coast, the first thing he did after reaching shore was to search for new plants.

This *Cattleya,* called flower of St. Sebastian in its native Guatemala, is found in the warmer parts of that country and along the Pacific shore. It flowers in March, producing blossoms that sometimes seem small and pale at first but which soon double their size and deepen in color. This trait, reminiscent of the wounds of St. Sebastian, may have given rise to the orchid's local name.

For cultivation see *Cattleya velutina* (page 16).

Lycaste virginalis

Before this orchid was given its present name it had been known under two others, *Lycaste skinneri* and *Maxillaria skinneri*. Perhaps the botanists may change it yet again, but if they do horticulturists needn't fret, since the plant continues to bc known by the stable and serviceable name of nun orchid. The flowers, some five to six inches in diameter and with a waxy look about them, bear a slight resemblance to the huge, winged head-dresses worn by some French and Belgian nuns. The generic name comes from the daughter of Priam, who was the last King of Troy and certainly one of its most prolific, for Lycaste was but one of his nineteen acknowl-edged children. The specific term, *virginalis*, is of course based upon the impression of unblemished beauty made by the orchid's blossoms, another reason for its popular name.

Of the thirty or more species of *Lycaste* that are known, this one is the most admired and widely known. Within a year of its introduction from Guatemala in 1842 (another of George Skinner's contributions) it was no longer a rarity, but could be found in almost every collection. Its instant popularity suggests that the plant is fairly easy to cultivate, and such is indeed the case. It produces long-lasting flowers from November through March, although James Bateman said in his *Orchidaceae of Mexico and Guatemala* that it blossomed in every season in the collection of a Manchester clergyman, the Reverend Clowes.

For cultivation see *Lycaste virginalis* varieties *delicatissima, picturata, purpurata* (page 66).

Masdevallia veitchiana

This genus was dedicated to Dr. Jose Masdeval, a Spanish physician and botanist, by Ruiz and Pavon in the course of compiling their *Flora of Peru and Chile*. As it so happens, the plant upon which Ruiz and Pavon established the genus, *Masdevallia uniflora*—the only species they had ever seen—has remained elusive down to present times, and may even be extinct. They did say that it could be found "in rocky places near Huassahuassi," but that location has been equally invisible since Ruiz and Pavon left it behind them. Luckily, numerous other species have been found since then that validate the existence of such a genus, proving that Ruiz and Pavon were not hallucinating from altitude sickness or from sampling some of the local plant products.

Masdevallia veitchiana, like most of its relatives, is alpine in habit, and is found growing happily at an elevation of eleven to thirteen thousand feet near Cuzco, Peru. That height, of course, is well above the snow line in many places, but since it is so near the equator little snow can persist through the day; even at twelve thousand feet temperatures reach 45° F. or a bit more.

The species was named in 1868 for James Veitch, owner of the Royal Exotic Nursery, Chelsea, London, at the time of its first published description, made by the great German orchidologist Reichenbach in the *Gardener's Chronicle*. Its flame-shaped and flame-colored flowers have kept it in the foreground ever since.

Growth: 50°–60° F., ample watering and humidity necessary. Food is obtained from compost. Give dilute 30–10–10 once a month. *Flowering:* Since masdevallias have no truly inactive season this will probably happen in late fall through winter. No change in temperature, feeding, or humidity. Simply give more water in summer, less in winter. *Maturity:* None. *Rest:* None. *Light:* Very bright. *Compost:* Pots two-thirds full of broken crockery, layered over with 1 part sphagnum moss and 1 part fibrous peat to rim level.

Houlletia brocklehurstiana

This dignified orchid, with its quietly elegant coloration, was discovered near Rio de Janeiro by Monsieur Houllet, Chief Horticulturist of the Jardin des Plantes in Paris. He returned it to France in live condition and brought it into flower shortly afterwards, when it was recognized as a new genus by the eminent French botanist Adolphe Brongniart. Brongniart named the orchid for its discoverer but forgot to attach a specific name to this first *Houlletia*, an incredible oversight that was immediately filled by the English Dr. Lindley. He named the species after Mr. Brocklehurst of Macclesfield, who was the first man to bring it into blossom in England. But Houllet was not left entirely at a loss, for he was made Assistant Curator of the Jardin des Plantes, and was then in a good position to see to it that no such slight would recur in matters of Anglo-French rivalry.

For cultivation see *Stanhopea wardii* (page 112).

Huntleya meleagris

It takes very little imagination to envisage a pixie laughing up at one out of the center of this flower while impishly sticking out its tongue. Very likely the target of its ridicule is the poor, innocent taxonomist who has the thankless task of placing this miscreant among orchids in its proper classification. In the past it has been listed as *Batemania burtii* and *Zygopetalum burtii,* and is now called *Huntleya meleagris;* but whether or not it is ready to submit to a permanent name remains an open question. Presently there are only four species in the genus, but they range over such a wide territory and have such extremely variable components that botanists just know trouble with labeling lies ahead. The plant's vegetative structure closely resembles three other plants, one of which is not even remotely related to it! The plant also turns out to be genetically compatible with at least eight genera; so while the hybridizers are certain to have a field day, taxonomists will have to reach for the headache tablets.

Named for the Rev. J. T. Huntley, *H. meleagris* was discovered in Costa Rica in 1867, and flowered (and was depicted) for the first time in cultivation in 1872. Its official pedigree, however, began with a description in Volume III of Bentham's *Genera Plantarum* in 1883. It is a very fragrant flower, whose aroma rises not from a separate scent-bearing organ but from the tissue of its labellum, the orchid's conspicuous central part. It lacks the pseudobulbs that most other epiphytic orchids have for food and water storage; when growers say they have trouble keeping it in fine condition, they are probably understating the case.

For cultivation see *Huntleya wallisii* variety *major* (page 74).

Disa uniflora variety *superba*

The common name for this orchid is "pride of Table Mountain," and after seeing the intense brilliancy of its pink and crimson blossoms one can easily understand how it came to be called by that name. Because its seed cannot live more than a month after its release and because it lacks mechanisms to delay germination until favorable conditions prevail, it could easily become extinct without governmental protection. Its conspicuous beauty is also a threat to its survival, so South African law now prohibits its exportation. It is extremely difficult to raise from seed, and usually takes over three years of unremitting care to bring it into flower. It is therefore best to leave it in its native place, for only a few botanical institutions have the necessary skill and equipment to be successful with it.

First brought into cultivation in 1825, this South African beauty created a sensation with its glorious, glowing color, and when an equally lovely sky-blue variety was found the genus *Disa* joined the most-wanted lists. Unluckily, disas require a long period of very dry warmth while in dormancy, and will not tolerate any change in those conditions. This, of course, is the reason that the range of these terrestrial orchids is limited to Table Mountain and similar areas of the Cape peninsula. Some day the genetic keys that will open other regions to its beauty may be found, but for now we must rest content to have the plant at all.

Growth: 60°–70° F., feed dilute 30–10–10, give ample water and spray plant often. Maintain high humidity by dampening growing area or with evaporating water. *Flowering:* Generally June and July. Maintain temperature and watering, but feed dilute 10–20–10 when buds appear. *Maturity:* After flowering resume 30–10–10 formula, and maintain water supply and temperature. *Rest:* In winter. 50°–55° F., keep compost moist, no food. *Light:* Semishade. *Compost:* 3 parts fir bark, 2 parts sphagnum moss, ½ part oak leaf humus over perlite and lump charcoal, filling pot one third full. *Note:* These plants are only rarely available and are *very* difficult to raise in practice.

Miltonia candida

Most members of this genus resemble large pansies, but here is another exception to prove that orchids continually do the unexpected. This particular orchid, *Miltonia candida,* more nearly resembles a cattleya (to which it is not related) than anything else. Even the term *candida*, which stands for white, is misleading, for the most prominent feature of the flowers is their irregular network of yellow lines on reddish brown sepals and petals. In any case its bold appearance makes a memorable tribute to Viscount Milton, the generous patron of horticulture for whom the genus was named.

The blossoms on this Brazilian orchid are about three inches wide and appear in the fall, unlike most of the group, which flower in May. Though it was first found about 1830, it took some time to realize that these miltonias, as well as all the others from Brazil, have somewhat different requirements for cultivation from Colombian species—still another aberration in this contrary orchid.

For cultivation see *Miltonia spectabilis* variety *moreliana* (page 22).

Coelogyne pandurata

Discovered in 1852 in the steaming jungles of Sarawak, this orchid has ever since epitomized the exotic, unusual, and surrealistic aspects of the entire orchid family. Even its botanical description comes under a faintly sinister influence, as in this quote from Veitch's *Manual of Orchidaceous Plants:* ". . . the side lobes erect, yellow-green streaked with black, the middle lobe crisped [curled] and covered with black warty asperities [rough patches] and traversed by two longitudinal toothed keels." One hopes that the botanist who wrote that escaped unscathed by those teeth.

Despite the malign atmosphere implied in this description, *Coelogyne pandurata* is an attractive and fantastically formed plant sometimes called the fiddle-shaped orchid. Since its stigma is set in a depression it was given the Greek name *Coelogyne,* meaning "hollow" and "female," while the specific name *pandurata* refers to the violinlike shape of its conspicuous streaked labellum, the organ that attracts pollinators. Its green petals and sepals, some four inches wide and set along twenty-inch stems, look like so many dancing hobgoblins. When these orchids first bloomed in the prosaic precincts of Hackney, London, in 1853, it must have seemed as if all the little green men we have heard about had come to remind Cockney-dom that another trip to the local pub might be one too many.

Growth: 65°–75° F., dilute 30–10–10 twice weekly. Keep compost thoroughly moist while plants remain active. *Flowering:* Usually in June. Feed 10–20–10 from appearance of buds to end of flowering. Maintain temperature and watering as above. *Maturity:* In fall. As plants lessen activity diminish water supply, but maintain temperature. *Rest:* In winter. 60° F., no food. Keep compost barely moist. *Light:* Shaded in summer; can be bright but indirect in autumn, winter, and spring. *Compost:* In wire or slat baskets. Coarse fir bark 3 parts, 1 part sphagnum moss over layer of broken crockery.

Cattleya exoniensis

Cattleyas were among the very earliest orchids to be used for purposes of hybridization, and this one, *Cattleya exoniensis*, did not result simply from two species but possibly crossed generic lines as well. Records of early hybrids (this example dates from 1863) were not as perfect as they might have been, so the true parentage of *C. exoniensis* can only be surmised by analyzing the traits it exhibits. Actually the possible parents are few in number; either *C. labiata* var. *mossiae* crossed with *Laelia purpurata*, or *L. crispa* and *L. purpurata*; general consensus leans to the first of these combinations.

The man who created this hybrid, John Dominy of the Exeter branch of Veitch and Sons Royal Exotic Nursery, was the first ever to succeed in hybridizing orchids. The specific name *exoniensis* commemorates Dominy's home city of Exeter, where he lived and worked for most of the seventy-five years of his life. In 1853 he crossed two species of *Calanthe*, sowed the resultant seed in 1854, and saw the flowers bloom in 1856 (hybridizers, it seems, need a great deal of patience). Dominy continued his plant-breeding experiments for the next twenty-two years, giving his firm a tremendous lead in crossbreeding. In fact, for the first fifteen years of that period no other orchid nursery could even supply a hybrid orchid. Horticulturists cheered his success, but Dr. Lindley simply said, "You will drive the botanists mad!"

For cultivation see *Cattleya velutina* (page 16).

Oncidium crispum

Many of the oncidiums seem to have come from a jeweler's bench rather than from the forest, and *Oncidium crispum,* the curly-edged oncidium, is no exception. Generous in its flower production, it bears from fifty to sixty or more blossoms, all of them two to three inches wide. Its thirty- to forty-five-inch stalks, however, do not begin to approach the prodigality of some species, which have flower stalks that wind on for several yards and are capable of displaying thousands of blooms.

This species originated in Brazil's Organ Mountains near Rio de Janeiro, an area that seems to have been a veritable orchid factory in the early nineteenth century. The first record of the plant appeared in Loddiges's *Botanical Cabinet* during 1832, where it was depicted after having flowered in that year. Incidentally, that journal was an outgrowth of the famous Hackney nursery of Messrs. Conrad Loddiges and Sons, who, together with the firm of James Veitch and Sons, gave nineteenth-century England a commanding lead in the commercial importation and culture of orchids.

The date of earliest cultivation of this orchid is somewhat unclear. Loddiges's gave an illustration of it in 1832, but five years later Dr. Lindley wrote in the *Botanical Register* that it had flowered for the Loddiges firm shortly after his discovery (no date mentioned) of a dried specimen in Sir William Hooker's herbarium. Elsewhere it is recorded that two amateur orchid fanciers in Liverpool, a Mrs. Horsfall and a Mr. Harrison, both of whom had direct commercial links with Brazil, were among the earliest cultivators of *On. crispum* in England. All we can be sure of is that it was and still is cultivated there.

For cultivation see *Oncidium lanceanum* (page 78).

Anguloa ruckeri

First discovered about 1788 by the Spanish explorers Ruiz and Pavon, this orchid has a rather small range—about forty miles on the eastern slopes of the Andes, some two hundred miles north of Bogota. Its discoverers dedicated it to Don Francisco de Angulo, then Director General of Mines in Peru; and they might have had good reason to do so, for his operations produced the wealth that financed their somewhat sumptuous expedition. Ruiz, for example, possessed an extensive wardrobe, which included a silk suit, three pairs of velvet breeches, two dressing gowns, and such necessary explorer's equipment as hair nets, nightcaps, plated dining service, and a silver chamberpot.

Anguloa ruckeri is one of a genus of about nine species, only three of which are regularly cultivated. It has the very suitable common name of tulip orchid because of the form of its fragrant, waxy blossoms, but is also known as boat orchid from the shape of its leaves. The plants are generally found growing on damp mossy rocks or in shady woods. Lost for a time, *A. ruckeri* was rediscovered in 1846 by Jean Linden, who purposely said little about its location, hoping to profit later from his secret. As a result the flower was lost again, but the third time it was lucky; Mr. Blunt, who made the final rediscovery in 1870, carefully documented his find. One of the handsomest orchids known, it is not apt to drop out of sight again, but if it does the damage will be slight, for it is now in many collections, and has been crossbred as well.

For cultivation see *Maxillaria luteoalba* (page 58).

Dendrobium superbum

This superb orchid was discovered in the Philippine Islands by one of England's most proficient collectors of natural materials, Hugh Cuming, born in Devonshire in 1791. In his youth, his interest in natural history was strongly encouraged despite the fact that other areas of his education were badly neglected; he could write his name but not much else. Nonetheless, by 1832 his business acumen had provided him with funds to build and outfit a yacht for the express purpose of collecting and storing materials gathered along the coasts of South America and Mexico. By 1835 he became more venturesome and sailed to Southeast Asia and the Philippines. There he found *Dendrobium superbum*, and it became one of the first orchids to be shipped live from Manila to England.

About 3500 other orchid species were gathered by Cuming, some of them new to science, and his name quite naturally became part of orchid nomenclature, appearing in such species as *Liparis cumingii, Coelogyne cumingii,* and *Podochilus cumingii*. By the time Cuming, a beaming, florid, full-faced man who always wore a ruffled stock, had left the Philippines, he had sent back home some 30,000 kinds of shells (his major interest), and 130,000 specimens of dried plants for the herbaria at Kew Gardens and other places. He vastly enriched our knowledge of the flora of Southeast Asia and neighboring archipelagos during the course of his adventurous seventy-four years.

For cultivation see *Dendrobium superbum* variety *giganteum* (page 12).

Odontoglossum cordatum

In a sense this might be called the anatomical orchid, for its scientific name refers to tooth, tongue, and heart. Yet when one searches for those forms, which botanists profess to see so clearly, the tooth and tongue diminish to a minute bump on the lip of the flower, and the heart bears a long point somewhat like the tail of a kite.

This species, a native of the Central American highlands, was among those discussed by the orchidologist James Bateman in his *Monograph of Odontoglossums,* a work that helped many to realize that temperate and cool conditions often benefited orchids far more than the tropical heat that had been almost Holy Writ until then. Orchid fanciers quickly learned that odontoglossums, and the closely related miltonias and oncidiums, could tolerate a considerable amount of benign neglect, and they soon became the Victorian era's favorite orchids.

For cultivation see *Odontoglossum nevadense* (page 42).

Laelia grandis

The astounding progress of orchid culture and propagation in just over one hundred years may perhaps best be illustrated by the experiences of two Frenchmen who were probably not related by anything more than their common interest in orchids, though both were named Morel. The earlier Morel received a specimen of *Laelia grandis* in 1849 from Brazil. When it flowered the following year it proved to be of great beauty, having a color combination of nankeen-yellow and white veined with rose-violet. Unaccountably, it dropped out of sight for the next fourteen years, until a few more plants were brought to England. M. Morel at that time had no certain means of continuing the species in cultivation, but time brings changes; in 1956 Dr. George Morel found a way to increase and perpetuate orchids by cloning.

Dr. Morel's method involved removing a section of tissue called the meristem apex from developing buds. When placed in the proper nutritive culture, that tissue, which contained all the genetic information needed to produce an entire plant, continued to grow and gradually create cells that differentiated out of a simple (!) mass of living matter. Eventually they formed an identical replica of the original plant, which they *had* to do since no other genetic information or material was available to them.

With this discovery, commercial suppliers could at last propagate orchids on a massive scale—as many as four million a year from a single plant—but it took until 1964 for the good news to spread. Luckily, Dr. Morel lived until 1973, long enough to see his work internationally acclaimed. Thanks to him orchids will never again be solely for the rich, nor entirely at the mercy of sexual reproduction.

For cultivation see *Cattleya velutina* (page 16).

Catasetum laminatum

The orchid family is in the very forefront of evolutionary development among plants, and the catasetums are the most highly developed of orchids. Small wonder, then, that nineteenth-century plant hunters and botanists were constantly faced with baffling puzzles created by the catasetums. Their male, female, and perfect (hermaphroditic) forms, which could all appear on a single plant, often caused the collector to mistake the various sexual forms for entirely different species or even genera. And the surprises continue, for now the crafty catasetums seem to be learning how to eliminate dependence on the mycorrhiza that furnish all other developing orchid embryos with the nutrition that is totally lacking in their seeds.

In the past catasetums have been called *Myanthus, Monacanthus*, and in some cases *Mormodes*. Accordingly, the history of their introduction and culture becomes something of a case for Sherlock Holmes. For instance, the horticultural introduction of the present species, *Catasetum laminatum*, has been variously reported as prior to 1841, in 1860 (although Moore's *Illustrations of Orchidaceous Plants* had listed it in 1857), and some even mention 1906! No definitive history of orchids will ever be written until *all* data are correlated, compared, corrected, and checked against specimens in the world's herbaria—a process that can easily consume another century of research. But that needn't hinder our enjoyment of them in the meantime.

For cultivation see *Catasetum macrocarpum* (page 28).

Schomburgkia tibicinis

Small boys the world over have always enjoyed noisemakers, and this is an orchid that can satisfy any one of them to his heart's content. When either end of the plant's fairly long pseudobulbs (its food and water storage organs) are cut off, it is transformed into a highly serviceable trumpet. True, it sounds a flat and unmusical note, but that is no flaw to juvenile ears; in fact, it is more of an advantage.

The trumpeter's plant, or cow horn orchid, as it is sometimes called, is a spring-flowering species with a range from Honduras to Panama. In southern Mexico, where it is the commonest of orchids, *S. tibicinis* is almost as popular with fire ants as with children. The hollow interiors of its pseudobulbs house huge colonies of those fiercely biting insects, who have long since learned to seek them out as shelter. There they live busily and happily until some ignorant intruder disturbs them, whereupon they charge out by the thousands and give a fiery baptism of formic acid to whatever bodily parts their jaws can bite. George Skinner, who first collected this orchid, made that interesting and painful discovery on his way down from the tree trunk where he had spotted the flower growing about twenty feet above the ground. No doubt he approached other orchids with considerably greater caution thereafter.

For cultivation see *Cattleya velutina* (page 16).

Phaius tankervilliae

This is a terrestrial orchid from the tropical regions of south China, and has been known under various names from time to time, including *Phaius bicolor* and *Bletia tankervilliae*. The generic term *Phaius,* meaning swarthy in Greek, is a bit misplaced here; many species of *Phaius* are dark-colored, but certainly not this one.

P. tankervilliae was one of the first two Asiatic orchids to reach England, brought there in 1780 by Dr. John Fothergill. He placed it in his botanic garden at Upton (near Stratford), an establishment famed throughout Europe. Some few years later, in 1789, it appeared on the first list of plants grown at Kew, and was one of the fifteen "exotics" cultivated there at that time. By 1860 it had migrated to Hawaii, in the company of some Chinese emigrants who longed to bring a touch of home along with them.

For cultivation see *Phaius tuberculosus* (page 86).

Laeliocattleya elegans

A great many orchid hybrids have been created by man, but nature is also busy crossbreeding on its own. The entire genus *Laeliocattleya,* as its name implies, results from a cross between the genera *Laelia* and *Cattleya*. Ordinarily, hybrids are bred to produce better flowers for cutting, but here nature sought to combine bright color with large size—and succeeded admirably.

As it so happens cattleyas and laelias are among the orchids best suited to the breeder's purpose, a fact which had already been manifested long before the first artificial generic cross was made in 1861. In fact, it was not until 1859 that the very first species hybrids of orchids were displayed, for most orchid fanciers had believed up to then that such a feat was an impossibility. Today there are countless hybrids, which proves once again that widely held notions often bear no relation to the facts.

The whole technique of crossbreeding has become more and more sophisticated with time, and it is no longer confined to crossing only two genera. Three, four, or more genera can now be combined, their chromosomes altered by colchicine, x-rays, and radioactive isotopes; and breeders are approaching the stage where they may soon be able to blueprint special orchids for particular purposes.

For cultivation see *Cattleya velutina* (page 16).

Sobralia macrantha

This is a terrestrial orchid often found by collectors prior to its introduction into cultivation in 1841, but somehow neglected by them. Since its roots often lie submerged for two to three months at a time in its natural habitats throughout Mexico, Guatemala, and Costa Rica, perhaps the collectors feared that it might not adapt to greenhouse conditions. Eventually, though, the colorful display made by its blossoms enticed two orchid gatherers, one of them the redoubtable George Skinner, to bring it in from the wild. A specimen first flowered outside of its native territory in the garden of the Horticultural Society at Chiswick, from May through July of 1841.

Despite its three-month period of bloom, *S. macrantha* is of no use as a cutting plant, for the blossoms last only an average of twelve hours. Several bloom in quick succession, however, so flowers are always present. Their five- to six-inch spread of a somewhat magenta hue, produced at regular intervals through early summer, more than makes up for the brief duration of the individual blossoms.

Growth: 60°–70° F., feed dilute 30–10–10 twice weekly; water abundantly, insuring that the roots are kept consistently moist. *Flowering:* Generally May through July. Maintain temperature, water, and feeding as above. *Maturity:* Continue as above, since plants will remain active until onset of dormancy in late fall. *Rest:* December through February. 50°–55° F., no food, keep compost moist but not wet. *Light:* Bright, but no direct sun. More light in autumn. *Compost:* Use large pots, since these plants grow from 4 to 7 feet high and have flowers 9 inches wide. Use humus rich in loam, over a deep layer of mixed perlite and charcoal lumps. Keep upper soil mixture open and porous.